# RECORDS

OF

# SALEM WITCHCRAFT,

COPIED FROM THE

## ORIGINAL DOCUMENTS.

### VOL. II.

PRIVATELY PRINTED FOR
W. ELLIOT WOODWARD, ROXBURY, MASS.
MDCCCLXIV.

# Woodward's

# Historical Series.

## No. II.

# SALEM
# WITCHCRAFT.

*Sarah Vibber v. Jno. Willard.*

june the 3. 1692.

SARAH Vibber aged 36 yeares or theara-
bouts teftifie and faith the day before
Jno Willard was examined at the uilleg
I being in Left Ingerfols Chamber I
faw yᵉ aporition of john willard com to mary wolcot and mary luis and hurt them griuofly and almoft choked Them Then I tould of it and emediatly yᵉ faid wiliard fel upon mee and tormented
me greuefly and pinched me and threw me down.
Sarah uibber ownid this har teftimony before us the
Jurrers for Inqweft this 3 of June 1692.

Jurat in Curia.

*Eliz Hubbard v. Jno Willard.*

The depofiftion of Elizabeth Hubburd agged about
17 years who teftifieth and faith that on the 11

May 1692 I faw the Apperifhtion of John Willard
of Salem Village who did Immediatly torment me
and urged me to writ in his book : but on the 18th of
May being the day of his examination John Willard did moft grevioufly tortor me during the time
of his examination for if he did but look upon me
he would Immediatly ftrick me down or allmoft
choak me and allso during the time of his examination I faw the Apperifhtion of John Willard goe
from him and afflict the bodys of Mary Walcott
mircy lewes Abigaill Williams and Ann putnam
Junᵣ.

Elizabeth Hubburt did one this teftimony after the
Reding of it before vs the Jurres for Inqweft this
3 day of June : 92.

### *Eliz Booth. v. Jno Willard.*

The Depofiftion of Eliz Booth agged about 18
yeares who teftifieth and faith that feverall times
fence the later end of June 1692. I have been moft
grevioufly afflicted and tormented by John Willard
or his Apperance by pinching pricking and almoft
choaking me to death. alfo I have often feen John
Willard or his operance, moft grevioufly tormenting
and afflicting my Brother George Booth almoft
Redy to kill him.

Sufannah Shelden alfo teftfieth that within this
fortnight fhe hath feen John Willard or his Appearance moft grevioufly torment and afflict George
Booth almoft Redy to prefe him to death.

*Lydia Nichols Margaret Knight v. Jno Willard.*

The depofition of Lydia Nicoles aged 46 yeares & of Margaret Knight aged 20 yeares, who teftify and fay, That the wife of John Willard being at her fathers houfe when the faid Willard lived at Groton fhe made a lamentable complaynt how cruelty her hufband had beaten her ; fhe thought herfelfe that fhe fhould neuer recouer of the blows he had giuen her, the next morninge he was got into a litle hole vnder the ftayres and then fhe thought fome thinge extra ordinary had befallen him, then he ran out at the dore and ran vp a fteep hill almoft impoffible for any man to run vp as fhe fayd then fhe tooke her mare and rid away, fearing fome euil had been intended as againft her and when fhe came to the houfe of Henery or Benjamin Willard fhe told how it was with her and the fayd Henery Willard or both went to looke after him and met him running in a ftrange diftracted manner.

*Sam^ll Wilkins v. Jno Willard.*

The Depofiftion of Samuell Wilknes agged about 19 years who teftifieth and faith that fence Jno Willard has been in prizfon I have been afflicted in a ftrange kind of maner for about the later end of June or begining of July as I was a weaving the yarn broak exceeding faft and as I was a tying a thread I had a ftroak on my hand like a knife the blood being almoft Redy to come out and I was alfo pinched feueral times by an unfeen hand alfo

Riding to Marble head Juſt as I came to forriſt Ri-
uer Bridge I was immediatly ſeized with a violent
wait on my back and I ſaw a black hate and was
immediatly pulled ofe my horſe or mare and almoſt
pulled into the Rivere but holding faſt as laſt I gott
vp againe awhile affter as I was once in the woods
and agoing hom and a little boy with me I thought
I muſt run and I ſaid to the by let us Run and as
ſoon as I ran there was a black hate ran along by
me a while affter one morning about an hour by
ſun I was afflicted and I ſaw John Willard or his
Appearance with a darke collored coot and a black
hate very like that hate which I formerly ſaw : a
little while affter this one night as ſoon as I was
a bed John Willard whom I very well knew or his
Appearance cam into the Room where I was a bed
and another man and woman along with him which
I did not know and they tould me they would carry
me away before morning.

Jurat in Curia.

*Thomas Bailey v. John Willard.*

The depoſition of Thomas Baly aged 36 yeares
who teſtifieth and ſaith.

That I being at Groton ſome ſhort tyme after John
Willard as the report went, had beaten his wife I
went to call him home and comeinge home with
him in the night I heard ſuch a hideous noyſe of
ſtrange createres I was much affrighted for I never
had heard the like noyſe. I fearinge they might be
ſome evil ſpirits I enquired of the ſaid Willard what
might it be that made ſuch a hideous noyſe the

fayd Willard fayd they ware Locuft. the next day
as I fuppofe the fayd Willards wife with a young
childe and her mother being upon my mare ridinge
betweene Groaton mil and Chemsford they being
willing to goe on foote a litle defired me to ride:
then I taking my mare being willing to let her feed
a litle there as I remember I aprehend I heard the
fame noyfe agayne where at my mare ftarted and
got from me

Jurat in Curia.

*Eliz: Bailey v. Jno Willard.*

The teftimonie of Elizabeth Bayly aged twenty fo-
uen yeares ore there-abouts teftifyeth and faith that
John Willard lookeing his oxen met w^{th} this deponent and told her that all the way from Francis
Elliotts houfe to his owne home he veryly thought
that the Deuell came before him or behind him all
the way which dreadfully frighted him, the faid
Deponent afked him why he thought fo he anfwered hee could not tell and emediatly fell a
finging.

The marke of + Elizabeth Bayley
Jurat in Curia.

*Rebecca Wilkins v. Jno Willard.*

The teftomony of Rebeckah Wilkins aged ninteen
years Doe teftifie that 29^{th} July at night fhee fe
John Wilard feting in the Corner and hee faid that
hee wold afflict me that night and forthwith hee
did afflick me and the nax day I ded fe him afflick
me foer by choaking and Polling one ear into Pea-

fes the nax day being the Lords day I being going
to meeting I fe John Willard and hee afflickted
me uery foer.

Jurat in Curia.

*Thos. Putnam & Edward Putnam v. Jno Willard.*

The depofiftion of Thomas putnam agged 40 years
and Edward Putnam agged 38 years who teftifie
and fay that we haueing been conuerfant with feueral of the afflicted parfons, as namly Mary Walcott mercy lewes Elizabeth hubbert abigail Williams and Ann Putnam Jun[r] and we haue feen them
moft grevioufly tormented by pinching and pricking
and being all moft choaked to death moft grevioufly
complaining of John Willard for hurting them but
on the 18th day of May 1692. being the day of his
examination the aforefaid afflicted parfons were
moft grevioufly tormented dureing the time of his
examination for if he did but caft his eies upon
them they were ftrochen down or all most choak
alfo feuerall times fence we have feen the Afforefaid
afflicted parfons moft grevioufly tormented as if
their bones would have been difjoyned grevioufly
complaining of John Willard for hurting them,
and we veryly beleue that John willard the priz-
foner at the bar has feuerall times tormented and
afflicted the afforefaid parfons with acts of witchcraft.

Thomas Putnam
Edward putnam.

Jurat in Curia.

*Henry Wilkins jr. v. John Willard.*

The depofition of Henery Wilknes fen aged 41 yeares, who teftifieth and fayth that upon the third of May laft, John Willard came to my houfe and very earneftly entreated me to go uith him to Boftton w^ch I at length confented to go with him. my fon Daniel comeinge and underftandinge I was goinge with him to Bofton and feemed to be much troubled that I would go with the faid Willard and he fayd he thought it were wel if the fayd Willard were hanged w^ch made me admire for I never heard fuch an expreffion come from him to any one beinge finc he came to yeares of difcretion, but after I was gone in a few days he was taken ficke and grew every day worfe and worfe whereupon we made aplication to a phyfitian who affirmed his ficknes was by fome preter natural caufe and would make no aplication of any phificke Some tymes after this our neighbours coming to vifit my fon Mercy Lewis came w^th them and affirmed that fhe faw the apparition of John Willard afflicting him quickly after came An Putnam and fhe faw the fame apparition and then my eldeft daughter was taken in a fad manner and the fayd An faw the fayd Willard afflicting her at Another tyme mercy lewes and mary Walcott came to vifit him and they faw the fame apparition of Willard afflicting him and this not but a little tyme before his death. Sworne in Court.

*Benj^m. Wilkins & Tho^s. Flint v. John Willard.*

The teftimony of benjamin Wilkins aged about
         and Thomas fflint aged about 46 years tefti-
fieth that one y^e 16 day of May laft 1692, we being
at the hous of henry Wilkins where we faw his fon
daniell Wilkins         as we judged at y^e point of
death and marcy lues and Mary wolcot being with
us Tould us That John Willard and goody buckly
were upon his throat and upon his breaft and
preffed him and choked him and to our bes judgment he was preffed and choked         time we
faw him almoft to death,
and the faid benjamin wilkins continued with him
till         was about 3 hours after and he altered not
in the         manner condifthtion only grew wors and
wors till he died.
         Jurat in Curia by Ben Wilkins

*Bray Wilkins v. John Willard.*

The depofition of Bray Wilkins of Salem Village aged about eighty and one years with reference
to John Willard of sd Salem lately charged with
witchcraft, when he was at firft complained of by
the afflicted perfons for afflicting of them he came
to my houfe greatly troubled defiring me with
fome other neighbours to pray for him. I told him
I was then going from home and could not ftay,
but if I could come home before night I fhould not
be unwilling, but it was near night before I came
home and fo I did not anfwer his defire, but I
heard no more of him upon that account whether

my not anfwering his defire did not offend him, I
cannot tell I was jealous afterward that it did A little after my wife & I went to Bofton at the laft
Election when I was as well in health as in many
yeares before & the Election day coming to my
brother Left Richard Way's houfe at noon there
were many friends to dine there, they were fat
down at the Table Mr. Lawfon and his wife & feverall more John Willard came into the houfe with
my fon Henry Wilkins before I fat down & fd Willard to my apprehenfion look'd after fuch a fort
upon me as I never before difcerned in any. I did
but ftep into the next room & I was prefently taken
in a ftrange condition fo that I could not dine nor
eat any thing. I cannot exprefs the mifery I was
in for my water was fuddenly ftopt & I had no benefit of nature but was like a man in a Rock and
I told my wife immediatly that I was afraid that
Willard had done me wrong my pain continuing
and finding no relief my jealoufie continued : Mr.
Lawfon and others there were all amazed & knew
not what to do for me. There was a woman ac-
counted fkilful came hoping to help me and after
fhe had ufed means fhe afked me whether none of
thofe evil perfons had done me damage I faid I could
not fay they had but I was fore afraid they had
fhe anfwered fhe did fear fo too as near as I remember I lay in this cafe 3 or 4 dayes at Bofton and afterwards with the jeopardy of my life (as I thought)
I came home and then fome of my friends coming
to fee me (and at this time John Willard was run
away) one of the afflicted perfons mercy Lewes

came in with them & they afked whether fhe faw
any thing: fhe faid yes, they are looking for John
Willard but there he is upon his Grandfathers Belly
(and at that time I was in grievous pain in the
fmall of my Belly) I continued fo in greevous pain
and my water much ftopt till sd Willard was in
chains and then as near as I can guees I had confiderable eafe, but on the other hand in the room of a
ftoppage I was vexed with a flowing of water fo
that it was hard to keep myfelf dry. On the 5 July
laft talking with fome friends about John Willard
fome pleading his innocenfy and myfelf and fome
others arguing the contrary, within about 1-4 of
an hour after that I had faid it was not I nor my
fon Benj Wilkins, but the teftimony of the afflicted
perfons and the jury concerning the murder of my
grandfon: Dan: Wilkins, that would take auay
his life if any thing did and within about 1-4 hour
after this I was taken in the foreft diftrefs & mifery
my water being turned into real blood, or of a
bloody colour and the old pain returned exceffively
as before which continued for about 24 hours together.

*Philip Knight & Thoˢ Nichols. v. John Willard.*

The depofition of Philip knight aged 46 yeares and
of Thomas Nicols 22 years who do teftify and fay,
That Some tyme in April laft there was difcourfe
at the houfe of the fayd Philip knight about feueral of the village that were taken vp vpon fufpition

of witchcraft., John Willard being prefent then replyed, hang them, they are all witches

*Mercy Lewis v. John Willard.*

The depofiftion of Mircy Lewes who teftifieth and
faith that I have often feen the Apperifhtion of
John Willard amongft the witches within this three
weeks, but he did not doe me much hurt till the
11<sup>th</sup> of May 1692 and then he fell upon me moft
dreadfully and dis moft grevioufly afflect me allmoft
Redy to kill me urging me moft vehemently to
writ in his book, and fo he hath continued euer
fince at times tortoring me moft dreadfully beating
and pinching me and allmoft Redy to choak me
threatning to kill if I would not writ in his book
alfo I being carried to wills hill on the 14<sup>th</sup> of may
at euening to fee the afflicted parfons there. I faw
there the Apperifhtion of John Willard grevioufly
afflicting his grandffather wilknes and I alfo faw the
apperifhtion of John Willard there grevioufly afflecting the body of Daniell Wilknes who laid
fpeachles and in a fad condition and John Willard
tould me he would kill Daniell Wilknes within
Two days if he could alfo I was at Henry Wilknes
the 16 May a little before night and their I faw the
apperifhtion of John Willard a choaking Daniell
Wilknes alfo on the 18<sup>th</sup> May being ing the day
of his examination I was moft grevioufly tortured
by him dureing the time of his examination for if
he did but look upon me he ftruck me down or
almoft choaked me to death and feveral times fence

the Apperifhtion of John Willard has moft greviouſly affected me by beating pinching and allmoft choaking me to death, alfo dureing the time of his examination I faw the Apperifhtion of John Willard goe from him and afflict the bodyes of Mary Wolcott Abigail Williams Elizabeth Hubbard and Ann Putnam Jun[r.]

### *Benj[m]. Wilkins v. Jno Willard.*

The teftimony of benjamin Wilkens aged about 36 years faith That about y[e] 12 of May laft Mary lues being at my father's houfe tould us that fhe faw John wilard and goody buckly upon my father wilknes preffing his belly and my father complained of extreme paine in his bely at y[e] fametime, then John putnam ftruck at y[e] aperiftions then marcy lues fell down and my father had eafe emidiatly.

### *John Putnam v. John Willard.*

John putnam teftifieth to y[e] fame above written.

### *Indictment v. Ann Pudeater.*

Effex in the Province of ⎫ Annog3R. R[d]& Reginee
the Maffachufetts Bay ⎬ Gulielmi & Mariee An-
Jn New England fs ⎭ glice & c Quarto. Anno-
gu Dom. 1692 . . .

The Juriors for our Sou[s] Lord and Lady the King and Queen Pfent, That Ann Pudeator of Salem in the County of Effex, aforefaid widdow, The fecond day of July in the yeare aforefaid and diuers othere

days and times as well before as after certaine deteftable arts called witchcraft & Sorceries Wickedly
Mallitioufly and fellonioufly hath ufed practifed and
exercifed At and within the Townefhip of Salem
aforefaid in & upon and againft one Mary Warren
of Salem aforefaid fingle woman by which faid
wicked arts the faid Mary Warren the fecond day
of July aforefaid and diuers other days and times
both before and after was and is tortured Afflicted
Pined Confumed wafted and tormented and alfo
for fundry other acts of witchcraft by the faid Ann
Pudeater Committed and done before and Since that
time Agft the peace of oᵗ Souⁿ Lord and Lady the
King and Queen theire Crowne and Dignity and
agft the forme of the ftatute in yᵗ Cafe made and
Provided.

    Witneffes          Mary Warren Jurat.
Sarah Churchel Jurat.   Ann Putnam Jurat.

### *Warrant. v. Ann Pudeater.*

To the Marfhall of Effex or Conftable in Salem.

    You are in theire Majefᵗˢ names hereby required
forthwith to apprehend and bring before vs Allic
Parker the wife of John Parker of Salem and Ann
Pudeater of Salem widdow who ftand charged with
fundry acts of witchcraft by them committed this
day Contrary to yᵉ Laws of our Souⁿ Lord and Lady. ffaile not. Dated Salem May the 12ᵗʰ 1692.

    Jvs.     JOHN HATHORNE     } Affifts.
             JONATHAN CORWIN  }

May 12ᵗʰ 1692. I have apprehended the above

named perfons and Brought them att yᵉ place apointed by youʳ honors

       P mee   GEORGE HERRICK Marfhall
                         of Effex

### *Sarah Churchill Confeffion.*

Sarah Churchwell confeffeth that Goody pudeater
brought the book to this examinaᵗ and fhe figned
it but did not know her at that tyme, but when fhe
faw her fhe knew her to be the fame and that
Goody Bifhop als Oliver appeared to this Examinant and told her fhe had killed John Trafks child
(whofe child dyed about that tyme) and faid Bifhop
als Oliver afflicted her as alfoe did old George Jacobs and before that time this Examinᵗ being afflicted could not doe her fervice as formerly and her
fᵈ Mafter Jacobs called her bitch witch and ill
names and then afflicted her as above and that
pudEater brought 3 Images like Mercy Lewis Ann
Putnam Elizᵃ Hubbard and they brought her
thornes and fhe ftuck them in the Images and told
her the perfons whofe likenefs they were would be
afflicted and the other day faw Goody Oliver fate
vpon her knee.

Jurat in Curia by Sarah Churchill.

   this confeffion was taken before John Hathorne
and Jonathan Corwin Esqʳˢ 1. Juni 1692. as atteft.
                      Thᵒ Newton.

### Examination of Ann Pudeator.

An Pudeater examined before y^e Majeftrates of Salem July 2. 1692

Sarah Churchwell was bid to fay what fhe had to fay of her.

You have charged her with bringing y^e book to you.

A : Yes faid Churchwell.

have you feen her fince.    A : no.

Goodwife puddeater, you have former ly bin complayned of we now further enquire : here is one perfon faith you brought her y^e book which is Sarah Churchell look on y^e perfon fes. Churchill :

you did bring me y^e book : I was at Goodman Jacobfes.

Pudeater fd I never faw y^e woman before now. it was told puddeater this mayd charged you with bringing her y^e book at y^e laft examinat^n Puddeater fd I never faw y^e Devils book, nor knew that he had one.

L^t Jer Neal was afked what he could fay of this woman. Neal fd fhe had been an ill carriaged woman and fince my wife has been fick of y^e fmall pox this woman has come to my houfe pretending kindnes and I was glad to fee it fhe afked whether fhe might ufe our morter which was ufed for my wife : and I confented to it, but I afterward repented of it : for y^e nurs told me my wife was y^e wors fenc fhe was very ill of a flux which fhe had not before.

When the officer came for puddeater, y^e nurs fd you

are come to late for my wife grew worſe till ſhe dyed : ſd Pudeater had often threatened my wife.

Eliz Hubbard ſd ſhe had ſeen ſdPudeater    ſd Mary Wolcot but ſhe had not hurt her ſhe had ſeen her with Goodwife nurs.

goody puddeater what did you do with yᵉ ointments that you had in yᵉ hous ſo many of them, ſhe ſd I never had ointment or oyl but meat tried out in my houſe ſince my huſband dyed : but the conſtable Joſeph Neal affirmed ſhe had ſhe had near 20 that had oyntment or greas in them, a little in a thing : ſhe ſde ſhe never had any ointment but neats foot oyˡ in yᵉ hous, but what was in theſe things yᵉ conſtables ſpeakes of.

A. It was greaſe to make ſope of. but why did you put them in ſo many things, when one would have held all but anſwered not to yᵉ porpoſe, but the conſtable sd oyntments were of ſeveral ſorts.

Sarah Vibber did you ever ſe this woman before now, anſwered no. An putnam sd ſhe had never ſeen her, but ſince ſhe come to Salem Town láſt : ſd Putnam fell into a fitt and sd Puddeater was commanded to take her by yᵉ wriſt, and did and ſd Putnam was well preſently.

mary warin fell into two fitts quickly after one another and both times was helped by ſd Puddeators taking her by yᵉ wriſt.

*Summons to witneſſes v. Ann Pudeator.*

Wm & Mary by yᵉ Grace of God of England,
  Scottland ffrance & Ireland King and Queen,
  defendˢ &c.
    To yᵉ Sheriff of Eſſex or deputy.
L. S.                                             Greeting.
  Wee commond you to warn John Weſgate John
Bullock, Martha Dutch Suſanna Dutch Lt. Jeremiah Neale John Beckett John Beſt Junʳ Jno
Loader, Sarah parott. that they and every of them
appear at yᵉ next Court of Oyer & Terminer holden
at Salem on yᵉ next Tueſday at twelve of yᵉ clock
there to Teſtify yᵉ truth to yᵉ beſt of theire knowledge on certain Indictments to be exhibited againſt
Alice Parker and Ann Pudeater, hereof make return
fail not
  Dated in Salem Septʳ 5ᵗʰ 1692. in yᵉ fourth year
of our Reigne.        STEPHEN SEWALL cler

  Sept 5ᵗʰ 1692. I have ſumoned and have warned
all the within named perſons John Beſt Junʳ Except 2ᵈ Beſt being Removed to Ipſwich that thay
and every of them appeare to Giue in their Euid
&c att time and place within written.
    P me      GEORGE HERRICK depᵗ Sheriff.

*Sarah Churchill v. Ann Pudeater.*

Sarah Churchel affirmed to yᵉ Jury of inqweſt that
Ann Puddeator has greatly afflicted her ſd Churchel
by choaking her pinching her and sticking pinſe
into her and by preſſing of her and making her ſett

C

her hands to y^e book upon y^e oath fhe hath taken
Sept. 6^th 1692.

Sworn in Court.

& brought poppits to her to ftick pins to w^ch fhe
did & y^e Pfons afflicted by it.

### *Mary Warren v. Ann Pudeator.*

Mary Warin upon her oath y^t fhe hath taken affirms to y^e Jury of Inqweft that Ann Puddeator
hath often afflicted me by biting me, pinching me,
fticking pins in me and choaking me and particularly on y^e 2 day of July att her examination fd
Puddeator did afflict me greatly alfo fhe on her Apperifhtion did offer me the book to fign to, fhe told
me alfo y^t fhe was y^e caufe of Jno Turners ffalling
off y^e cherry tree : to his great hurt and which
amazed him in his head and almoft kiled him, fhe
told me alfo fhe was the caus of Jeremiah Neals
wifes death and I faw her hurt Eliz Hubbard,
Mary Walcott and An Putnam y^e laft night fhe
afflicted me alfo laft night by her witchcraft and I
doe verily beleev fd Ann Puddeater is a witch; fhe
affirms Puddeator told her fhe kiled her hufband
Puddeator and his firft wife and that fhe was an
inftrument of John Befts wifes death

Sept^r 7 : 1692. Sworne in Court.

### *Eliz Hubbard v. Ann Pudeator.*

Eliz Hubbard affirmed upon y^e oath fhe hath taken
that fhe hath feen Ann Pddeator afflict Mary War-

rin and that fhe or her Apperiftion did hurt me and
Mary Warin y<sup>e</sup> laft night. before y<sup>e</sup> Jury of Inqueft
Sept<sup>r</sup> 7. 1692. & that fhe hath afflicted her fince
fhe came into Court.

Jurat in Curia.

### *Ann Putnam v. Ann Pudeator.*

An Putnam affirmed upon her oath, to y<sup>e</sup> Jury of
Inqueft that fhe hath feen Ann Puddeater afflict
Mary Warin Mary Walcott and Eliz Hubbard of-
ten and particularly att y<sup>e</sup> time of her laft examination before y<sup>e</sup> MaJeftrates at Mr. Tho Beadles, fhe
alfo hath afflicted me both then and at other times
Sept<sup>r</sup> 7. 1692.

Owned her Euidence in Court.

### *Sarah Vibber v. Ann Pudeator.*

Sarah Vibber upon her oath affirmed to y<sup>e</sup> Jury of
inqueft that fhee hath feen An Puddeator afflict
Mary Warin Mary Walcot and An Putnam both
at y<sup>e</sup> time of her examination at Mr. Tho Beadles
and y<sup>e</sup> laft night fhe together with Goodwife Parker did afflict y<sup>e</sup> fornamed Warin Walcot and Putnam ; fd Puddeator hath afflicted me to, and i do
believe fhe is a witch.   Sept<sup>r</sup> 7. 1692.

### *Mary Walcott v. Ann Pudeator.*

Mary Walcot upon oath affirms to y<sup>e</sup> Jury of Inqueft that fhe hath feen An Puddeator afflict Mary
Warrin An Putnam and Eliz Hubbard at y<sup>e</sup> time

of her examination at Mr Tho Beadles : and alfo yᵉ laft night I faw her afflict Mary Warin An Putnam and Eliz Hubbard by witchcraft and I verily beleiv sd Puddeator is a witch September 7 : 92. & that this day fhe hath afflicted this deponent.

Jurat in Curia.

Sept⸱ 10. 92.                    Atteft. S. Sewall.

I find by my characters : which I took : at yᵉ Examination of An Puddeator, that it was in yᵉ 2 day of July that fhe was examined at Mr. Tho. Beadles thay bearing date fo.

Septʳ 7. 1692.                    Simon Willard.

### *Samˡˡ Pickworth v. Ann Pudeater.*

The teftimony of Samuell Pickworth whow teftifieth that a bowt fix weeks agoo : I this deponant was coming along Salem Strete between Ann Pudeatres hous and Captin higifon hous it being in the ewening and J this deponant faw a woman neare Captin higifonn corner., the which I fuppofed to be Ann Pudeatar and in a moment of time fhe pafid by me as fwift as if a burd flwe by me and I faw faid woman goo into Ann Pudeaters hows.

Jurat in Curia.

S. Sewall cle.

Samˡˡ Pickworth affirmeth yᵗ yᵉ above written euidence is yᵉ truth : upon oath to : yᵉ Jury of Inqueft Septʳ⸱ 7. 92.

### *Ann Putnam v. Ann Pudeater.*

Septʳ⸱ 7. 92. Ann Putnam afarmed to the grand

Jnqueſt that ann Pudeatar : tould har that ſhe flu by a man in the neight into a hous

### *John Bert Sr. v. Ann Pudeater.*

The Teſtimony of Jnº Bert Senior aged about 48 yeres Teſtifieth & ſaith yᵗ ſome yeers paſt yᵗ I this deponant did often hear my wife ſaye yᵗ Ann Pudeater would not Lett her alone vntill ſhe had killd her By her often pinching & Bruſeing of her Till her Earms & other parts of her Body Looked Black by Reſon of her ſoer pinching of her in yᵉ Time of her ſickneſs of my wife did affirm agᵗ itt woes an pudeater yᵗ did afflict her & ſtood in yᵉ Belefe of itt as Long as ſhe Lived.

Jurat in Curia.

Sept 7. th 92. S. Sewall. cler.

Jno Beſt affirmed to yᵉ truth of yᵉ aboue written before ye Jury of Inqueſt. Septʳ 7 ; 1692.

### *Jno. Beſt v. Ann Pudeater.*

The teſtimony of John beſt Jwnear how teſtifieth uppon his. oath before the grant Inqweſt, that his mother did ſeuerall tims in har ſicknis complain of ann pudeater of Salem the wife of Jacob pudeater how ſhe had bewitched har and that ſhe did belieue ſhe would kill hor before ſhe had dun and ſoo ſhe ſaid ſeuerall tims dueing hear ſicknis vntill har death allſo I this deponant did ſeuerall tims goo in to the woods to fech my fathers Cowes and I did driue goode pudeaters cow bak from our Cowes and I being all alone ann pudeater would chide me when J came howm for turning the cow bak by Refon of which I this deponant did couclude faid pudeater was a witch

Jurat in Curia.

### Petition of Ann Pudeator.

The humble Petition of Ann Pudeater unto yᵉ honoured Judge and Bench now Setting in Judicature in Salem humbly Sheweth.

That whereas your Poor and humble Petitioner being condemned to die, and knowing in my own confcience as I fhall fhortly anfwer it before yᵉ Great God of heaven, who is the fearcher and knower of all hearts : That the Euidence of Jnᵒ Beft Senʳ and Jnᵒ Beft Junʳ and Samᵘ Pickworth wᶜʰ was given in againft me in Court were all of them altogether falfe and untrue, and befides the abouefaid Jno Beft hath been formerly whipt. and likewife is recorded for A Lyar, I would humbly begg of yoʳ honowrs to Take it into your Judicious and Pious confideration, That my life may not be taken away by fuch falfe Evidences and witneffes as thefe be likewife yᵉ Euidence given in againft me, by Sarah Church and Mary Warren I am altogether ignorant off and know nothing in yᵉ leaft meafure about it, nor nothing elfe concerning yᵉ crime of witchcraft for wᶜʰ I am condemned to die as will be known to men and angells, att the great day of Judgment, begging and imploring your prayers att the throne of grace in my behalfe and your poor and humble petition<sup>r</sup> fhall for ever pray as fhe is bound in duty for you<sup>r</sup> hon<sup>rs</sup> health and happinefs in this life and eternall felici<sup>ty</sup> in y<sup>e</sup> world to come.

*Warrant v. Rebecca Jacobs.*

To the Conftable in Salem.

You are in theire Majef<sup>ts</sup> names hereby required to Apprehend and bring before vs, on Tufday next being the feauenteenth day of this Jnftant month of May aboute ten of y<sup>e</sup> clocki n the forenoon at y<sup>e</sup> houfe of L<sup>t</sup> Nathaniell Ingerfons, of Salem Village Daniell Andrews, of Salem Village Bricklayer George Jacobs Jun<sup>r</sup> of Salem Village hus bandman and Rebecka Jacobs the wife of faid George Jacobs and Sarah Buckley the wife of W<sup>m</sup> Buckley of Salem Village Cordwayner And Mary Withridge the daughter of faid Buckley who all ftand charged in behalfe of theire Majefties with high fufpition of fundry acts of witchcrafts by them donne or committed on y<sup>e</sup> Bodys of Ann putnam Marcy Lewis Mary Walcot, and Abigail Williams and others of Salem Village (Lately) Whereby great hurt hath been donn them. And hereof you are not to faile.

Dated Salem May the 14<sup>th</sup> 1692.

JOHN HATHORNE ⎫ Affifts.
JONATHAN CORWIN ⎭

In profecution of this Warrant I have apprehended and brought the bodyes of Sarah Buckley and Mary withridg and Rebekah Jacobs all of Salem velage

according to the tenor of the within written warrant, and haue likewife made delegant farch at the
houfe of Daniell Andrew and at the houfe of Georg
Jacobs for them likewife but cannot find them.

P me Jonathan Putnam Conftable in Salem.

### Indiɛtment *v. Rebecca Jacobs.*

Effex in the Prouince | Anno R. Rˢ & Reginee Gu-
of the Maffachufetts | lielmi & Mariee Anglice &cᶜ
Bay in New England | Quarto Annog 3 Domini
| 1692.

The Juriors for our Souᵉ Lord and Lady the King
and Queen doe Pfent, That Rebeccah Jacobs the
wife of George Jacobs of Salem Villadge in the
County of Effex aforsᵈ hufbandman In the year
aforefaid In Salem Villadge in the County of Effex
aforefd Wickedly and fellonioufly a Couenant with
the Euil Spiritt the Devill did make Contrary to
the Peace of our Souᵉ Lord and Lady the King and
Queen theire Crowne and Dignity. And the forme
in the Stattute in that Cafe made and Provided.

### *Eliz Hubbard v. Rebecca Jacobs.*

The depofiftion of Eliz Hubbard who teftifieth
and faith that one the begining of May 1692. I was
afflided by Rebecah Jacobs the wife of George
Jacobs, but on the 18ᵗʰ May 1692. being the day
of hir examination I faw Rebekah Jacobs or hir
apperance moft grevioufly afflid Mary Walcott
Abigail williams and Ann putnam tho when fhe
began to confefs fhe left ofe hurting of us but feueral

times fenc that fhe has moft grevioufly afflicted me and I beluee in my heart that Rebeckah Jacobs is a wicth and that fhe has often afflected me and the aforefaid parfons by acts of wicthcraft.

Eliz : Hubbard owned yᵉ truth of yᵉ aboue written evidence before yᵉ Jury of Inques. Septʳ 10, 1692.

### *Warrant v. Roger Toothaker.*

To the Marfhall of Effex or his dept or Conftables in Salem

You are in theire Majeſ\*\* names hereby required to apprehend forthwith and bring before vs, (Roger Toothaker of Bilrica who ftands charged with fundry acts of witchcraft by him committed or donne on yᵉ bodyes of Eliz Hubert, Ann Putnam Mary Walcot &c of Salem Village in order to his examination Relateing to yᵉ premifes. faile not

Dated Salem May 18ᵗʰ 1692.

JOHN HATHORNE  }
JONATHAN CORWIN }

J order of the Goverʳ and Councill.

the perfon fpicefied in this warrant was Apprehended this day and brought before the corte Acordinge to ye tennor of this warrant by mee

JOSEPH NEAL.

Conftable Jn Salem May 18 1692.

**D**

*Mittimus v. Roger Toothaker.*

To the Keeper of Theire Majesᵗˢ Goale in Boston.

You are in theire Majesᵗˢ names hereby required to take into your care and safe Custody the Bodys of Roger Toothaker of Bilrica John Willard of Salem Village, husbandman Thomas ffarrer of Lyn husbandman and Elizabeth Hart the wife of Isaac Hart of Lyn husbandman who all stand charged with Sundry acts of witchcraft, by them and Euery one of them Committed on the Bodys of Mary Walcot Abigail Williams Mary Lewis Ann Putnam and others of Salem Village or farmes whom you are well to secure in order to theire tryall for the same and vntill they shall be deliuered by due order of Law and hereof you are not to faile.

Dated Salem May 18ᵗʰ 1692.

JOHN HATHORNE } by order of yᵉ
JONATHAN CORWIN } Gouernʳ & Councill.

*Tho Gage v. Roger Toothaker.*

The Deposition of Thomas Gage Aged aboute thirty six years. This Deponant saith & doth testifie that sometime this Last spring of yᵉ year, that Doctor Toothaker was in his house in Beuerly (vpon some occasion) & we discoursed aboute John Marstons Childe of Salem, that was then sich and haue-ing vnwonted fitts and Likewise another Childe of Phillip Whites of Beuerly who was then strangely sick. I perswaded sd Toothaker to goe and see sd

Children and fd Toothaker anfwered he had feen
them both already and that his opinion was they
were vnder an Evill hand And farther fd Toothaker
fd that his Daughter had Kild a witch and I afked
him how fhe did it and fd toothaker anfwered rea-
dily that his daughter had Learned fomething from
him J. afked by what means fhe did it and he fd
that there was a a certaine perfon be witched and
fd perfon complained of beeing afflicted by another
perfon, that was fufpected by y^e afflicted perfon &
further fd Toothaker fd that his fd Daughter gott
fome of y^e afflicted perfons urine and put it into an
Earthern pott and ftopt fd pott uery clofe and putt
fd pott *into* a hott oven and ftopt vp fd oven and
y^e next morning fd *childe* was dead, other things I
haue forgotten and farther faith nott.

ias Pickworth Aged aboute thirty foure years
teftifieth to all that is aboue written.

Sworne by Thomas Gage. Salem Village May.
20*th* 1692

befor vs. $\left.\begin{array}{l}\text{JOHN HATHORNE}\\\text{JONATHAN CORWIN}\end{array}\right\}$ Affifts.

*Complaint of Mary Eafty.*

Salem May the 20^th 1692.

There being complaint this day made before mee
by John Putnam Jun^r and Benjamin Hutchefon
both of Salem Village for themfelfes and alfo for
theire Neighbours in behalfe of theire Majefties
againft Marah Eafty the wife of Ifaac Efty of Topffield for fundry acts of witchcraft by her Commit-

ted yefterday and this prefent day of the date hereof vpon the bodys of Ann putnam Marcy Lewis, Mary Walcot and Abigail Williams of Salem Village to y^e urong and Jnjury of theire bodys therefore crave Juftice.

John Putnam Jun.
Beniamin Hutchinfon.

*Warrant v. Mary Eafty.*

To the Marfhall of the County of Effex or dept or Conftables of Salem.

You are in theire Majef^ts names hereby required to apprehend and forthwith bring before me at ye houfe of Mr. Thomas Beadles in Salem, the Body of Mary Eafty the wife Ifaac Eafty of Topffield to Be Examined Relating to fundry acts of witchcraft. by her committed yefterday and this prefent day according to Complaint abouefd. and hereof you are not to faile. Dated Salem May 20^th 1692.

JOHN HATHORNE Affift
May 20^th 1692. J order of ye Councill.

I have taken the body of the abouenamed Mary Eftiee and brought her at y^e time and place abouenamed.

P^e me. GEO HERRICK Marfhall of Effex.

*Indictment v. Mary Eafty No. 1.*

| Province of y^e Maffachu fetts, Bay In New England Effex fs. | Anno Regni Regis et Reginee Gulielmi et Mariee nunc Anglice J^" Quarto Annog Dom. 1692. |

The Jure for our Sovereigne Lord and Lady the

King and Queen P$^r$fents that Mary Eafty wife of
Ifaack Eafty of Topsfield hufbandman—on the
twenty third day of May in the fourth year of our
Sovereigne Lord and Lady William and Mary by
the Grace of God of England Scottland ffrance and
Ireland King and Queen Defenders of the faith &c.
and divers other Day and times as well before as after certaine Deteftable arts called Witchcrafts and
Sorceries wickedly and ffellonoufly hath vfed Practifed and Exercifed at and within the Townefhip of
Salem in the County of Effex aforefaid in Vpon and
againft one Marcy Lewis of Salem Village Single-
woman by which faid wicked Arts the faid Marcy
Lewis the Twenty third day of May in the year
abovefaid and Divers other Days and times as well
before as after, was and is Tortured Afflicted Pined
Confumed wafted and Tormented ag$^t$ the Peace of
our Sovereigne Lord & Lady the King and Queen
and ag$^t$ the forme of the Statute in that cafe made
and Provided—
Witneffes

 Marcy Lewis Jurat Eliz Hubbard Jurat.
 Ann Putnam Jurat Mary Wolcott Jurat.

*Indictment v. Mary Eafty No.* 2.

Province of the Maffa- Anno Regni Regis et Re-
chufetts Bay in New ginee Gullielmiet Mariee
England Effex, fs. nunc Anglice &c Quarto
        Annog Dom 1692.
 The Juro$^s$ for our Sovereigne Lord and Lady the
King and Queen p$^r$fents That : Mary Efty wife of

Ifaack Efty of Topsfield hufbandman the twenty third day of May—in the fourth year of the Reigne of our Sovereigne Lord and Lady-William and Mary by the Grace of God of England Scottland ffrance and Ireland King and Queen Defenders of the faith &c and Divers other Dayes and times as well before as after certaine Deteftable Arts called Witch-crafts & Sorceries Wickedly and ffellonioufly hath Vfed Practifed and Exercifed at and within the Townfhip of Salem in the County of Effex aforef^d in vpon and ag^t one Elizabeth Hubbard of Salem Single women by which faid Wicked Arts the faid Elizabeth Hubbard the twenty third Day of May in the fourth year aboues^d and Divers other Dayes and times as well before, as after was, and is, Tor-tured Afflicted Pined Confumed wafted and Tor-mented ag^t the Peace of our Sovereigne Lord and Lady the King and Queen and ag^t the fform of the Statute in that cafe made and Provided.

Witneffes

 Eliz: Hubbard Jurat Marcy Lewis Jurat.
  Ann Putnam Jurat.

### *Geo: Herrick v. Mary Eafty.*

May 20^th 1692. The teftimone of Geo: Herrick aged thirty four or thereaboutes and John Puttnam Jun^r of Salem Village agid thirty five yeares or there aboutes teftifieth and faith y^t beeing att the houfe of y^e aboue fd John Puttnams both faw Mercy Lewis in a very Dreadfull and Solemn Condition : So y^t to our aprehention fhee could not continue

long in this world without A mittigation of thoes
Torments wee faw her which Caufed us to Expediate
A hafty difpatch to apprehend Mary Esftick in hopes
if poffable it might faue her Life and Returneing
y^e fame night to fd John Puttnams houfe aboute
middnight wee found y^e fd Mercy Lewis in a
Dreadffull fitt but her reafon was then Returned
Againe fhe faid what haue you brought me y^e winding Sheet Goodwife Esftice, well J had rather goe
into y^e winding Sheet then Sett my hand to ye Book
but affter that her fitts was weaker and weaker but
ftill Complaining y^t Shee was very fick of her Sto-
make aboute break of Day She fell a Sleep but ft.ll
Continues Extream fick and was taken w^th A Dread
fitt Juft as wee left her fo y^t wee perceaued life in
her and that was all. Jurat in Curia.

Sep^r 9^th 92. Ateft. Geo. Herrick.

John putnam Jun.

*Jonathan Putnam, James Darling, Benj^a Hutch-
infon & Sam. Braybrook v. Mary Eafty.*

The depofition of Jonathan Putman, James Darling, Benj^a Hutchinfon & Sam : Braybrook w^o teftify and fay that we together with divers others the
20 : May. 1692. between eight and eleven oclock
at night being with Mercy Lewes whom we found
in a cafe as if death would have quickly followed,
and to whom Eliz: Hubbard was brought (faid Mercy
being unable to Speak moft of the day) to difcover
what fhe could fee did afflict faid Mercy, heard and
obferved that thefe two fell into fits by turns, the

one being well whilft the other was ill, and that each of them complained much of Mary Eaftie, who brought the book to faid Mercy feverall times as we heard her fay in her trances, and vexed and tortured them both by choking and feemingly breathlefs fits and other fits, threatning faid Mercy with a winding fheet &, afterwards with a Coffin if faid Mercy would not figne to her book, with abundance more of vexations the both received from her.

### *Examination of Mary Eafty.*

The Examination of Mary Eaftie.

At a Court held at Salem village 22 : Apr. 1692.

By the Wop. John Hathorne & Jonathan Corwin.

At the bringing in of the accufed feverall fell into fits.

Doth this woman hurt you.

many mouths were ftopt, and feveral other fits feized them

Abig : Williams faid it was Goody Eaftie, and fhe had hurt her, the like faid Mary Walcot, & Ann Putman, John jackfon faid he faw her with Goody Hobbs.

What do you fay, are you guilty ?

I can fay before Chrift Jefus, I am free.

You fee thefe accufe you.

There is a God.

Hath fhe brought the book to you ?

Their mouths were ftopt.

What have you done to thefe children?

I know nothing.

How can you fay you know nothing, when you fee thefe tormented, and accufe you that you know nothing?

Would you have me accufe myfelf?

Yes if you be guilty.

How far have you complyed w<sup>th</sup> Satan whereby he takes this advantage ag<sup>t</sup> you?

Sir, J never complyed but prayed againft him all my dayes, J have no complyance with Satan, in this.   What would you have me do?

Confefs if you be guilty.

J will fay it, if it was my laft time, J am clear of this fin.

Of what fin?

Of witchcraft.

Are you certain this is the woman?

Never a one could fpeak for fits.

By & by Ann Putman faid that was the woman, it was like her, and fhe told me her name.

It is marvailous to me that you fhould fometimes think they are bewitched, and fometimes not, when feverall confefs that they have been guilty of be-witching them.

well Sir would you have me confefs that J never knew?

Her hands were clinch<sup>d</sup> together and then the hands of Mercy Lewis was clincht.

Look now you hands are open, her hands are open.

E

Js this the woman ?

They made fignes but could not fpeak, but Ann Putman afterwards *Betty Hubbard* cryed out Oh. Goody Eafty, Goody Eafty you are the woman, you are the woman

Put up her head, for while her head is bound the necks of thefe are broken.

What de you fay to this?

Why God will know.

Nay God knows now.

I know he dos.

what did you think of the actions of others before your fifters came out, did you think it was Witchcraft?

I cannot tell.

Why do you not think it is Witchcraft ?

Jt is an evil fpirit, but wither it be witchcraft J do not know, Severall faid fhe brought them the Book and then they fell into fits.

Salem Village March 24ᵗʰ 169⅟.

Mr Samˡ parris being defired to take in wrighting the Examination of Mary Eaftie hath deliuered itt as aforefaid.

Upon heareing the aforefaid, and feeing what we did then fee, together with the Charge of the perfons then prefent, Wee Committed fd Mary Eaftie to theire Majefᵗˢ Goale.

JOHN HATHORNE } Affifts.
JONATHAN CORWIN

### Sarah Vibber v. Mary Eafty.

Sarah Viber : afirmed vpon her oath : that fhe faw Mary yᵉ wife of Ifaac Efty upon Jnᵒ Nortons bed ; when fd Norton was ill : and fd goody Efty flew out upon her : and afflicted her : fd Vibber : and fd Vibber affirmed : that fince yᵉ time of the laft examination of fd Efty : fd Efty has hurt and afflicted mercy Lewis : and mary walcot and Ann Putman : fhe or her Apperition : and fhe fd Efty has fome times hurt and afflicted her : fd Vibber alfo fince fd, Efty her laft examination : alfo : fd Vibber fd that fd Efty or her apperition has Afflicted Elis. Hubbard : this fd Vibber owned to be yᵉ truth : before yᵉ Jury of Inqueft

Augˢᵗ : 3 : 1692.

### Mary Warin v. Mary Eafty.

Mary Warin affirmed before the Jury of Inqueft : that Goodwife Efty of Topsfield has afflicted her fhe or her Apperition : and that fd Efty hath af- flicted Marcy Lewis : Elizabeth Hubbard & Mary Walcot and Ann Putman : upon ye oath : yᵗ fhe has taken. Augˢᵗ 3 : 1692.

### Mary Walcott v. Mary Eafty.

The Depoeftion of Mary Walcott : who Tefti- fieth and faith on the 20ᵗʰ of may 1692 : about twelve of the clock : I faw the Apparition of good-

dy Eaftleck come and pinch and choake me : and
terrified me much and fhe told me that fhe had
blinded al our eyes, that ware afflicted only merfy
Lewis for fhe faid that fhe had not power anought
to doe itt on that day fhe was cleared : on this 20ᵗʰ
Inftante of may : 92 about an hour by fun J went
to mʳ John Putnams to fee merfey Lewis : and
their J faw the apparition of the aboue faid gooddy
Eafteck : a choaking of merfy Lewis and preffing
upon her breaft with her hands and J faw hur put
a chane aboute her neck and choaked her : and all
the while J was their J faw her hurting of her grevioufly : and fhe told me that fhe would kill her
this night if fhe could.

    Sworne Salem Village May 23ᵈ 1692.

before vs $\left. \begin{array}{l} \text{JOHN HATHORNE} \\ \text{JONATHAN CORWIN} \end{array} \right\}$ Affifts.

mary Walcott ffurther teftifieth yᵗ on 23 may
1692. mary Eftick did moft grevioufly torment me
during the time of hir examination alfo ye day J faw
hir or hir Apperanc moft grevioufly torment mercy
lewes Eliz : Hubbrt and ann putnam and I veryly
beleve in my hart that Mary Eftick is a moft dreadfull wicth and that fhe hath very often moft dreadfully tormented me and perfons aboue named by
her acts of witchcraft.

    Mary walcot declared before yᵉ Jury of Inqueft
yᵗ yᵉ above written evidence and that on yᵉ other
fide of this paper is ye truth, upon oath : Augˢᵗ 4 :
1692.

The Depofiftion of Abigaill williams Ann Putnam who teftifieth and faith that we both goeing
along with goodman Abby and Sarah Trafk the
20th of may 1692. to the houfe of Conftable Jno
Putnam to fe Mercy lewes as we ware in the way
we both faw the Apperifhtion of Gooddy Eftick
the very fame woman that was fent whom the other
day : and alfo the apperifhtion of that woman that
was with hir the other day : and the Apperifhtion
of Gooddy Eftick tould us both that now fhe was
afflecting of mrcy lewes becaufe fhe would not clear
hir as others did and wn came to nircy lewes who
laye fpeachlefs and in a fad condition we faw there
the Apperifhtions of gooddy Eftick and Jno willard
and mary witheridge afflecting and choaking mercy lewes in a moft dreadfull maner, which did moft
grevioufly affright us and jmmediately gooddy Eftick did fall upon us and tortor us, allfo Redy to
choake us to death.

Abigail Williams and An putnam Teftified to ye
truth of ye aboufd Evedence.

Salem Village May the 23d. 1692.—

Before vs JOHN HATHORNE  } Affifts.
JONATHAN CURWIN }

Ann putnam further teftifieth   on 23 may 1692.
being the laft day of the examination of Mary Eftick fhe did moft grevioufly torment me dureing
the time of hir examination alfo on the fame day J
faw Mary Eftick or hir Apperance moft grevioufly
torment and afflecd mary walcott, mercy lewes Eliz.
Hubbard and abigail william and J veryly beleue

in my hart that mary Eftick is a moft dreadfull
width and that fhe hath very often afflected me and
the perfons affore named by hir acts of witchcraft.

Ann Putnam declared to y<sup>e</sup> Jury of Inqueft y<sup>t</sup>
y<sup>e</sup> her above written evidence: is y<sup>e</sup> truth upon her
oath.    Aug<sup>st</sup>. 4: 1692.

### *Eliz. Hubbard v. Mary Eafty.*

The Depofiftion of Elizabeth Hubburt who teftifieth and faith J being caryed vp to Conftable
Jn<sup>o</sup> putnams houfe on the 20<sup>th</sup> of may 1692 to fe
Mircy lewes who laid fpeachlefs and in a fad con-
dition J faw there the apperifhtions of gooddy eftick the very fame woman that was fent whom the
other day: and  Jn<sup>o</sup> willard and mary witherridge
Afflecting and tortoring of Mircy lewes in a moft
dreadfull maner which did affright me moft grevioufly and jmmediately gooddy Eftick did fett upon
me moft dreadfully and  tortoree me almoft Ready
to choak me to death and urged me vehemently to
writ in his book.

Sworne Salem Village May the 23<sup>d</sup>: 1692.

    Before vs.  JOHN HATHORNE   } Affifts.
             JONATHAN CORWIN }

we whofe names are under writen  heaving been
along with Elizabeth Huburd this time aboue mentioned herd hir  declare what is aboue writen  and
we read it to hir when we came away and fhe faid
it was all true    this 21 may 1692.

    Thomas putnam       John putnam Jun.
Jurat in Curia Sept<sup>m</sup> 9<sup>th</sup> 1692.

Eliz. Hubburd further teftifieth that on the 23 may 1692, being the laft day of the examination of mary Eftick fhe did moft grevioufly afle&t and torment mary walcott mercy lewes Abigail williams and ann putnam by twifting and allmoft choaking them to death and I verily beleve in my heart that Mary eftick is a moft dreadfull witch and that fhe hath very often affle&ted and tormented me and perfons aboue named by hir a&ts of witchcraft.

Eliz. Hubbard declared y^e two aboue written evidences : in this paper before ye Jury of Inqueft to be y^e truth upon oath : Auguft 4. 1692.

### *Excufe of Mary Towne.*

To the Honered Court now Seting in Salem

Right honered : the Conftable of Topsffild hath farved a warant on me and too of my dafters ; to Apere this day at Salem I humby baig that your honer will not Impuet anything concerning our not coming as Contempt of athority for ware I myfelf or any of my famely fent for in any capafete of Coming we would com but we are in a ftraing condition and moft of vs can fcars, git of of our beds we are fo wake and not abell to Reid at all : as for my dafter Rebeka fhe hath ftraing fitts fometimes fhe is knoked downe of a fodin :

Mary Towne.

Date y^e 7^th of September 1692.

*Summons of Mary Town.*

W<sup>m</sup> & Mary by y<sup>e</sup> Grace of God of England
  Scotland ffrance & Ireland King & Queen de-
  fend<sup>rs</sup> of y<sup>e</sup> faith.
L. S.  To  Mary  Towne Widow and Rebecka
Towne her daughter.—Greeting :
Wee Comand you all Excufes Set apart to be and
appear at ye Court of Oyer and Terminer holden
at Salem to morrow morning at Eight of y<sup>e</sup> Clock
precifely there to Teftify y<sup>e</sup> truth to y<sup>e</sup> beft of your
knowledge on Seuer<sup>ll</sup> Jndictments Exhibited againft
Mary Eafty hereof fail not at your vtmoft perill
    Dated in Salem  Sep<sup>r</sup> 8<sup>th</sup> 1692 and in y<sup>e</sup> fourth
yeare of our Reign.
                    STEPHEN SEWALL cler


To y<sup>e</sup> Conftable of Topsfield hereof make return
  fail not.
I have warned the Widow town and her dafter
to apear at the corte acording to time fpoken of in
the warant as atefted.
        by me EPHRAIM WILDES
                        conftable of Topsfield

*Thomas Ffoffe & Elizabeth Ffoffe for Mary Eafty.*

    this may fartifie home it may cun*cern*
that wee hows names are vnder Rit*ten*
Being dafired by fome of the Realeations of
mary eftwcke to giue our abfarvations how

ſhe behaued hurſelf while ſhe Remained
in Ipſwech priſon we dow afarme that
wee ſawe noe ell carreg or behaviour in
hure but that hure daportment woſi
Sobor and civell as witnes own hands this
5 Saptem. 92.　　　thomos F[ ffoſſe

his mark

eleſebeth F[ ffoſſe

hur m

*Samuel Abby v. Mary Eaſty.*

The Depoſiſtion of Samuell Abby aged about 45
years who teſtifieth and ſaith that on the 20th of
may 1692 I went to the houſe of conſtable Jnᵒ
putnam about 9 a clock in the moring and when J
came there : Mircy lewes lay on the bed in a ſad
condition and continueing ſpeachleſs for about an
hour : the man not being at whom : the woman
deſired me to goe to Tho : putnams to bring Ann
putnam to ſe if ſhe could ſe who it was that hurt
Mircy lewes : accordingly J went : and found Abigail williams along with ann putnam and brought
them both to ſe mercy lewes : and as they ware
a goeing along the way both of them ſaid that they
ſaw the Apperiſhtion of Goody Eſtick and ſaid it
was the ſame woman that was ſent whom the other
day : and ſaid alſo that they ſaw the Apperiſhtion
of the other woman that appered with gooddy eſtick the other day, and both of them allſo ſaid that
the Apperiſhtion of gooddy Eſtick tould them that
now ſhe was affleċting of mircy lewes and when
they came to Mircy lewes both of them ſaid that

F²

they faw the Apperifhtion of gooddy Eftick and
Jn° willard and mary witheridge afflecting the body
of mircy lewes : and J continueing along with mircy
who contineued in a fad condition the greateft part
of the day being in fuch tortors as no toungue can
exprefs ; but not able to fpake : but at laft faid
Deare lord Received my foule and againe faid lord
let them not kill me quitt, but at laft fhe came to
hir felf for a little whille and was very fenfable and
then fhe faid that goody eftick faid fhe would kill
hir before midnight becaufe fhe did not cleare hir
fo as the Reft did, then againe prefently fhe fell
very bad and cried out pray for the falvation of my
foule for they will kill me.

Jurat in Curia Sep<sup>r</sup> 9<sup>th</sup> '92.

### *Sarah Trafk v. Mary Eafty.*

Sarah Trafk aged about 19 years teftifieth that
fhe went along with Abigaill williams and Ann
putnam and alfo hard them fay what is aboue writ-
en they faid : and alfo hard mercy lewes declare
what is aboue writen fhe faid.

### *Edward Putnam v. Mary Eafty.*

the depofiftion of Edward Putnam aged abought
38 years he teftifieth and faith abought 18 day of
may 1692. mary eafty the prifner now at the bar
being then feat at liberty but one the 20 and 21
days of may marcy lues was fo greuioufly aflicted
and tortred by her (as fhe herfelf and mary walcott
ann putnam Elizabeth hubbart abigel williams)

faid) I myfelf being ther prefent with feueral others
with marcy lues looked for nothing elfe : but prefent death with marcy lues for all moft the fpace
of two days and a night fhe was choked allmoft to
death in fo much we thought fumtimes fhe had
banded her mouth and teath fhut and all this uery
often untill fhuch time as we under ftood mary
eafty was laid in Jrons, allfo upon the fecond day of
mary eftys examination at the uilag marcy lues
mary wallcott elizabeth hubbart ann putnam mary
warin and abigell williams when mary eafty came
to the mar was choked in fhuch a moft greuious
maner that the honred mageftrats cold not profeed
to her examination untell they defired me$^{nd}$ haile to
go to prayer and in prayer time and fumtime after
it they remaned in this fad condition of being allmoft choked to death and when they ware abul
againe to fpeak they all with one Confent charged
her that fhe did them that mifchief. J all fo haue
hard fum of them Complain uery often of hur
hurting them with the fpindall of a wheel.

Jurat in Curia. Edward Putnam.

### *Samuel Smith v. Mary Eafty.*

The depofiftion of Samuell Smith of Boxford
aged about 25 yers who teftifieth and faith that
about fiue years fence J was one night at the houfe
of Ifaac Eftick fen$^r$ of Topsfield and J was as farr
as I know to Rude in difcorfe and the aboue faid
Efticks wife faid to me J would not haue you be fo
rude in difcorfe for J might Rue it here after and as

J was agoeing whom that night about a quarter of a mille from the faid Efticks houfe by a ftone wall J Received a little blow on my fhoulder with I know not what and the ftone wall rattled uery much which affrighted me my horfe alfo was affrighted very much but I cannot give the refon of it.

### *Margaret Redington v. Mary Eafty.*

the depefiafion of margret Redengton aged about feuenty yees teftifieth and faith that about three yers a gow J was at goodman Efties and tallking with his wife about an Jnfermety J hade and prefently after J fell jnto a moft follom condifion and the threfday before the thankfgiuing that wee hade laft Jn the afternone J was exfeding elle and that night godey Eftiey apered to mee and profered me a pece of frefh mete and J tolld hare twas not fete for the doges and J woulld haue non of ite and then fhe vanifhed awaye.

### *Petition of Mary Eafty.*

The humbl petition of mary Eaftick unto his Excellencyes S$^r$ W$^m$ Phipps and to the honour$^d$ Judge and Bench now Stting Jn Judicature in Salem and the Reuerend minifters humbly fheweth.

That wheras your poor and humble Petition being condemned to die Doe humbly begg of you to take it in your Judicious and pious confiderations that your Poor and humble petitioner knowing my own Jnnocencye Blifed be the Lord for it and fee-

ing plainly the wiles and fubtility of my accufers by
myfelfe cannot but Judg charitably of others that
are going ye fame way of myfelfe if the Lord ftepps
not mightily in i was confined a whole month upon
the fame account that J am condemed now for and
then cleared by the afflicted perfons as fome of your
honours know and in two dayes time J was cryed
out upon by them and have been confined and now
am condemned to die the Lord aboue knows my
Jnnocencye then and likewife does now as att the
great day will be known to men and Angells—I
Petition to your honours not for my own life for J
know J muft die and my appointed time is fett but
the Lord he knowes it is that if it be poffible no
more Jnnocent blood may be fhed which undoubt-
idly cannot be Anoydd Jn the way and courfe you
goe in J queftion not but your honours does to the
uttmoft of your Power in the difcouery and Select-
ing of witchcraft and witches and would not by
gulty of Jnnocent blood for the world but by my
oun Jnnocencye I know you are in the wrong way
the Lord in his infinite mercye direct you in this
great work if it be his bleffed will that no more
Jnnocent blood be fhed J would humbly begg of
you that your honors would be pleafed to examine
theis Aflicted Perfons ftrictly and keep them apart
fome time and Likewife to try fome of thefe con-
fefing wiches J being confident there is feverall of
them has belyed themfelves and others as will appeare if not in this word J am fure in the world to
come whither J am now agoing and J Queftion not

but youle fee an alteration of thei things they fay myfelfe and others haueing made a League with the Divel we cannot confeffe J know and the Lord knows as uill fhortly appeare they belye me and fo J Queftion not but they doe others the Lord aboue who is the Searcher of all hearti knowes that as I fhall anfwer it att the Tribunall feat that I know not the leaft thinge of witchcraft therefore. J cannot J dare not belye my own foule J beg you honers not to deny this my humble petition from a poor dying Jnnocent perfon and J Queftion not but the Lord will giue a blefling to yor endeuers.

To his Excellencye S$^r$ W$^m$ Phipps. Gouern$^r$ and to the honoured Judge and Magiftrates now fetting in Judicature in Salem.

### Petition of *Mary Eafty & Sarah Cloys.*

The humble Requeft of Mary Efty and Sarah Cloys to the Honoured Court.

Hambly fheweth, that whereas we two Sifters Mary Efty and Sarah Cloys ftand now before the Honoured court charged with the fufpition of Witchcraft, our humble requeft is firft that feing we are neither able to plead our owne caufe, nor if councell alowed to thofe in our condicion, that you who are our Judges, would pleafe to be of councell to us, to direct us wher in we may ftand in neede, Secondly that wheras we are not confcious to our-felves of any guilt in the leaft degree of that crime, wherof we are now accufed (in the prefence of ye Living God we fpeake it, before whofe awfull Tribunall we know we fhall ere Long appeare) nor of any other fcandloufe evill, or mifcaryage inconfiftant with Chriftianity, Thofe who have had ye longeft and beft knowledge of vs, being perfons of good report, may be fuffered to Teftifie upon oath what they know concerning each of vs, viz Mr. Capen the paftour and thofe of y^e Towne and Church of Topsfield, who are ready to fay fomething which we hope may be looked upon, as very confiderable in this matter : with the feven children of one of us, viz Mary Efty, and it may be produced of like nature in reference to the wife of Peter Cloys, her fifter, Thirdly that the Teftimony of witches, or fuch, as are afflicted, as is fuppofed, by witches may not be improved to condemn us, without other Legal evidence concurring, we hope the honoured Court and Jury will be foe tender of the lives of fuch as we are who have for many yeares lived vnder the vnblemifhed reputation of Chriftianity as not to condemne them without a fayre and equall hearing of what may be fayd for us, as well as againft us, And your poore fupplyants fhall be bound always to pray &c.

### Complaint v. Sarah Proctor.

Salem May the 21^st 1691. Thomas putnam and John Putnam of Salem Village yeomen made Complaint (before vs) on behalfe of theire Majes^ts againft Baffet ye wife of      Baffet of Lyn hufband-man and      Roote of Beverly widow, and Sarah proctor of Salem ffarms daufter of John procter of fayd place for Sundry acts of Witchcraft by them doune and Committed on the Bodys of Mary Walcot Abigail Williams, Marcy Lewis, ann putnam and others Lately whereby great hurt and Jnjury hath benne donne them therefore Craves Juftice.

Thomas putnam<br>John putnam Jun.

This Comp<sup>lt</sup> was Exhibited Salem 21<sup>st</sup> may 1692.

Before vs. JOHN HATHORNE JONATHAN CORWIN

J ord<sup>r</sup> of y<sup>e</sup> Govern<sup>r</sup> and Councill.

### *Eliza Booth v. Sarah Procter.*

May. 20<sup>th</sup> : 1692. Elizabeth Booth aged 18 years or thereabouths Teftifieth and Saith. That Sarah Procter apeared vnto her and brought her a Book and bid her fett her hand to it, this Deponent told her that fhe would not, ever fence this Deponent hath been grevioufly afflicted by her y<sup>e</sup> faid Procter, and John Procter and his wife hath Pinch<sup>t</sup> and Pricked this Deponent Likewife feverall times : and ftill continues to do fo: day

### *Eliz<sup>a</sup> Booth v. Sarah Procter & Mary Derifh.*

May y<sup>e</sup> 23. 1692. Elizabeth Booth aged 18 years or thereaboutes depofeth and faith. That Sarah Procter and Mary Derifh the wife of Michell Derifh apeared to this deponent in the night and called her Jade, Mary Derifh afked her what made her fay any thing about Sarah Procter, faid it was

well fhe did not come to the Village that Day : and
with all afflicted, and Pinched her, this Deponent
moft grevioufly and fo Continues to afflict her this
Deponet ftill, and John Procter and his wife Likewife whos name is Elizabeth Procter :

*Mary Walcott v. Sarah Procter.*

The Depoeftion of mary Walcott who teftifieth
and faith on the 20th omay 1692. faw the apparition of Sarah Procter : come and choake me and
pincht me and terrified me much and urged me
greuioufly to write in her book : but J told her I
would not touch it and then fhe tormented me
dreadfully.
Sworne Salem Village May 23d, 1692.

before vs. JOHN HATHORNE   }
          JONATHAN CORWIN } Affifts.

*Sufanah Sheldon v. Sarah Procter.*

The complaint of Sufanah Shelden of Mr andras
and Sarah Procter 20 of this may they both a flicted
me the next day Sarah Procter brought the book to
me and Sarah Procter and andres and·irog yato fo
they mad me def and dumb and blind al nigh and
the next day teh 10 of clock then cam inges and
brought his book and drod his knife and faid if I
would not touch it he would cut my throt, then
thar A pered to me a ded man hè told me his name
was Jofeph rabfon then he looked upon ingles and
told him that he murdered him and drounded him
in the fe thar was a nother man in the boot A long
Ga

with me and the boot tofed vp and doun and turend
ouer and my hand es ware clunched that J could
not lay hold, the other man layd hold and was fa-
ued then he told me that J muft tell mufter hath-
eren and told me that J fhould not reft tel J had
told it then inglifh told me that if J did he would
cut my leges of then ther a pered to me a fhinging
and told me J fhould tell of it to morah then inglefh
told me that he would go kill the gouernor if he
could he would go try he was the gretes innemy he
had then he fayd that he would kil 10 folck in
bofton before next fix day if he was not tacken up.
the greter weemen a flict me ftil not.

*David Ferneax & Jonᵃ Walcott jr. v. Sarah Procter.*

The Depofition of David Furneax Aged 23 or
their abouts and Jonathan Walcott Junior aged 21 :
who teftifieth and faith yᵗ on the 20ᵗʰ of may 1692.
about 12 of the clock we hearde mary Walcott in
one of her fitts fay that fhe faw the apparition of
Sarah Procttor come and hurte her by choaking
and pinching of her we both alfo heard her fay that
fhe brought the book to her and urged her to write
in her book we ware then both prefante and heard
her fay J would not write in your book though you
kill me.

David Furneax
Jonathan Walcott Junior.

*John Putnam jr. v. Sarah Procter.*

John putnam Juner teftifieth that very latly he hath hard Elizabeth Huburd complaine of Sarah procter that fhe hath tortored hir very much and urgeth her vehemently to writ in hir book.

*Thomas Putnam v. Sarah Procter.*

The Depofiftion of Thomas putnam who teftifieth and faith that within thefe few days I have hard Elizabeth Hubbard and Ann putnam Two of the afflected perfons grevioufly complaine of Sarah procter that fhe did tortor them very much and urged them vehemently to writ in hir book.

*Warrant v. Sufannah Roots.*

Salem May 21—1692.

To yᵉ Conftables of Beuerly.

Whereas, Complaint hath been this day made before us by Sergent Thomas Puttnam and John Puttnam both of Salem village yeomen againft Sufannah Roots of Beuerly widdow for Sundry acts of witchcrafft by her commited on the bodys of Mary wallcott Abigal williams Marcy Leuis Ann Puttnam and others. You are therefore in their Majefties names hereby Required to apprehend and forthuith bring before us Sufannah Roots of Beuerly widdow who ftands charged with Committing Sundry acts of witchcraft, as abou fᵈ to the wrong and Jnjury of the bodys of the abouenamed perfons, in order to her Examination Relating to y<sup>e</sup> abou<sup>sd</sup> premifes faile not. Dated Salem, May the 21<sup>st</sup> 1692.

> JOHN HATHORNE
> JONATHAN CORWIN

To the Marfhall of Effex or his Deputy.
pr order of y<sup>e</sup> Gouerner & Councell.

vera Copia atteft
> GEO. HERRICK Marfhall of Effex,

May 21. 1692. J doe apoint m<sup>r</sup> Jonathan Biles to bee my Lawffull Deputy to ferve this warrant.
> GEO. HERRICK Marfhall of Effex,

I haue prefented the within written warant and haue aprehended the perfon of the within men-tioned Sufanah Roots and Brought her before authority.

By me          JONATHAN BILES
> Cunftible of Beuerly.

*Andrew Elliott v. Sufannah Roots.*

An " information if it might be any help in the examination of y<sup>e</sup> perfon before you goode Roots, J being in y<sup>e</sup> houfe of m<sup>r</sup> Lauvonco Dennis fome time fince fhe was fufpected for what fhe is now before you and there was Likewife Leonard Auften of our Town of Beuerly fd Auften then fd that he thought fhe was a bad woman, his reafon was that he Living in ye houfe with f<sup>d</sup> Roots not Long Since and when he went to prayer at any time with his wife and thought fd Roots would accompany them in fd Duty but did not at any time but would with-

draw and abſent herſelfe and farther when my ſelf
and wife were gone to bed and ſhe vnto her bed
ſhe would riſe in ye night and we could hear her
talk in yᵉ roome below J lying in ye Chamber over
ſᵈ roome a if there were 5 or ſix perſons with her
more ſd Auſten might ſpeak if called therevnto as
far as know more concerning Roots

Andrew Eliott.

### *Complaint v. Benjᵃ Procter.*

Lᵗ Nathanell Ingerſall and Thomas Rayment
both of Salem village yeoman Complained on behalfe of theirs Majesᵗˢ againſt Benjamin procter the
ſon of John Procter of Salem ffarmes, and Mary
Derich yᵉ wife of Michall Derich and daufter of
William Baſſet of Lyn and        peaſe the wife of
Robert peaſe of Salem weaver for Sundry acts of
Witchcraft by them Committed on yᵉ bodys of
mary Warren Abigaile Williams and Eliz. Hubbard &c of Salem Village, whereby great hurt is
donne them therefore Craues Juſtice.

Salem May 23ᵈ 1692.        Nathannil Jngerſoll

the mark of

Thomas c Rayment

### *Warrant v. Benjᵃ Procter & als.*

To the Marſhall of Eſſex or depᵗ or Conſtables in
    Salem.

You are in theire Majesᵗˢ names hereby required
to apprehend and forthwith bring before us Benjamin procter the ſon of John Procter of Salem
farmes and Mary Derich the wife of micˡ Derich

of Salem ffarmes hufbandman, and Sarah peafe the wife of Robert peafe of Salem Weaver who all ftand charged of haueing Committed Sundry acts of Witchcraft on the Bodys of Mary Warren Abigail Williams and Eliz. Hubbert of Salem Village whereby great hurt is donne them Jn order to theire examination Relating the abouefaid premifes and hereof you are not to faile. Dated Salem May the 23ᵈ 1692.

JOHN HATHORNE,
JONATHAN CORWIN.

J order of yᵉ Gouʳ & Councill

I doe apoint mʳ John Putnam to bee my lawffull Deputy to ferue this warrant
pʳ   GEO HERRICK Marſhall of Eſx.

I haue feſed the body of Beniemin prokter and haue brought him to the place wᵗin expreſſed.
by me,   JOHN PUTNAM marſhell Debety.

*Complaint v. Martha Carrier.*

Salem May the 28ᵗʰ 1692. Joſeph Houlton and John Wallcot both of Salem village yeoman made Complaint in behalfe of theire Majesᵗˢ againſt Carrier of Andover the wife of Thomas Carrier of ſᵈ Towne hufbandman      ffoſdick of maulden or charleſtown      Reed of Marblehead the wife of Samull Reed of ſd place      Rice of Reding the wife of Nicholas Rice of ſd Towne      How the wife of James How of Topsfield Capt. John Alden of Boſton mariner, William procter of Salem ffarmes.

Capt. John fflood of Rumney marſh mariner, Mary Toothaker, the wife of Roger toothaker of Belrica and            Toothaker the dauſter of ſ<sup>d</sup> Roger Toothaker     Abbott y<sup>t</sup> liues between Jp<sup>s</sup> Topsfield & wenham ffor ſundry acts of Witchcraft by them and every one of them Committed on the bodys of Mary Walcot, Abigail Williams Marcy Lewis Ann putnam and others belonging to Salem Village or farmes Lately to the hurt and Jnjury of theire bodys therefore Craues Juſtice.

Joſeph houlton<br>John Walcott.

### *Warrant v. Martha Carrier.*

To the Marſhall of Eſſex or his dep<sup>r</sup> or to the Conſtables of Andover

You are in theire Majeſt<sup>s</sup> names hereby required to apprehend and forthwith ſecure, and bring before us martha Carrier the wife of Thomas Carrier of Andover on Tueſday next being the 31<sup>st</sup> day of this Jnſtant month of Maye about ten of the clock in the forenoon or as ſoon as may be afterwards at the houſe of L<sup>t</sup> Nathaniell Jngerſalls in Salem Village who ſtands charged with haueing Committed Sundry acts of Witchcraft on the Bodys of Mary Walcot and abigail Williams of Salem Village to theire great hurt and injury in order to her Examnation Relating to y<sup>e</sup> premiſes aboueſaid faile not.

Dated Salem May 28<sup>th</sup> 1692.

J vs.   JOHN HATHORNE   } Aſſiſts.
        JONATHAN CORWIN  }

J haue apprehended the w^tin named parſon and brought her to the place appointed.

by me    JOHN BALLARD. conſt and ouer.

### *Examination of Martha Carrier.*

The Examination of Martha Carrier 31 May. 1692.

Abigail Williams w° hurts you ?

Goody carrier of Andover.

Eliz. Hubbard who hurts you ?

Goody carrier

Suſan Shelden who hurts you ?

Goody carrier, ſhe bites me pinches me, and tells me ſhe would cut my throat if I did not ſigne her book.

Mary Walcot ſaid ſhe afflicted her and brought the book to her.

What do you ſay to this you are charged with ?

I have not done it.

Sus: Sheldon cried ſhe looks upon the black man.

Ann Putman complained of a pin tuck in her.

What black man is that ?

J know none.

Ann Putman teſtifyed there was.

Mary Warrin cryed out ſhe was prickt

What black man did you ſee ?

J ſaw no black man but your own preſence.

Can you look upon theſe and not knock them down ?

They will diſſemble if I look upon them.

You fee you look upon them and they fall down.

Jt is falfe the Devil is a liar.

J lookt upon none fince I came into the room but.

Sufan Sheldon cryed out in a Trance J wonder what could you murder 13 perfons?

Mary Walcot teftifyed the fame that there lay 13 Ghofts. All the afflicted fell into moft intollerable out cries and agonies.

Eliz Hubbard and Ann Putman teftifyed the fame that fhe had killed 13. at Andover.

Jt is a fhamefull thing that you fhould mind thefe folks that are out of their wits.

Do not you fee them?

Jf J do fpeak you will not believe me?

You do fee them faid the accufers.

You lye, I am wronged.

There is the black man wifpering in her ear faid many of the afflicted.

Mercy Lewes in a violent fit, was well upon the examinants grafping her arm.

The Tortures of the afflicted was fo great that there was no enduring of it, fo that fhe was ordered away and to be bound hand and foot with all expedition the afflicted in the meanwhile almoft killed to the great trouble of all fpectators Magiftrates and others.

Note. As foon as fhe was well bound they all had ftrange and fodain eafe. Mary Walcot told the Magiftrates that this woman told her fhe had been a witch this 40 yeares.

H<sup>a</sup>

### *Indictment v. Martha Carier.*

Anno Regis et Reginee Willm et Maria nune
   Anglia &c. Quarto :

Effex fs.   The Juro$^{rs}$ of our Sovereigne Lord and
Lady the King and Queen p$^{r}$fents That Martha
Carier wife of Thomas Carier of Andover in y$^{e}$
county of Effex hufbandman the 31 day of May
in the forth year of the Reigne of our Sovereigne
Lord and Lady William and Mary by the Grace of
God of England, Scottland ffrance and Ireland
King and Queen, defenders of the faith &. c. And
divers other Dayes and Times as well before as after, certaine deteftable Arts called Witchcraft and
Soceries,  Wickedly and ffellonioufly hath vfed
Practifed and Exercifed at and within the Townefhip of Salem in the County of Effex afores$^{d}$ in,
and Upon and ag$^{t}$ one Elizabeth Hubbard of Salem
in y$^{e}$ County of Effex afores$^{d}$ by which faid Wicked
Arts the faid Elizabeth hubbard the thirty firft day
of May in the fforth year abouefd and Divers other
Dayes, and times, as well before as after was and
is Tortured Afflicted Pined Confumed Wafted and
Tormented ag$^{t}$ the  Peace of our Sovereigne Lord
and Lady the King and Queen : and ag$^{t}$ the fforme
of the Statute in that cafe made and Provided.

   Witneffes.

| | |
|---|---|
| Elizabeth Hubbard | Jurat. Ann Putnam |
| Mary Walcutt Jurat. | Mary Warren Jurat. |

*Summons to witneſſes v. Martha Carrier.*

Wᵐ & Mary by ye Grace of God of England
Scotland ffrance & Ireland King and Queen
defendʳˢ of yᵉ faith &cᵃ

L. S.   To ye Conſtable or Conſtables of Andover Greeting.

Wee Comand you to Warn and give Notice vnto
Allen Toothaker Ralph ffarnum Junʳ John ffarnum
ſon of Ralph farnum ſenʳ Benjamin Abbot and his
wife Andrew ffoſter Phebe Chandler daughter of
Wᵐ Chandler : Samˡ Holt Senʳ Samuel Preſton
Junʳ that they and Euery of them be and perſonaly
appear at ye Court of Oyer and Termina to be hed
by adjournment on Tueſday next at Ten of ye
clack in yᵉ Morning there to teſtifye yᵉ truth to yᵉ
beſt of their knowledge on certain Jndictment to
be Exhibited againſt Martha Carrier of Andover
hereof fail not at your vtmoſt perill and make return of your doings herein.

Dated in Salem  July 30ᵗʰ 1692.
          STEPHEN SEWALL Cler.

Jn obedence to this writ J haue timely warned
the perſons hoſe names are herein written and euery
one of them this 1 day of Auguſt 1692.

By me JOHN BAILAY conſtable of Andover.

*Benjᵃ Abbott v. Martha Carier.*

The teſtymony of Beniamin Abbutt aged about
31 years Saith : laſt march was twelfe months, then

haueing fome land granted to me by the Towne
of Andover near to goodman Carriers his land,
and when this land came to be laid out goodwiffe Carrier was very Angery, and faid fhe would
ftick as Clofs to Benjamin Abbut as the bark Stooke ·
to the Tree and that J fhould Repent of it afore
feuen yeares Came to an End and that docter prefcott could neuer cure me : Thefe words were heard
by Allin Toothaker fhe alfo faid to Ralph farnam
Jun^r that fhe would hold my nofs fo Clofe to the
grindftone as Ever it was held Since my name was
Beniamin Abbut prefently after J was taken with
a Swelling in my ffoot and then was taken with a
payne in my fide Exkfedingly Tormented, wich
bred to a fore, which was lancit by docter prefcott
and Seuerall gallons of Corruption did run out as
was Judged and fo Continued about fix weeks very
bad, and then one other fore did breed in my grine
wich was lancit by doct. prefcott alfo and Continued very bad awhile and then another fore breed in
my grine which was alfo cutt and putt me to very
great miffery, So that it brough me almoft to
Deaths doore, & Continued, untill goodwiffe Carrier was Taken and Carried a waye by the Conftable, and that very day J began to grow better, my
foers grew well and J grew better Every day and
fo haue been w^ell ever fince and have great caufe
to think that the f^d Carrier had a great hand in my
ficknefs and mifery.

beniamin Abbut.

Jurat in Curia Aug^t 3^d 1692.

Atteft  STEP. SEWALL Cler.

### *Sarah Abbott v. Martha Carrier.*

The depofition of Sarah Abbott aged about 32 years teftifieth that fince my hufband had a parcell of land granted by yᵉ Towne, lying near ye land of Thomas Carrier, (which as J have heard) his wife martha Carrier was greatly troubled att and gaue out threatning words that my hufband Benjamin Abbott has not been only afflicted in his body, as he teftifies, but alfoe that ftrange and unufuall things has happened to his Cattle, for fome have died fuddenly and ftrangely, which we could not tell any naturall reafon for, and one Cowe Cleaned a fourthnight before fhe Calved but yᵉ Cowe died afterwards ftrangely though fhe calved well foe far as we could perceive, and fome of ye Cattle would come out of ye woods wᵗʰ their tongues hanging out of their mouths in a ftrange and affrighting manner, and many fuch things, which we can giue noe account of ye reafon of, unlefs it fhould be yᵉ effects, of martha Carrier threatings.

Jurat in Curia. Sarah + Abbott
her mark
Augᵗ 3ᵈ 1692. atteft. STEPH. SEWALL Cler.

### *John Roger v. Martha Carrier.*

The depofition of John Rogger of Billreca aged 50 yeares or Thereabouts Saith, That about Seven yeares Since Martha Carrier being a Nigh Neighbour vnto this dponᵗ and there hapening fome difference betwixt vs, She gave forth feueral threatñing words as ſhe often vſed to doe and in a ſhort time after this deponent had two large luſty ſowes wᶜʰ frequented home daily that were loſt and this deponent found one of them dead nigh yᵉ ſᵈ Carriers houſe wᵗʰ both Eares cut of and yᵉ other ſow J Neuer heard of to this day, and yᵉ ſame ſummer to yᵉ beſt of my rembrance J had a Cow wᶜʰ vſed to give a good Mess of milk twice a day and of a ſudden She would giue little or none Every Morn⋅ing though a Night ſhe gaue as formerly and this continued about ye ſpace of a month in wᶜʰ time J had three meals milke on three Severall Mornings not Succeſſively and no more though One Night three of vs Watched yᵉ Cow all night yet J could have no milke in yᵉ morning of her and about yᵉ monthes End She gave milke as formerly ſhe vſed by all wᶜʰ J did in my Conſcience belieue then in yᵉ day of it and have ſo done euer ſince and doe yet belieue that Martha Carrier was yᵉ occaſion of thoſe Jll accidents by Meanes of Witchcraft ſhe being a very Malicious woman and further ſaith not.

John † Rogger
marke of

*Phebe Chandler v. Martha Carrier.*

The depoſition of Phebe Chandlʳ aged about 12 years. Teſtifieth that about a fourtnight before Martha Carrier, was ſent for to Salem to be examined, upon yᵉ Sabbath day when ye pſalm was ſinging, ſᵈ Martha Carrier took me ſd deponent by ye

fhoulder and fhaked me, in ye meeting houfe and
afked me where I lived, but J made her no anfwer,
(not doubting but that fhe knew we, hauing liued
fome time the next door to my futhers houfe, on
one fide of y<sup>e</sup> way) and that day that f<sup>d</sup> Martha
Carrier was ceafed, my mother fent me to Carry
fome bear to y<sup>e</sup> folks y<sup>t</sup> were att work in ye lott,
and when I came within y<sup>e</sup> fence, there was a voice
in ye bufhes (which J thought was Martha Carriers uoice, which J know well) but faw noe body,
and y<sup>e</sup> voice afked me what J did there and whether J was going : which greatly frighted me, foe
that J run as faft as J could to thofe att work, and
told them what J had heard, about an hour & half
or two hours after, my mother fent me again upon
y<sup>e</sup> fame occafion, to y<sup>e</sup> workmen abouf<sup>d</sup> and Com-
ming home, near y<sup>e</sup> place abouf<sup>d</sup> where I heard
that voice before, J heard y<sup>e</sup> fame uoice, as J judged, ouer my head, faying J fhould be poyfoned
within two or three days, which accordingly happened, as J conceiue, for J went to my fifter Al-
lens farm ye fame day, and on friday following,
about one half of my right hand was greatly fwo-
len and exceeding painfull, and alfoe part of my face,
which J can give no account how it came and Continued uery bad fome days, and feueral times fince
J haue been troubled with a great weight upon my
breaft, and upon my leggs, when J haue been going about, fo that J could hardly goe, which J haue
told my mother of : And y<sup>e</sup> laft fabbath day was
feauennight, J went to meeting very well in y<sup>e</sup>

morning, and went to my place where J ufed to
fitt (ye minifters not being come) and Richard Carrier fon of abouefd Martha looked uery earneftly
upon me, and imediately my hand which had formerly been poyfoned as abouefd began to pain me
greatly, and J had a ftrange burning att my ftom-
ake and then was ftruck deaf that J could not hear
any of ye prayer, nor finging till ye two or three
laft words of ye finging.

Jurat in Curia      Phebe † Chandler.
her mark

### *Bridget Chandler v. Martha Carrier.*

Bridget Chandler aged 40 years mother ye fd
Phebe Teftifieth yt in ye day of it her daughter
Complained as aboue is expreffed.

Jurat in Curia.

### *Allen Toothaker v. Martha Carrier.*

The Depofition of Allin Toothaker aged about.
22 years Saith, J heard martha Carrier fay that
Beniamin Abbutt would wifh he had not medled
with that land fo Near our houfe for She would
ftick as Cols to him as the barck to the tree afore
feauen years Com a but, and that docter prefcott
fhould Neuer Cure him, and about laft march
Richard Carrier and my felfe had Som difference
and faid Richard pulled me downe by the hair of
my head to the ground for to beat me, J defired
him to lett me Riffe, when J was up J went to
ftrike at him, but J fell down flatt upon my back

to the ground and had not power to ſtir hand Nor
foote then J toold ſayd Richard J would yeald to
him and owne him the beſt man and then J ſaw
Martha Carrier goe of from my breſt, butt when
J was Riſen up J ſaw non of her, J was Wounded
in the Warre, Martha Carrier tould me J ſhould
never be Cured, afore ſhe was Aprehended J could
thruſt in my Wound a knitting nedle four Jnches
deep but, ſince She have been taken J am tho-
roughly healed, and haue had more Eaſe then J
haue had in halfe a year before Sometimes when
Martha Carrier and J had ſome difference ſhe would
Clap her hand at me and ſay J ſhould get nothing
by it, and ſo with in a day or two J loſt a three year
old heffer : Next a yealin, and then a Couw, and
then had ſom little difference againe and loſt a
yearlin, And J know not of any naturall Cauſes of
ye death of the abouſᵈ Creatures, but haue always
feared it hath been ye effect of my Aunt Martha
Carrier her malice :

Jurat in Curia.        *Allen* ✝ *Toothaker*
                                   his mark

*Samuel Preſton v. Martha Carrier.*

Samuel Preſton aged about 41 years Saith yᵗ about
2 yeares Since J had ſome difference wᵗʰ Martha
Carrier wᶜʰ alſo had hapened Seuerˡˡ times before
and ſoon after J loſt a Cow in a Strange manner
being Caſt upon her back wᵗʰ her heels vp in firm
ground when ſhe was very Luſty it being in June

Iª

and within abo^t month after this ye f^d martha and
J had fome difference again at which Time fhe told
me J had loft a Cow lately and it fhould  not or
fhould not be long  before  J fhould  loofe another
w^ch accordingly came to pafs,  for J had a Cow y^t
was well kept w^th Englifh Hay and J could not
pceive y^t fhe aild any thing and y^t fhe pined and
quickley lay downe as if fhe was afleep and dyed.
    Jurat in Curia.                                    .

*Francis Dane Sen^r for Martha Carrier.*

R.^vd S^r Whereas there haue been divers reports rayf-
ed, how and by what hands J know not, of the Towne
of Andover, and the Jnhabitants, J thought it my
bounden duty to giue an account to others,  fo farr
as J had the vnderftanding of any thing amongft
us. Therefore do declare that, J beleeue the reports
haue been Scandalous, and unjuft neither will bear
y^e light.   As for that, of the Sine, and bifers J never heard of it, till this laft Summer, and the Sab-
both after J fpake publiqly concerning it finçe
which J beleeue it hath not been tryed, As for fuch
things of Charmes, and ways to find their cattle,
J never heard, nor doe J know any Neighbour that
ever did fo, neither have J any grounds to beleeue
it, I haue lived above Fortie foure yeares in the
Towne, and haue been frequent among y^e Jnhabitants, and in my healthfull, yeares oft at their ha-
bitations, and fhould certainly heard if fo it had
been. That there was a fufpicion of Goodwife Carrier among fome of us before fhe was apprehended,

J know. As for any other perfons, J had no fufpicion of them, and had Charity been put on the
Diuel would not haue had fuch an advantage againft
us, and J beleeve many Jnnocent perfons haue been
accufed, and Jmprifoned yᵉ Conceit of Speƈtre Evidence as an infallible mark did too far prevaile with
us Hence we fo eafily parted with our neighbours
of honeft and good report, and members in full
Comunion, hence we fo eafily parted with our
Children, when we knew nothing in their liues,
nor any of our neighbours to fufpeƈt them and thus
things were hurried on, hence fuch ftrange breaches
in families, feverall that came before me, that fpoke
with much fobriety, profeffing their innocency,
though through the Devils Subtilty they were to
much urged to confeffe, and we thought we did doe
well in fo doing, yet they ftood their ground profeffing they knew nothing, never fay ye deuil, never
made a Covenant with him, and ye like, and fome
children that we haue caufe to feare that dread has
overcome them to accufe themfelves in that they
knew not. Stephen Johnfon Mary Barker yᵉ
daughters of Lieftenant Barker, and fome others by
what we had from them with fuitable affeƈtions we
haue caufe to beeleeve they were in the truth, and
fo held to it, if after many indeavours they had not
been overcome to fay wᵗ they never knew. This
hath been a trouble to me, confedering how oft it,
hath been fayd, you are a witch, you are guilty,
and who affliƈts this maid or the like, and more
then this hath been fayd, charging perfons with

witchcraft, and what flatteries haue paſt from ; and threats and telling them they muſt goe to priſon and this I feare haue cauſed many to fall, our Sinne of Jgnorance wherein we thought we did well, will not excuſe us when we know we did amiſſe but whatever might be a ſtumbling block to others muſt be removed, elſe we ſhall procure divine diſpleaſure, and Euills will unavoidably breake in upon us.

    Yours Sʳ who am though unworthie a friend to them yᵗ are friends to Sion.

    Andever Jan 2. 92.

                    Francis Dane Ser.

    Concerning my Daughter Elizabeth Johnſon, J never had ground to ſuſpeɛt her neither have J heard any other to accuſe her, till for Speɛtre evidence ſhe was brought forth, but this J muſt ſay, ſhe was weake, and incapacious, fearfull, and in that reſpeɛt J feare ſhe hath falſely accuſed herſelf and others Not long before that ſhe was ſent for ſhe ſpake as to her owne particular, that ſhe was ſure ſhe was no witch, and for her daughter Elizabeth, ſhe is but ſimpliſh at ye beſt, and J feare the common ſpeech that was frequently ſpread among us, of theire liberty, if they would confeſſe, and the like expreſſion, uſed by ſome, haue brought many into a ſnare, the Lord direɛt and guide thoſe that are in place, and giue us all ſubmiſſiue wills, and let the Lord doe with me, and mine, what ſeems good in his owne eyes.

*Warrant v. Elizabeth How.*

To ye Conſtable of Topsfield

You are in theyre Majeſtyes Names hereby Required to Apprehend and bring before us Elizabeth How yᵉ wife of James How of Topsfield Huſbandman, on Tueſday next being yᵉ thirty firſt day of May about Ten of yᵉ Clock in yᵉ forenoon at yᵉ houſe of Levᵗ Nathaniell Ingerſolls of Sallem Village, Whoe Stand Charged wᵗʰ Sundry Acts of Witchcraft done or Committed on yᵉ bodyes of Mary Walcott, Abigall Williams and others of Salem Village, to theyr great hurt, in order to hir examination, Relateing to yᵉ abouefᵈ premiſes, and hereof you are nott to fayle.

· Datᵈ Salem May 28ᵗʰ 1692.

J vs. JOHN HATHORNE } Aſſiſts.
JONATHAN CORWIN }

In obedence to this warrant J have apprehended Elizabeth How the wife of Jems how on the 29ᵗʰ of May 1692, and haue brought har unto the houſe of leftenant nathaniell englofons according too to warant as ateſted by me.

EPHRAIM WILDES conſtabell
for the town of Topsfield.

Dated may 31ˢᵗ 1692.

*Examination of Elizabeth How.*

The examination of Eliz. How. 31. May 1692.

Mercy Lewis and Mary Walcot fell in a fit quickly after the examinant came in.

Mary Walcot faid that this woman the examinant had pinch<sup>d</sup> her and choakt this month. Ann Putman faid fhe had hurt her three times. What fay you to this charge ? Here are them that charge you with witchcraft.

If it was the laft moment I was to live, God knows J am innocent of any thing in this nature.

Did not you take notice that now when you lookt upon Mercy Lewis fhe was ftruck down ?

J cannot help it,

You are charged here, what doe you fay ?

J am innocent of any thing of this nature.

Js this the firft time that ever you were accufed ? Yes S<sup>r</sup>

Do not you know that one at Ipfwich hath accufed you ?

This is the firft time that ever J heard of it.

You fay that you never heard of thefe folks before.

Mercy Lewis at length fpake and charged this woman with hurting and pinching her. And then Abigail Williams cryed fhe had hurt me a great many times, a great while and fhe hath brought me the book, Ann Putman had a pin ftuck in her hand.

What do you fay to this ?

J cannot help it.

What confent have you given ?

Mary Warren cryed out fhe was prickt

Abig Williams cryed out that fhe was pincht, and great prints were feen in her arm.

Have not you feen fome apparition?

No, never in all my life.

Thofe that haue confeffed, they tell us they ufed images and pins, now tell us what you haue ufed.

You would not haue me confefs that which J know not.

She lookt upon Mary Warren, and faid Warren violently fell down. Look vpon this maid viz: Mary Walcot, her back being towards the Examinant, Mary Warren and Ann Putman faid they faw this woman upon her, Sufan Sheldon faith this was the woman that carryed her yefterday to the Pond, Sus. Sheldon carried to the examinant in a fit and was well upon grafping her arm.

You faid you never heard before of thefe people.

Not before the warrant was ferved upon me laft Sabbath day, John Jndian cryed out O fhe bites, and fell into a grevious fit; and fo carried to her in his fit and was well upon her grafping him,

What do you fay to thefe things, they can not come to you?

Sr I am not able to give account of it.

Cannot you tell what keeps them off from your body?

J cannot tell, J know not what it is?

That is ftrange that you fhould do thefe things and not be able to tell how.

This a true account of the examination of Eliz: How taken from my charaćters written at the time thereof. Witnefs my hand

Sam. Parris.

*Witneffes v. Elizabeth How.*

Witneffes againft goody How.

| | |
|---|---|
| Samuel Pearly & his wife. | Deborah Pearly |
| Timothy Pearly | Sarah Andrews |
| deacon Cumnins his wife | Thomas Heafons wife |
| Sofeph Andrews & his wife | of boxford |
| Boxford | John fherring of Ipf- |
| Jofeph Safford Jpfwich | wich |
| | Abram Howe wife |

*Indictment v. Elizabeth How.*

Anno Regis et Reginee Willm et Mariee nune
   Anglice &c Quarto.

Effex fs.   The Juror⁵ for our Sovereigne Lord
and Lady the King and Queen Prfents That Elizabeth How wife of James How of Ipfwich the thirty firft day of May in the forth year of the Reigne
of our Sovereigne Lord and Lady, William & Mary
by the Grace of God of England Scottland ffrance,
and Jreland King and Queen defenders of the
ffaith &c. and Divers other dayes and times as well
before as after Certaine Deteftable Arts called witchcraft, and forceries wickedly and ffellonioufly hath
vfed Practifed and Exercifed at and within the
Townefhip of Salem in the county of Effex aforefaid in upon and againft one Mary Wolcott of Salem Villiage finglewoman by which faid wicked
arts the faid Mary Walcott the 31ˢᵗ day of May in
the forth year as abouefaid and Divers other Dayes
and times as well before as after was and is Tor-

tured Afflicted Pined Confumed wafted and Tormented and alfo for fundrey other Acts of witchcraft
by faid Elizabeth How Committed and Done before and fince that time, agt the Peace of our Sovereigne Lord and Lady the King and Queen, and
againſt the forme of the Statute in that cafe made
and Provided.

| | |
|---|---|
| Mary Wolcott Jurat, | Jofeph Andrews & wife |
| Ann Putman Jurat, | Sarah Jurat |
| Abigall Williams | Jno. Sherrin Jurat. |
| Sam$^{ll}$ Pearly & wife | Jos. Safford Jurat |
| Ruth. Jurat | ffrancis Lane Jurat. |
| Abraham ffofter wife Jurat | Jfack Cumins Jun$^r$ Jurat. |

*Timothy Perley & Deborah Perley v. Elizabeth How.*

the firſt of iune 1692. the depofition of timothi
Perley and Deborah Perley his wife, timoth Perley
aged about 39 and his wife about 33 there being
fom diferance betwene goode how that is now
feifed namely Elizabeth How wife of James How
Jun$^r$ and timothi Perli abouefaid about fom bords
the night folowing thereof our cous lay out and
finding of them the next morning we went to milk
them and one of them did not give but two or
thre fpoone fuls of milk and one of the other cous
did not give above halfe a Pinte and the other gave
aboute a quart and thefe cous ufed to give three or
four quarts at a meale two of thes cous continued
to giue litle or nothig four or five meals and yet
thai went in a good inglefh pafture and within four

K²

.

dais the cous gave ther full Proportion of milk that
thai ufed to give.

furder deborah Perley teftifieth and as confern-
ing hanah Perley Samuel Perleys daughter that was
fo fore afflicted her mother and fhe coming to our
houfe hanah Perley being fuddinli fcared and f<sup>d</sup>
the<sup>r</sup>s that woman fhe goes into the oven and out
againe and then fell into a dredful fit and when J
have afked her when fhe faid that woman what
woman fhe ment fhe tould me ieams howfwife
fometime hanah Perley went along with me to
ieams hows an fone fell into a fitt goode how was
ueri loving to her and when the garl and J came
away i afked whi fhe talked fo of goode How being
fhe was fo louing to her fhe tould me that if i were
aflicted as fhe was that i would talk as bad of her
as fhe did at another time i faw goode how and
hanah Perley together and thai were veri louing
together and after goode How was gone i afked her
whi fhe was fo louing to goode how when thai
were together fhe tould me that fhe was afraide to
doe other wife for then goode how would kil her.

deborah Perley.

Timothy Pearly And Deborah his wife declared
to y<sup>e</sup> Jury of inqueft to all of y<sup>e</sup> above written evidence, on this fide of this paper, that it is y<sup>e</sup> truth
upon oath : June 30<sup>th</sup>

*Sam<sup>l</sup> Perley & ux v. Elizabeth How.*

the firft of iune 1692. the depofition of Samuel
Perley and his wife aged about 52 an his wife about

46 years of age we hauing a dafter about ten years
of age being in a forowful condition this being fone
after a faling out thai had bene betwen ieams how
and his wife and and mifelf our daughter told us
that it was ieams hows wife that afflicted her both
night and day fomtimes complaining of being
Pricked with Pins and fometimes faling doun into
dredfull fits and often fai i could never aflict a dog
as goode how aflicts me mi wife and i did often
chide her for naming goode how being loth her
name fhold be defamed but our daughter would
tell us that though we would not beleue her now
yet you wil know it one day we went to feveral
docters and thai tould us that fhe was under an
evil hand our daughter tould us that when fhe came
nere the fire or water this witch Puls me in and
was often foreli burnt and fhe would tel us what
cloaths fhe wore and would fai there fhe goes and
there fhe goes & now fhe is gone into the ouen and at
thefe fights faling down into dredful fits and thus our
daughter continuing about two or three years con-
ftantli afirming to the laft that this goode how that
is now feifed was the caufe of her forows and fo
Pined a wai to Skin and bone and ended her forowful life, and this we can ateft vpon oath nith Perleys mark

Sam[ll] Pearly and his wife declared y[e] above
written to be y[e] truth upon oath, after this the
abouefaid goode how had a mind to wyn to ipfwich church thai being unfatisfied fent to us to
bring in what we had againft her and when we had
declared to them what we knew thai fee caufe to

Put a Stop to her coming into the Church within a few days after J had a cow wel in the morning as far as we knew this cow was taken ftrangli runing about like a mad thing a litle while and then run into a great Pon—and drouned herfelf and as fone as fhe was dead mi fons and mifelf towed her to the fhore and fhe ftunk fo that we had much a doe to flea her. As for the time of our daughters being taken ill it was in the yere of our lord 1682.

Sam⁰ Pearly Declared to ye Jury of inqueft that all ye above written is yᵉ truth upon oath, June 30ᵗʰ 92.

### Samuel Phillips for Elizabeth How.

The teftimony of Samuel Phillips aged about 67, minifter of the word of God in Rowly, who fayth, that mr payfon (minifter of gods word alfoe in Rowley) and myfelf went, being defired to Samuel pearly of ipfwich to fe theire young daughter who was vifeted with ftrang fitts and in her fitts (as her father and mother affirmed) did mention good wife How the wife of James How Junior of Ipfwich, as if fhe was in the houfe and did afflict her : when we were in the houfe the child had one of her fitts but made noe mention of goodwife how : and when the fitt was over and fhe came to herfelf, goodwife how, went to the child and took her by the hand and afkt her whether fhe had ever done her any hurt And fhe anfwered noe never and if J did complain of you in my fitts J knew not, that J did foe : J further can affirm vpon oath that young

Samuel Pearly, Brother to the afflicted girle looking out of a chamber window (I and the afflicted
child being without dores together) and fayd to his
fifter fay goodwife How is a witch, fay fhe is a
witch, and the child fpake not a word that way,
but I lookt up to the window where the youth
ftood and rebuked him for his boldnefs to ftir up
his fifter to accufe the faid goodw : How when as
fhe had cleared her from doing any hurt to his
fifter in both our hearing, and J added no wonder
that the child in her fitts did mention Goodwife
How, when her neareft relations were foe frequent
in expreffing theire fufpitions in the childs hearing
when fhe was out of her fitts that the fayd Goodwife How, was an Inftrument of mifchief to the
child.

    Rowley 3 June 1692.    Samuel Phillips.

  I Edward Paifon of ye Towne abovef$^d$ tho' prefent at y$^e$ place and time aforef$^d$ yet cannot evidence
in all the particulars mentioned : Thus much is yet
in my remembrance, viz$^t$ being in ye abovef$^d$ Pearleys houfe fome confiderable time before ye f$^d$
Goodw How came in : their Afflicted Daughter
upon fomething that her mother fpake to her with
tartnefs, prefently fell into one of her ufual ftrange
fitts, during which fhe made no mention (as I obferved) of ye above f$^d$ How her name, or any thing
relating to her, fometime after, the f$^d$ How came in,
when f$^d$ Girl had recovered her capacity, her fitt
being over f$^d$ How took f$^d$ Girl by ye hand, afked
her whether fhe had ever done her any hurt ? y$^e$

child anfwered no never : with feveral expreffions
to y$^t$ purpofe which I am not able particularly to
recount, &c,

Rowley, June 3 1692.        Edward Paifon.

### *Deborah Hadley v. Elizabeth How.*

The Depofition of Debory Hadley aged about
70 yeares : this Deponant teftifieth and f$^{th}$ that J
have lived near to Elizabeth How (ye wife of James
How Junior of Ipfwich) 24 year and have found
her a Neighbourly woman Confciencious in her
dealing, fatthfull to her pmifes and Chriftianlike in
her Converfation fo far as I have obferved and further faith n$^t$

June 24. 1692.        Deborah Hadley.

### *Daniel Warner John Warner & Sarah Warner for Elizabeth How.*

from Jpfwich Ju- y$^e$ 25 : 1692.  this may fer-
tify hom it may conferne we being defired to wright
fome thing in y$^e$ behalfe of y$^e$ wife of Jeams how
Junior of Ipfwich hoe is aprehended upon fuffpition
of being gilty of ye Sin witchcraft and now in Salem priffon upon ye fame acount for ouer oun partes
we haue bin well aquainted w$^t$ hur for aboue twenty yeers we never fee but y$^t$ fhe cared it very wel
and y$^t$ both hur wordes and actions wer always fuch
as well become a good criftian : we ofte fpake to
hur of fome things y$^t$ wer reported of hur y$^t$ gave
fome fuffpition of y$^t$ fhe is now charged w$^t$ and fhe

always profeffing hur Inofency y<sup>r</sup> in offen defiring
our prayers to god for hur y<sup>t</sup> god would keep hur
in his fear and y<sup>t</sup> god would fupport her under hur
burdin we have offen herd hur Speaking of thos
perfons y<sup>t</sup> raifd thos reports of hur and we never
heerd hur Speake badly of y— for ye fame, but in
ouer hering hath offen faid y<sup>t</sup> fhe defired god that
he would fantify y<sup>t</sup> afflicttion as well as othars for
hur fpiritual good.

    .     Daniel Warner fen<sup>r</sup>    John Warner fen<sup>r</sup>

*Simon Chapman & Mary Chapman for Elizabeth*
*How.*

Ipfwich June the 25<sup>th</sup>, 1652. The teftimony
of Simon Chapman agid About 48 years teftifieth
and fayth that he hath ben Aquainted with the wiuef
of James how iunr as a naybar for this 9 or 10 yers
and he never faw any harm by hur but that That
hath bin good for J found hur Jouft Jn hur delling
faythfooll too hur promicifis I haue had ocation to
be in the compiny of good wief howe by the fortnight togathar at Thayar hous : and at othar times
and I found at all Tims by hur difcors fhee was a
woman of afliktion and mourning for fin in hur
felves And othars and when fhe met with eny
Afliktion fhe femid to ioftifi god and fay that Itt
was all better than fhe deffufid that it war. By falls
aqufations from men and fhe yuft To bles god that
fhe got good by afliktions for it med hur exfamin
hur oun hart. I neuar herd hur refil any perfon
that hath akufid hur with wichcraft but pittied

them and fayid i pray god for giue them for thay
harm them felues more then me Thof i am a gret
finar yit i am cler of that fayid fhe and fuch Kind
of afliktions doth but fet me a exfamining my oun
hard and J find God wondarfolly feportining me
and comfarting me by his word and promifis fhe
femid to be a woman thron in that gret work of
conuiktion and conuertion which J pray god mak
us all.

Simon Chapman
my wiuef Mary Chapman cane Teftifi to the
moft of this abou retan as witnes my hand

Mary Chapman.

### *Ifaac Cummins Sr v. Elizabeth How.*

Jvn 27. 1692. The difpofition of Ifaac commins
fyne^r aged about fixty years or thare abouts who
teftyfyeth and faith that about aight yers agon
James how ivn^r of ipfwech came to my hous to
borow a hors J not being at home my fon ifaac,
told him as my fon told me whan i cam home i
hade no hors to ride on bot my fon ifaac did tell the
faid how that his father hade no hors to ride on
but he hade a mare the which he thovght his father wovld not be wiling to lend this being vpon a
thvrfday the next day being fryday J took the mare
and my felf and my wif did ride on this maer abvte
half a mile to an naighbours hovs and home again
and when we came home J tvrned the maer out
the maer being as well to my thinking as ever fhe

was next morning it being faterday abovt fun rifing
this faid maer ftood neer my doore and the faid
maer as i did aperehend did fhow as if fhe had bin
much abvfed by riding and here flefh as J thovg
mvch wafted and her movth mvch femenly to my
aperehantion mvch abvfed and hvrt with y^e bridel
bits J feing ye maer in fvch a fad condition J toke
vp the faid maer and pot her into my barn and fhe
wold eate no maner of thing as for provender or ary
thing w^c i gave her then J fent for my brother thomas andros which was living in boxford the faid
Anderos came to my hovs, J not being at home
when J came home a letil afore night my brother anderos told me he head giving the faid mear fonthing
for the bots bvt as he coold pvrfeve it did do her no
good bvt faid he J cannot tell but fhe may have the
baly ach and faid he i wil try one thing more my
brother anderos faid he wold take a pipe of tobaco
and lite it and pot itt in to the fvndement of the
mare J told him that I thought it was not lawfvll
he faid it was lawfvll for man or beaft then I toke
a clen pipe and filled it with tobaco and did lite it
and went with the pipe lite to the barn then the
faid anderos vfed the pipe as he faid before he wold
and the pipe of tobaco did blaze and bvrn blew then
I faid to my brother anderos you fhall try no more
it is not lawfvl he faid I will try again once mor
which he did and then thar arofe a blaze from the
pipe of tobaco which feemed to me to cover the
bvtocks of the faid mear the blaz went vp ward towards the roof of the barn and in the roof of the
**L**ᵃ

barn thar was a grate crackling as if the barn wovld
have falen or bin bvrnt which femed fo to vs which
ware within and fom that ware with ovt and we
hade no other fier in the barn bvt only a candil and
a pipe of tobaco and then J faid I thought my barn
or my mear muft goe the next day being Lords day
J fpoke to my brother anderos at noone to come to
fee the faid mear and faid anderos came and what
h did J fay not the fame Lords day at night my
naighbour John Hvnkins came to my hovs and he
and J went into my barn to fee this mear faid hvnkins faid and if I ware as you i wolvd cut of a pece
of this mear and burn it J faid no not to day bvt if
fhe lived til to morrow morning he might cut of a
pece off of her and bvrn if he wovld prefentely as
we hade fpoken thefe words we ftept ovt of the
barn and emedeiatly this faid mear fell down dade
and never ftvred as we coold pvrfeve after fhe fell
down but lay dead.

Jfac Comings fenr declared to ye Jury of Inqueft
that ye above written evidence is ye truth upon
oath June 30th 1692.

*Jofeph Knowlton for Elizabeth C. How.*

from Ipfwich June 27, 1692. Jofeph knoulton
being acquainte with the wife of James How Junr
as a neighbour and fomtims bording in the houfe,
and at my firft coming to live in thofe parts which
was about ten years ago J hard a bad Report of
her about Samuell perleys garle which caufed me
to take fpefhall noates of her life and converfation

ever fence and I have afked her if fhe could freely
forgive them that Raifed fuch Reports of her fhe
tould me yes with all her heart defiering that God
would give her a heart to be more humble vnder
fuch a prouidences and further fhe fayd fhe was
willing to doe any good fhe could to them as had
don vnneighbourly by her alfo this I have taken
notes of that fhe would deny herfelf to doe a neighbour a good turn and alfo J have known her to be
faithfull in he word and honeft in her dealeings as
fare as ever I faw

Jofeph knoulton aged forty tu
mary knowlton aged thury tu

*James How fen for Elizabeth How.*

information for Elizebeth How the wife of Iames
How Iun Jams How Sen aged about 94 fayth
that he liuing by her for about thirty years hath
taken notes that fhe hath caried it well becoming
her place as a daughter as a wife in all Relation feting a fide humain infurmitys as becometh a Chrif-
tion with Refpect to myfelf as a father very duty-
fully and a wifife to my fon uery Carefull loveing
obediant and kind confidering his want of eye fight
tenderly leading him about by the hand now defiering god may guide your honours to fe a differans
between predigous and Confentes.  I Reft yours to
Sarve                     James How fen of Ipfwich.
Dated this 28 day of June 1692.

### *Isaac Cummins jr v. Elizabeth How.*

June 28<sup>th</sup> 1692. The teftimony of Jfack Comings Juner aged about 27 years Teftifieth and faith
y<sup>t</sup> James Hough Juner came to my fathers houfe
when he was not at home he afked me if my father
had ever a hors and J told him no he afked me if
he had Ever a maer and I told him yefh he afked
me if J Thought my father would lend him his
maer and J told him J did not Think he would
vpon w<sup>ch</sup> in a fhort Tyme after my father and mother Ridd their maer to Their Neighbours houfe
y<sup>e</sup> fame maer w<sup>ch</sup> fd hough would have Borowed
w<sup>ch</sup> femingly was well when my fath<sup>r</sup> and moth<sup>r</sup>
came home J feeing ye fame f<sup>d</sup> maer y<sup>e</sup> nex morning could Judge noe other butt y<sup>t</sup> fhe had bin Rid
ye other part of y<sup>t</sup> night or oth<sup>r</sup> ways horibly abu-
fed vpon w<sup>ch</sup> my fath<sup>r</sup> feeing w<sup>t</sup> a condition his
maer was in fent for his Broth<sup>r</sup> Thomas Andros
w<sup>ch</sup> when he came he gin her feuerall Things w<sup>ch</sup>
he Thought to be good for her butt did her not
any good upon w<sup>ch</sup> he faid he would try one thing
moer w<sup>ch</sup> was a pipe and fome Tobaco w<sup>ch</sup> he ap-
plid to her Thinking itt might doe her good againft
ye Belly ake Thinking y<sup>t</sup> might be her difçeafe w<sup>ch</sup>
when they vfed y<sup>e</sup> pipe w<sup>th</sup> Tobaco in itt abought
y<sup>e</sup> fd maer y<sup>e</sup> pipe being Litt itt Blazed fo much
y<sup>t</sup> itt was as much as two perfons could putt itt
ought w<sup>th</sup> both of Their hands, vpon w<sup>ch</sup> my father
faid we will Trye no more brother my vncle f<sup>d</sup> he
would trye once more y<sup>e</sup> w<sup>ch</sup> he did ye pipe be-

ing Litt ye fyed Blazed out of ye fame f<sup>d</sup> pipe more
vehemently than before vpon w<sup>ch</sup> my father anfwered he had Rather Loofe his maer yn his barn
ye uery next night follo--ing ye fd maer fulloing
my father in his barn from one fide to ye other fide
fell down imediately Dead againft ye fell of ye Barn
before my fath<sup>r</sup> had well cleered him felfe from her
—furth<sup>r</sup> faith not.

### *Mary Cummings v. Elizabeth How.*

Jvn 27, 1692. The difpofition of mary com-
mings y<sup>e</sup> wif of ifaac commins fen<sup>r</sup> aged aboot fixty
yers or thare abovts tefeifieth and faith my hufband
not being at home J was fent to by fom parfons of
ipfweg fent to me for to have me to write what J
cold fay of James how ivn<sup>r</sup> his wife elefebeth con-
fcarning her life or converfation and that J woold
fay what I cold fay for or againft her when the faid
hows wife fovght to aioyn with ythe church at
ipfweg and I fpoke to my fon Jfaac to write that
we hade vfed no brimfton nor oyl nor no combvf-
tables to give to our mear becavs thare was a report
that the faid hows wife hade faid that we hade
given the mear brim brimfton and oyl and the like
and a ftort time after J hade written my teftemony
confarning this hows wife my fon Ifaac his maer
was miffing that he coold not find her in to or thre
days and in a fhort time after my fon ifaacs maer,
came in fight not fare from the hovs and my fon
ifaac praid me to go ovt and look on his maer when
J came to her he afked me what J thovght on her

and J faid if he wold have my thoughts i covld not
compair it nothing elce but that fhe was riden with
a hot bridil for fhe hade divirfes brofes as if fhe had
bin runing over rocks an mvch wronged and where
the bridil went was as if it had been burnt with a
hot bridil then J bide Jfaac take y^e mare and have
her vp amongft the naghbors that peopl might
fee her for I hered that James how wn^r or his wife
or both hade faid that we kept vp ovr maer that
popel might not fee her and ifaac did fhow his
maer to faveril and then the faid how as i hered did
report that ifac had riden to Sin fpring and caryed
his gairl and fo fvrfited the maer the which was not
fo.

Mary Comins owned this har teftimony to be
truth before the Juryes for Inqueft this 29 of June
1692                           Jurat in Curia.

Jvn 27, 1692. J mary comins ageed abovt fixty
yers or thar abovts the wife of ifaac comins fyne^r J
being at my neighbour Samul parlys hovs samvel
parlys davgter hannah being in a ftraing condition
afked me if J did not fee godee how in the hovs
going round vpon the wall as the gvrl directed her
finger along rovnd in won place and another of the
hovs J teled her no J loked as dilegently as i cold
and i covld fee nothing of her the gorls mother
then did chek her and told her fhe was alwas fvll
of fvch kind of notions and bid her hold her tovng
then fhe told her mother fhe wovld belive it one
day and fomthing mor which fhold have bin man-
tioned as the garl poynted to fhow me whare goode

how was fhe afked me if J did not fe her go ovt
at that crak which fhe poynted at Mary Comins
owned this har teftimony one her oath to be the
truth before the Juriars of Inqueft this 29 of June
92. Jurat in Curia

Jvn 27-1692. The difpofi-tion of Mary commins aged abovt fixty yers or there aboots ho teftefieth and faieth that above too yeres agon J went to
vifet my naighbovr fherins wife and fhe told me
that James how ivn[r] had bin thare to give her a
vifet and he did fharply talk to her afking her what
hopes fhe hade of her falveation her anfwer was to
him that fhe did bild her hopes vpon that fver rock
Jefvs chrift this the faid ferins wife did tell me and
fhe told me alfo that fhe had never talked of the
faid how or his wife bot fhe was the wors for it afterwards, and fhe faid alfo when fhe lay fick of the
fame fiknefs whareof fhe dyed that the faid how
would come fom times into the roome to fee her
but fhe covld not tell how to bare to fe him nor
that he fhovld be in the hovs.

Mary Comins ownid that this har teftimony on
har oath before the Juryars for Jnques, this 29 of
June. 1692. Jurat in Curia.

### *Francis Lane v. Elizabeth How.*

Francis Lane g-ged 27 yeares teftifyeth and faith
that about feauen yeares agoe James How the hufband of Elizabeth How of Ipfwich farmes hired
f[d] Lane to get him a parcell of pofts and railes and
f[d] Lane hired John Pearly the fon of Samuell Pear-

ly of Ipfwich to help him in getting of them And
after they had got faid Pofts and railes, the faid
Lane went to the faid James How that he might
goe with him and take delivery of faid Pofts and
railes, and Elizabeth How the wife of fᵈ James
how told faid Lane that fhe did not beleiue that fd
Pofts and railes would doe becaufe that fᵈ John
Pearly helped him and fhe faid that if he had got
them alone and had not got John Pearly to help
him fhe beleived beleived that they would have
done but feing that faid Pearly had helped about
them fhe beleived that they would not doe, fo fᵈ
James How went with faid Lane for to take deliu-
ery of fᵈ Pofts and railes and the fᵈ James How
toke feverall of the faid railes as they lay in heaps
up by the end and they broke of, fo many of them
broke that faid Lane was forced to get thirty or
forty more and when faid How came home he told
his wife thereof and fhe faid to him that fhe had
told him before that they would not doe becaufe
faid Pearly helped about them which railes faid
Lane teftifyeth that in his Aprehention were good
found railes.

ffrancis Lane declared to ye Jury of inques to ye
truth of yᵉ above written evidence upon oath June
39ᵗʰ 1692.                    Jurut in Curia.

### *John How v. Elizabeth How.*

The Teftimony of John How aged about 50
yers faith that one that day that my brother James
his wife was Caried to Salem farmes upon exami-

nation fhe was at my houfe and would a have had
me to go with her to Salem farmes J tould hur :
that if fhe had ben fent for vpon allmoft any aCount
but witchcraft J would a have gone with hur bvt
one that aCount I would not for ten pounds, but
faid I If you are a witch tell me how long you have
ben a witch and what mifcheve you have done and
then J will go with you for faid I to hur you have
ben acufied by Samuell pearleys Child and fufpaĉt-
ed by Daken Cumins for witchcraft : fhe femed to
be aingry with me, ftell afked me to come on the
morow I told hur I did not know but I might com
to morow but my ocafhons caled me to go to Ipfwich one the morow and came whome a bout fun
faet and ftanding nere my door talking with one of
my Naibours, I had a fow with fix fmall pigs in the
yard the fow was as well fo fare as I know as ever
one a fuding fhe leaped up about three or fouer
foot hie and turned about and gave one fqueake and
fell downe daed I told my naibour that was with
me I thought my fow was bewitched for faied I
think fhe is daed he lafed at me but It proued true
for fhe fell downe daed he bed me cut of hur eare
the which I did and my hand I had my knif in was
fo numb and full of paine that night and fauerall .
days after that I could not doe any work and is not
wholy wall now and I fofpeĉted no other perfon by
my fd fifter Elizabeth How.

Capt Jnº How declared ye above written evidence to be ye truth before ye Jury of inqueft.
June 30th 1692. upon his oath in court,

### *Jacob Foster v. Elizabeth How.*

The depofion of Jacob foster aged about 29 yeares this deponant faith that fome years agoe good wife How the wife of James how was a bout to Joyne with the church of Ipfwich My father was an inftrumentall means of her being denyed admifion quickly after my mare was turned out to grafs on the tufday and on thurfday J went to feek my mare to go to lecture I fought my mare and could not find her I fought all friday and found her not on Saturday I fought till noon and I found my mare ftanding leaning with her butocks againft a tree I hit her with a fmall whip fhe gave a heave from a tree and fell back to the tree again then I took of her fetters and ftruck her again fhe did the fame again then J fet my fhoulder to her fide and thruft her of from the tree and moued her feet then fhe went home and leapt into the paufture and my mare lookt as if fhe had been miferably beaten and abu-fed  Jacob ffofter declared ye evidence to be ye truth before ye Jury of inqueft, on oath June 30. 92.

### *Jofeph Safford v. Elizabeth How.*

The depofiftion of Jofeph Safford aged about 60, he teftefyeth and faith that my wife was much afraid of Elizabeth how the wife of James how upon the Reports that were of her about Samuell perlleys child but upon a tim after thes Reportes James how and his wife coming to my houfe ne-

ther myfelfe nor my wife were at home and goodwife how afked my children wher ther mother was
and thay faid at the next nayboaers hovs fhe difired
them to Coll ther mother which they did, when
my wife cam whom my wife told me that fhe was
much ftartled to fe goode how but fhe took her by
the hand and faid goode Safford, J beliue that you
are not ignorant of the grete fcandall that I Ly under upon the euill Report that is Raifed upon me
about Samuell perlleys child and other things Jofeph
Safford faith that after this his wife was taken be-
yond Rafon and all parfwafion to tek the part of this
woman after this the wife of this Jams how pro-
pounded herfelfe to com into the church of Ipfwich wherupon fum objection aRofe by fum unfatisfied brethren wherupon ther was a meeting
apinted by our elders of the church to confidar of
things brought in againft her my wife was more
then ordenery ernift to goe to Lectur the church
meeting being on that day notwithftanding the many arguments I ufed to perfwed her to the Contrery
yet I obtained a promis of her that fhe would not
goe to the church meeting but meeting with fom
of the naybourhood they perfwaded her to go with
them to the church meeting at eldar pains and told
her that fhe need fay nothing ther, but goodwife
how then being Rether Rendred guilty than cleered my wife took her by the hand after meeting and
told her though fhe wer condemned before men
fhe was Juftefyed befor god, the next Sabath after
this my fon that caried my wife to Lectur was ta-

ken aftar a ftrang manar the Saturday aftar that
my wife was taken after a Raving frenzy manar
expref-ing in a Raging manar that goode how muft
Com into the church and that fhee was a precious
faint and though fhee wer condemned befor men
fhee was Juftefyed befor god and continued in this
fram for the fpace of thre or four hours after that
my wife fell into a kind of a tranc for the fpac of
two or thre minits fhee then coming to herfelfe
opened her eye and faid ha J was miftaken no anfwer was med by the ftandars by, and again fhee
faid ha J was miftaken majar appletons wife ftanding by faid wherein art miftaken J was miftaken
faid fhe for I thought goode how had bene a precious faint of god but now I fee fhe is a witch for
fhee hath bewitched mee and my child and we
fhall neuer be well till ther is teftemoney for her
that fhe may be taken into the church, after this ther
was a meeting of the eldars at my hous and thay
defired that goode how might be at the meeting
infign wallis went with myfelfe to inuite goode how
to this meeting fhe coming in difcours at that
time fhee faid two or thre times fhee was fory to
fe my wife at the church meeting at eldar pains
aftar this fhee faid fhe was aflicted by the aparifh-
tion of goode how a few dayes after fhe was taken
fhee faid the caus of her changing her opinion confarning goode how was becaus fhee apeared to her
throug a creuie of the clambouerds which fhe knew
no good perfon could do and at thre feuerall tims
after was aflicted by the aperifhtion of goode how

and goode olleuer and furdir this deponit faith that
Rifing erlly in the moring and kindling a fir in the
other Room in wife fhrickèd out I prefently Ran
into the room wher my wife was and as foon as
euer I opened the dore my faid ther be the evill one
take them wherupon I Replyed whar are they I
will take them if I can fhee faid you will not tak
them and then fprang out of the bed herfelfe and
went to the window and faid thar they went out
thay wer both biger than fhe and thay went out
ther but fhe could not then J Replyed who be thay
fhe faid goode how and goode olleuer goode olleuer
faid J you never faw the woman in your Life no
faid fhe I never faw her in my Life but fo fhe is
Reprefented to me goode ollever of Sallam that hurt
william ftace of Sallam the millar.

Jofeph Safford declared to ye Jury of inqueft
that ye evidence above written and on ye other fide
of this paper is ye truth upon oath,

June 30ᵗʰ 1692.    Jurat in Curia.

*Thomas Andrews v. Elizabeth How.*

July 1ˢᵗ 1692.
The Teftimony of Thomas Andrews of Boxford
aged· about 50 years this deponant Teftifieth and
faith yᵗ Jfiah Comings, fenioʳ of Topsfield fent for
me to help a mare yᵗ was not well and when I came
thare yᵉ mare was in fuch a condition yᵗ I could not
tell wᵗ fhe ailed for J never fawe ye like her lips
ware exceedingly fwelled yᵗ yᵉ Jnfides of Them

Turned outward and Looked Black and blew and gelled, her Tung was in ye fame Condition J told ye faid Comings I could not tell w$^t$ to doe for her J perceived fhe had not ye Botts w$^{ch}$ J did att firft think fhe had butt J faid fhe might have fome great heat in her Body and I would applie a pipe of Tobacco to her and y$^t$ was concented to and I litt a pipe of Tobaco and putt itt vnder her fundiment and there came a Blew flame out of ye Bowle and Run along ye ftem of f$^d$ pipe and took hold of ye haer of f$^d$ maer and Burnt itt and we tryed itt 2 or 3 times together and itt did ye fame itt femed to Burn Blew butt Run Liki fyer y$^t$ is fett on ye grafs to Burn itt in ye spring Tyme and we ftruck itt outt w$^{th}$ our hands and y$^e$ f$^d$ Comings f$^d$ y$^t$ he would trye no more for f$^d$ he J had Rather loofe my mare y$^n$ my barn and J this deponant doe teftifi y$^t$ to y$^e$ Beft of my vnderftanding was y$^e$ fame mare y$^t$ James Hough Junior Belonging to Ipfwich farmes hufband to Elizabeth Hough would have have Borowed of y$^e$ f$^d$ Comings.

Tho. Andrews.

*Warrant v. William Procter.*

To ye Conftable of Salem,

You are hereby required in theyr Majeftys Names to Apprehend and bring before us William procter of Salem ffarmes fon of John procter of f$^d$ ffarmes Hufbandman, upon Tuefday next being ye Thirty ffirft day of May about Tenne of the Clock in ye morning att ye houfe of Lev$^t$ Nath$^{ll}$ Jngerfolls in ſ<sup>d</sup> Village, Whoe ſtands charged w<sup>th</sup> Sundry Acts of Witchcraft done or Comitted upon the Bodys of Mary Walcott and Suſanah Shelden and others of Salem Village to theyr great hurt, in order to his examination, Relateing to ye above ſ<sup>d</sup> premiſes and hereof you are nott to fayle.

Dated Salem May 28<sup>th</sup> 1692.

J vs. JOHN HATHORNE } Aſſiſts.
JONATHAN CORWIN

I have apprehended the parſon above named and brought him to the place apinted

by me JOHN PUTNAN Cunt of Salem.

*Indictment v. William Procter No. 1.*

Eſſex in the Province of the Maſſachuetts, Bay in New England ſs. } Anno R R<sup>s</sup> & Reginee Guliel-mi & Mariee Angliee Quarto Annoq Domini 1692.

The Juriors for our Sou<sup>r</sup> Lord and Lady the King and Queen doe preſent that William Procter of Salem Jn the county of Eſſex Huſbandman Jn. and Vpon the Thirty firſt day of May Jn the yeare aforeſaid and divers other days and times as well before as after Certaine deteſtable arts called Witchcrafts, and Sorceries Wickedly Mallitiouſly and felloniouſly hath uſed practiſed and Exerciſed at and in the Towneſhipe of Salem aforeſaid in upon and againſt one Elizabeth Hobert of Salem aforeſaid Single Woman by which ſaid Wicked acts the ſaid Elizabeth Hobart the day and year aforeſaid and diuers other days and times both before and after, was and is Tortured Afflicted Confumed pined Wafted and Tormented and alfo for fundry other acts of Witchcraft by the faid William procter Comitted and done before and fince that time againft Our Sou<sup>r</sup> Lord and Lady the King and Queen theire Crowne and Dignity And the forme in the ftattute in that Cafe made and Provided,

     Witnefs,             Mary Warren,

*Indictment v. William Procter No. 2.*

Effex in the Province of the Maffachufetts Bay in New England fs. | Anno R R<sup>s</sup> & Reginee Gulielmi & Mariee &c. Quarto Annoq. Domini 1692.

The Juriors for our Sou<sup>r</sup> Lord and Lady the King and Queen doe prefent that William Procter of Salem Jn the county of Effex hufbandman in and vpon the thirty firft day of May Jn the yeare abovefaid and diuers other days and time as well before as after Certaine deteftable art called Witchcrafts and Sorceries Wickedly mallitioufly and ffelonioufly hath ufed practifed and Exercifed at and in the Towne- fhip of Salem aforefaid in upon and againft one Mary Warren of Salem aforefaid Single woman by which faid Wicked Acts Mary Warren aforefaid the day and year the aforefaid and diuers other days and times tothe before and after was and is Tortured aflicted Confumed Pined Wafted and Tormented and alfo for fundry other acts of Witchcraft by the faid William Procter Comitted and done before and fince that time againft Our Sou^r Lord and Lady the King and Queen theire Crowne and Dignity and the forme in the ftatute in that cafe made and Prouided.

   Wittnefs,      Eliz. Hobert.

### *Eliz^a Hobert v. William Procter.*

elizabeth hubart dooth teftify one har oath before the grand inqueft that William Procter did aflicte me this deponant the 31 day of may 92. at the time of his examination, and allfo I did fee faid William procter aflicte mary Warren at the time of his examination, and faid William Procter hath aflikted me this deponant feuerall tims fins :

feptember the 8 day 1692.

### *Warrant v. Willmot Reed.*

To the Conftables of Marblehead,

 You are in theire Majefts names hereby required to apprehend and bring before vs willmot Reed the wife of Samuell Reed of Marblehead, on Tuefday next being the 31^st day of this Jnftant month of May aboute ten of the cloak in the forenoon at ye houfe of L^t Nathaniell Ingerfalls in Salem Village; who ftands charged with hauing Committed Sundry acts of Witchcraft on ye bodys of Mary Walcot and Marcy Lewis and others of Salem Village to theire great hurt &c. in order to her Examination

      N²

Relateing to y<sup>e</sup> abovef<sup>d</sup> premifes and hereof you are not to faile.

Dated Salem May 28<sup>th</sup> 1692.

P vs. John Hathorne ⎫ Affifts.
Jonathan Corwin ⎭

Jn anfwer to ye within mentioned warrant J have apprehended Willmot Reed wife to Sam<sup>l</sup> Reed of Marblehead and brought her to ye houfe of L<sup>t</sup> Jngerfals, May ye 31<sup>st</sup>, 92.

James Smith Con<sup>st</sup> for Marblehead.

*Indictment v. Wilmott Reed No. 1.*

Effex in the Province ⎫ Anno R R<sup>s</sup> & Reginee Guli-
of the Maffachufetts ⎪ elmi & Mariee Anglice &c
Bay in New Englandfs. ⎪ Quarto Annoq<sup>z</sup> Domini
⎭ 1692.

The Juriors for our Sou<sup>r</sup> Lord and Lady the King and Queen doe prefent that Willmott Redd wife of Samuel Redd of Marblehead, Jn the County of Effex ffifherman vpon the Thirty firft day of May Jn the yeare aforef<sup>d</sup> and diuers other days and times as well before as after Certaine deteftable arts called Witchcraft and Sorceries Wickedly Mallitioufly and fellonioufly hath ufed practifed and exercifed At and in the Towne of Salem in the County of Effex aforefaid in upon and againft one Eliz<sup>a</sup> Booth of Salem aforefaid Single Woman by which faid Wicked acts ye faid Eliz<sup>a</sup> Booth the day and year aforefaid and diuers other days and times both before and after was and is Tortured Aflicted Confumed Pined Wafted and Tormented and alfo for

Sundry other acts of Witchcraft by the said Willmot Redd Comitted and done before and since
that time againt the peace of our Sou<sup>r</sup> Lord and
Lady the King and Queen theire Crowne and
Dignity and the forme of the Stattute in that cafe
made and Provided.

*Indictment v. Wilmott Reed No. 2.*

Effex in the province | Anno R R<sup>s</sup> & Reginee Guli-
of the Maffachufetts | elmi & Marie Anglice &<sup>c</sup>
Bay in New England fs. | Quarto Annoq Domini 1692.
    The Jvrors for our Sou<sup>r</sup> Lord and Lady the
King and Queen doe prefent that Willmott Redd
wife of Samuel Redd of Marblehead Jn the County of Effex ffifherman vpon the Thirty firft day of
May In the year aforefaid and divers other days
and times as well before as after Certaine Deteftable Arts called Witchcraft and Sorceries Wickedly Mallicioufly and fellonioufly hath vfed practifed
and Exercifed at and in the Towne of Salem in the
County of Effex aforefaid in Vpon and againt one
Eliz<sup>a</sup> Hobert of Salem aforefaid in the County of
Effex aforefaid Single Woman by which faid wicked
Acts the faid Eliz<sup>a</sup> Hobert the day and year aforefaid and Divers other dayes and times both before
and after was and is Tortured aflicted Confumed
Pined Wafted and Tormented and alfo for fvndry
other acts of Witchcraft by the faid Willmot Redd
Comitted and done before and fince that time
againt the peace of our Soueraigne Lord and Lady
the King and Queen theire Crowne and Dignity

And the forme of the Stattute in that Cafe made and Prouided.—

*Examination of Wilmott Reed.*

The examination of Wilmot Redd wife of Sam<sup>l</sup> Redd of marblehead ffifherman, 31 May 1692.

When this examinant was brought in Mercy Lewis Mary Walcot and Abigail Williams fell into fits.

Mercy Lewis faid this Woman hath Pinch<sup>t</sup> me a great many times Mary Walcot fais this woman brought the Book to her.

Ann Putman jun<sup>r</sup> Saith fhe never hurt her, but fhe hath feen her once upon Mercy Lewis and once upon Mary Walcot the laft faft day,

Eliz. Hubbard faid this Examinant had brought the book to her, and told her fhe would knock her in the head, if fhe would not write.

Ann Putnam faid fhe brought the Book to her juft now.

Eliz. Booth fell into a fit, and Mary Walcot and Ann Putnam faid it was this woman afflicted her,

Sufan Sheldon was ordered to go to the examinant but was knockt down before fhe came to her, and being fo carryed to faid Redd in a fit, was made well after faid Redd had grafpt her arm.

Eliz. Hubbard dealt with after the fame manner.

This examinant was bid by the Magiftrates to look vpon Eliz: Hubbard and upon the examinants cafting her eye vpon faid Hubbard, fhe the faid Hubbard was knoct down.

Abig. Williams and John Jndian being carried to the examinant in a grevious fit were made well by her grafping their arms.

This examinant being often urged what fhe thought thefe Perfons ailed, would reply, J cannot tell. Then being afkt if fhe did not think they were Bewitched: fhe anfwered I cannot tell, And being urged for her opinion in the cafe. All fhe would fay was: my opinion is they are in a fad condition.

### Summons v. Willmott Reed.

W$^m$ and Mary by y$^e$ Grace of God of England Scottland ffrance and Jreland King and Queen

L. S. defend$^{rs}$ of y$^e$ faith &c Effex fs. To y$^e$ Sheriff of Effex or deputy or Conftable of Marble-head. Greeting.

Wee Comand you to Warm and give notice vnto y$^e$ wife and daughter of Thomas Dodd y$^e$ Wife and Daughter of Thomas Ellis John Caley David Shapley wife and daughter John Chin Marthah Beale Elias Henly jun$^r$ and wiffe Benjamin Gale Joane Bubbee, Charitty Pittman, and Jacob Worm-wood, That they and Every of them be and perfo-naly appear at y$^e$ Court of Oyer and Terminer holden at Salem to morrow at Eight of y$^e$ clock in y$^e$ Morning there to Teftify y$^e$ truth to y$^e$ beft of your knowledge on Seuerall Indictments Exhibited againft Wilmot Redd hereof make return fail not dated in Salem Sept$^r$ 13$^{th}$ 1692. and in y$^e$ fourthe year of our Reign. STEPHEN SEWALL Ce.

J haue warn and fumoned all y<sup>e</sup> perfons within mentioned accordingly except John Calley and Ellis henly who are at fea, and beni. gale not well. Sep<sup>t</sup>ber y<sup>e</sup> 14<sup>th</sup> by 7 o'clock in y<sup>e</sup> morning.

P me JAMES SMITH Con<sup>t</sup> in Marblehead.

### Mary Walcott v. Willmott Reed.

The depofiftion of mary Walcott who teftifieth and faith J was for a confiderable time afflected by a woman which tould me hir name was Redd and that fhe came from marblehead but on the 31 of may 1692 being the day of the examination of willmott Redd then J faw that fhe was the very fame woman that tould me hir name was Redd, and fhe did moft dreadfully afflict and torment me dureing the time of hir examination for if fhe did but look upon me fhe would ftrike me down or almoft choak me, alfo on the day of hir examination J faw willmott Redd, or hir Aperance moft grevioufly affect and torment marcy lewes Eliz: Hubberd and ann putnam and J beleue in my heart, that willmott Redd is a witch and that fhe has often affleted and tormented me and the aforef<sup>d</sup> perfons by acts of witchcraft

Jurat in Curia.

Mary Walcot upon her oath Affirmed to y<sup>e</sup> grand Jnqueft y<sup>t</sup> y<sup>e</sup> above written evidence is y<sup>e</sup> truth, Sep<sup>t</sup> 14. 1692.

### Mary Warren v. Wilmott Reed.

The depofiftion of mary warren who teftifieth

and faith J canot fay that willmott Redd ever hurt
me but J faw willmott Redd on the 31 may 1692.
moft grevioufly affleƈt and torment mary walcott
Abigaill williams and Eliz. Booth and elizabeth
Hubard and Ann putnam and J verily beleue in
my heart that willmott Redd is a witch and that
fhe has often hurt the above faid perfons by aƈts of
wiƈthcraft.

Mary Warin vpon oath affirmed to yᵉ grand Inqueft to yᵉ truth of yᵉ above written evidence
Septʳ 14ᵗʰ 1692.

and this day fhe hath afliƈted this deponant
moft Grevioufly.

Jurat in Curia.

*Ann Putnam v. Wilmott Reed.*

The depofition of Ann putnam who teftifieth
and faith that J was for a confiderable time afleƈted
by a woman that tould me hir name was Redd
and that fhe çame from marblehead but on the 31
may 1692, being the day of the examination of
wilmott Redd then J faw that fhe was the very
fame woman that tould me hir name was Redd
and fhe did moft grevioufly torment me dureing
the tim of her examination for if fhe did but look
on me fhe would ftrick me down or almoft chook
me alfo on the day of her examination J faw willmott Redd or hir aperance moft grevioufly afflet
and torment mary walcott Eliz Hubbard Eliz Both
and Abigail williams and J very beleve that Willmott Redd is a witch and that fhe has often affle-

ted me and the aforefaid perfons by acts of witch-craff.

Ann Putnam ownd yᵉ truth of yᵉ above written evidence to yᵉ grand inqueft Septʳ. 14. 1692. upon oath   Jurat in Curia.

### *Elizᵃ Hubbard v. Wilmott Reed.*

The depofiftion of Eliz. Hubburd who teftifieth and faith that J was a confiderable time afflected by a woman wᶜᵗ tould me hir name was Redd and that fhe came from marblehead but on the 31 may 1692 being the day of the examination of willmott Redd then J faw that fhe was yᵉ very fame woman that tould me hir name was Redd, and fhe did moft grevioufly afflect and torment me during the time of hir examination for if fhe did but look upon me fhe would ftrick me down or almoft choake me, alfo on the day of hir examination J faw will-mott Redd or hir Apperance moft dreadfully afflect and torment mary walcott Abigail williams and Ann putnam and J beleue that willmott Redd is wicth and that fhe hath often affleted me and the affore faid perfons by acts of wicthcraft.

Eliz Hubbert upon her oath to ye grand inqueft to ye truth of ye above written evidence, Septʳ 14. 1692·   Jurat in Curia.

### *Charity Pitman v. Wilmott Reed.*

The Teftimony of Charity Pitman of Marblehead.
This deponent aged  twenty nine years affirms,

that about five years agoe, Mrs Syms of yᵉ Tovne haveing loſt ſome linen which ſhe ſuſpeċted Martha Laurence the girle which then lived with Wilmott Reed had taken up deſired the deponant to goe with her to Wilmott Redds, and demanding the ſame, having many words about the ſame, mrs Syms told her, that if ſhe would not deliver them, ſhe would go to Salem to mʳ Hathornes and gett a ſpeciall warrant for her ſervante girl, upon which the ſᵈ Redd told her in my hearing, that ſhe wiſhed ſhe might never mingere, nor cacare, if ſhe did not goe, and ſome ſhort time after the deponent obſerved, that the ſᵈ Mrs Syms was taken with the diſtemper of the dry Belly-ake and ſo continued many moneths dureing her ſtay in the Towne, and was not cured whilſt ſhe tarryed in the Countrey,

Jurat in Curia.

### *Sarah Dod v. Wilmott Reed.*

Sarah Dod Affirmed upon her oath to yᵉ grand Jnqueſt that ſhe heard Mʳˢ Simſe threatened to have Wilmot Redd before a Majeſtrate for ſome of ſᵈ Redds miſdemeanures ſᵈ Redd wiſht ſᵈ Simſe might never any wayes eaſe nature before ſhe did it, and ſoon aftar, to this depᵒnants knowledge it fell out with Mʳˢ Simſe, according ſᵈ Redds wiſh

this ſhe ownd before ſᵈ Jury of inqueſt, Septʳ 14 : 1692.

### *Ambroſe Gale v. Wilmott Reed.*

Mʳ Ambros Gale Affirmed that Mʳˢ Simſe was

Oª

abo^t that time or foon after fo aflicted; as was then reported. Septem^r 14, 1692.

Juriat in Curia.

*Complaint v. Eliz^a Fofdick & Eliz^a Paine.*

Salem May the 30^th 1602.
Lt Nathaniell putnam and Jofeph Whipple both of Salem Village made Complaint in behalfe of theire majes^ts againft Elizabeth ffofdick of Maulden the wife of John ffofdick aforef^d Carpenter & Elizabeth paine of Charlftown the wife of Stephen paine of f^d hufbandman for fundry acts of Witchcraft by them Committed Lately on the bodys of Marcy Lewis and Mary Warren of Salem Willage or farmes to theire great hurt therefore craues Juftice.

Nathanell Putnam<br/>Jofeph whipple.

The abouefayd Complaint was Exhibited before us Salem May the 30^th 1692.

JOHN HATHORNE<br/>JONATHAN CORWIN } Affift.

peter Tuft of Charlftowne alfo appeared before vs Salem June 2^d 1692 and alfo Complained againft both y^e abouef^d for acts of Witchcraft by them Committed on his negro Woman.

The mark of<br/>Peter ✝ Tufts

*Warrant v. Elizabeth Fofdick & Elizabeth Paine.*

To the Marfhall or Sheriff of the County of Mid-
dlefex or dep[t]

You are in theire Majeft[s] names hereby required
to apprehend and bring before vs at Salem forthwith
or as foon as may be Elizabeth ffofdick the wife of
John ffofdick of Maulden Carpenter and Elizabeth
paine the wife of Stephen paine of Charleftowne
hufbandman, for fundry acts of Witchcraft by them
Committed Lately on ye Bodys of Marcy Lewis
Mary Warren &c of Salem Village or farmes to
theire great hurt and Jnjury accord[s] to Complaint
Exhibited before vs appears, fail not, Dated Salem
June the 2[d] 1692 :

JOHN HATHORNE } Affifts.
JONATHAN CURWIN }

I doe Appoint Sam[ll] Gibfon of Cambridge To
Serue this warrant To Effect. June 2[d] 1692.
SAN[ll] GOOKIN Marfh[ll] for Mddx.

June 2[d] 1692. J haue Appehended the aboue
named Elizebeth paine and delivered her unto the
Sheriff of the County of Effex att Salem in ye County aforef[d] in order to her examination and waite in
expectation of the aboue f[d] Elizabeth Fofdick by
mee.

June 3, 92 J haue all fo apprehended the body
of Elizabeth ffofdick of mauldin and delivered her
to the aboue faid Sheriff of Effex,

SAM[ll] GIBSON ye mar[sh] dep.

Deacon Edward putnam and Thomas Rayment
both of Salem Village Complained on behalfe of
theire Majesfties againft Mary Irefon the wife of
Benjamin Jrefon of Lyn hufbandman for Sundry
acts of Witchcraft by her Committed Lately on ye
bodys of Mary Waren Sufana Shelden and Mary
Walcot and others of Salem Village whereby great
hurt hath beene donne to· theire bodys therefore
Craves Juftice,

Salem June 4ᵗʰ 1692.

| | |
|---|---|
| alfo | |
| Eliz both | Edward Putnam |
| Abe Williams | the mark of |
| Ann Putnam | Thomas **✝** Rayment |
| alfo | |

To the Sheriffe of the County of Effex or his deputie or conftable in Lyn.

You are in theire Majesᵗˢ names hereby required
to apprehend and brig before vs Mary Jrefon ye
wife of Benjamin Irefon of Lyn hufbandman on
Munday next about ten of ẏe Clock in the forenoon
at ye houfe of Thomas Beadles in Salem who
ftands Charged on behalfe of theire Majeftˢ with
hauing Committed Sundry acts of Witchcraft on yᵉ
bodys of Marry Warren, Sufanah Shelden Mary
Walcot and others whereby great hurt is donne to
theire bodys, in order to her Examination Relateing to the aboue fᵈ premifes faile not.

Dated Salem June 4ᵗ 1692.

| | |
|---|---|
| JOHN HATHORNE | |
| BARTHᵒ GEDNEY | Jpeace |
| JONATHAN CORWIN | |

### *Examination of George Burrough.*

The examination of Geo: Burrough. 9 May, 1692.

| By the Honourd | { Wᵐ Stoughton John Hathorne Sam. Sewall, Jonath. Corwin | } Eſqˢ |

Being aſkᵗ wᵐ he partook of the Lords ſupper, he being (as he ſaid) in full comunion at Roxbury.

He anſwered is was ſo long ſince he could not tell : yet he owned he was at meeting one Sab : at Boſton parᵗ of the day, and the other a Charleſtown part of a Sab : when that ſacrament happened to be at both, yet did not partake of either. He denyed that his houſe as Caſko was haunted, yet he owned there were Toads. He denyed that he made his wife ſwear, that ſhe could not write to his father Ruck without his approbation of her letter to her Father. He owned that none of his children, but the eldeſt was Baptized The above was in private none of the Bewitched being preſent, At his entry into the Room many (if not all of the Bewitched) were greviouſly tortured.

1. Sus. Sheldon teſtifyed that Burroughs two wives appeared in their winding ſheets, and ſaid that man killed them.

He was bid to look upon Sus. Sheldon,

He looked back and knockt down all (or moſt), of the afflicted wᵒ ſtood behind him.

Sus: Sheldon . . (one line gone)  the foldiers

2. Mary Lewes depofition going to be read and he lookt upon her and fhe fell into a dreadful and tedious fit,

3. Mary Walcot
4 Eliz Hubbard
Sufan Sheldon
} Teftimony going to be read and they all fell into fitts

Sufan Sheldon
5 Ann Putman junr
} affirmed each of them that he bought the Book and wd have them write.

Being afkt wt he thought of thefe things.  He anfwered it was an amazing and humbling Providence, but he underftood nothing of it and he faid (fome of you may obferve, that) when they begin to name my name, they cannot name it.

Ann Putman junr
Sufan Sheldon
} Teftifyed that his 2 wives & 2, Children were deftroyed by him.

The Bewitched were fo tortured that Authority ordered them to be taken away fome of them.

6. Sarah Bibber teftifyed that he had hurt her, tho fhe had not feen him perfonally before as fhe knew.

Abig. Hobbs.
Deliverance Hobbs
Elizar Keifer
} Teftimony read

Capt Willard
Jno Brown
Jno Wheldon
} Teftimony about his great ftrength and the Gun.

Capt Putman teftifyed about the Gun.

Cap.^t Wormwood teftifyed about the Gun and the Mallaffoes  He denyed that about the nalaf-foes  About the Gun he faid he took it before the lock and refted it upon his breaft,

John Brown teftifyed about a bbl Cyder.

He denyed that his family was affrighted by a white calf in his houfe

Cap.^t Putman teftifyed that he made his wife enter into a covenant.  11 May 1692.

Abig : Hobbs in prifon affirmed that Geo. Burroughs in his fhape appeared to her, and urged her to fet her hand to the Book, which fhe did, and after-wards in his own perfon he acknowledged to her, that he had made her fet her hand to the Book.

The original minutes (of which the above is a true copy) is in the poffeffion of I. F. Andrews Efq. and was found among Judge Hathornes papers.  Aug. 8. 1843.

I. B. Curwine

*Summons v. Geo. Burrough.*

Wm & Mary by ye Grace of God of England L. S. and Scotland ffrance & Ireland King defend^r of ye faith &c^a

To James Greenflit                    Greeting—

Wee comand you all Excufes fet apart to be and perfonaly app^r at ye next Court of Oyer and Termina held at Salem on y^e firft Tuefday in Auguft next There to Teftify y^e Truth on certain Jndictments to be Exhibited againſt George Burroughs and not depart ye Court without lycenſe or leave of ſ[d] Court hereof faile not on penalty of One hundred poundes money to be leuied on your Goods chattels &c[a] Dated in Salem July 26th 1692. To y[e] Sheriffe of Eſſex.      STEP. SEWALL, Cle.

July 26th 1692.   J haue Sumoned the within named James Greinſley according to this within Sub. pena to Give in his Euidence att the time and place within mentioned. by me
GEO HERRICK Dept. Sheriff.

*View of body of Geo. Burroughs.*

Wee whoes names are under written hauing received an order from y[e] freife for to ſearch ye bodyes of George Burroughs and George Jacobs wee find nothing upon y[e] body of y[e] above ſay[d] burroughs but w[t] is naturall, but upon ye body of George Jacobs wee find 3 tetts w[ch] according to y[e] beſt of our Judgments wee think is not naturall for wee run a pinn through 2 of y[m] and he was not ſinceible of it. one of them being within his mouth upon y[e] Inſide of his right cheake and 2nd upon his right ſhoulder blade an a 3rd upon his right hipp.

Ed. Welch ſworne      Tom flint Jurat
Will. Gill ſworne.      Tom Weſt ſworne
Zeb. Hill Jurat      Sam Morgan ſworne
John Bare Jurat.

## *Samuel Webber v. Geo. Burroughs.*

Samuell Webber aged about 36 yeares Teſtifieth and ſayth yᵗ aboute ſeauen or eight Yeares agoe J liued at Caſco Bay and George Burroughs was then Mineſter there, and haueing heard much of the great ſtrength of him ſᵈ Burroughs ; he Coming to our houſe wee ware in diſcourſe aboute the ſame and he then told mee yᵗ he had put his fingers into the Bung of a Barrell of Malaſes and lifted it vp, and carryed it Round him and ſett it downe againe. Salem Auguſt 2ᵈ 1692.

Jurat in Curia.                    Samuell Webber.

## *Ann Putnam v. Geo. Burroughs.*

The Depoſition of Ann putnam who teſtifieth and ſaith that on 20ᵗʰ of April 1692 at euening ſhe ſaw the Apperiſhtion of a miniſter at which ſhe was greviouſly affrighted and cried out oh dreadfull : dreadfull here is a miniſter com, what are Miniſters witches to : whence com you and What is your name for J will complaine of you tho you be A miniſter : if you be a wizzard : and Jmmediately i was tortored by him being Racked and allmoſt choaked by him : and he tempted me to write in his book which J Refuſed with loud out cries and ſaid J would not writ in his book tho he tore me al to peaces but tould him that it was a dreadfull thing : that he which was a Miniſter that ſhould teach children to feare God ſhould com to perſwad poor creatures to giue their ſouls to the de-

P⁴

vill: Oh, dreadfull dreadfull, tell me your name
yᵗ J may know who you are: then againe he tortored me and urged me to writ in his book: which
J Refufed: and then prefently he tould me that his
name was George Burroughs and that he had had
three wives: and that he had bewitched the Two
firſt of them to death; and that he kiled Miſᵗ Lawfon becaufe fhe was fo unwilling to goe from the
village and alfo killed Mʳ Lawfons child becaufe
he went to the eaftward with Sir Edmon and
preached foe to the fouldiers and that he had be-
witchɛd a grate many fouldiers to death at the eaft-
word when Sir Edmon was their, and that he had
made Abigail Hobbs a wiɗth and feuerall wiɗthes
more: and he has continwed ever fence; by times
tempting me to write in his book and grevioufly
tortoring me by beating pinching and almoſt choaking me feuerall times a day and he alfo tould me
that he was above a wiɗth he was a conjurer.

   Jurat in Curia.

*Thomas Putnam, Peter Prefcott, Robert Morrell &
   Ezekiel Cheever v. Geo. Burroughs.*

   wee whofe names are under writen being prefent
with Ann putnam att the time aboue mentioned
hard hir declare what is aboue writen what fhe faid
fhe faw and hard from the Apperifhtion of Mʳ
George Burroughs and allfo beheld hir tortors and
perceived her hellifh temtations by hir loud out
cries J will not J will not writ tho you torment me

al days of my life, and being converfant with hir euer fence have feen hir tortored and coplaining that Mr Burroughs hirt hir, and tempts hir to writ in his book,

Thomas putnam        peter prefcott
Roburt Morrell,

Ann Putnam declared her above written evidence to be ye truth before y^e Jury of Inqueft. Aug^{st} 3. 92. upon her oath

Ezekiel Cheever made oath to ye latter part of this paper. Jurat in Curia.

### *Ann Putnam v. Geo. Burroughs.*

The depofiftion of Ann putnam who teftifieth and faith that on the 3^{th} of may 1692, at euening J faw the Apperifhtion of M^r George Burroughs who grevioufly tortored me and urged me to writ in his book which J refufed then he tould me that his Two firft wives would appear to me prefently and tell me a grat many lyes but J fhould not belicue them, then Jmmediately appeared to me the forme of Two women in winding fheats and napkins about their heads, att which J was gratly affrighted, and they turned their faces towards M^r Burroughs and looked very red and angury and tould him that he had been a cruell man to them, and that their blood did crie for vengance againft him: and alfo tould him that they fhould be cloathed with white Robes in heauen, when he fhould be caft into hell, and immediately he vanifhed away, and as foon as he was gon the Two women turned their faces towards me and looked as pail as a white wall: and tould me that they were M^r Burroughs Two first wives and that he had murthered them: and one tould me that she was his first wife and he stabed her under the left Arme and put a peace of sealing wax on the wound and she pulled aside the winding sheat, and shewed me the place and also tould me that she was in the house M^r parish now lived w^r it was don, and the other tould me that M^r Burrough and that wife which he hath now kiled hir in the vessell as she was coming to see hir friends becaufe they would have one another: and they both charged me that J should tell these things to the Magisstrates before M^r Burroughs face and if he did not own them they did not know but they should appere their: thes moring. also Mi^s Lawson and hir daughter Ann appeared to me whom J knew, and tould me that M^r Burroughs murthered them, this morning also appered to me another woman in a winding sheat and tould me that she was goodman ffullers first wife and Mr Burroughs kiled hir becaufe there was sum differance between hir husband and him, also on the 9^th may dureing the time of his examination he did most grevioufly torment and affect mary Walcott mercy lewes Eliz. Hubberd and Abigail williams by pinching pricks and choaking them. Jurat in Curia.

*Edward Putnam and Thomas Putnam v. Geo. Bur-
roughs.*

we whofe names are under writen being prefent
with ann putnam at the times aboue mentioñed,
faw hir tortured and hard hir refufe to writ in the
book alfo hard hir declare what is aboue writen:
what fhe faid fhe faw and hard from the Apperifhtion of Mr George Burroghs and from thof which
accufed him for murthering of them.

Edward putnam   Thomas putnam

Ann putnam ownid this har teftimony to be the
truth uppon her oath before the Juriars of Jnqueft
this 3ᵈ of Aguft 92.

*Mercy Lewis v. Geo. Burroughs.*

the depofiftion of mircy Lewes who teftifieth
and faith that one the 7ᵗʰ of may 1692. att evening
J faw the apperifhtion of Mʳ George Burroughs
whom j very well knew which did grevioufly tortor me and urged me to writ in his book and then
he brought to me a new fafhon book which he
did not ufe to bring and tould me J might writ in
that book: for that was a book that was in his
ftuddy when J lived with them: but J tould him
J did not beleve him for I had been often in his
ftuddy but J never faw that book their: but he
tould me that he had feverall books in his ftuddy,
which J never faw in his ftuddy and he could raife
the diuell: and now had bewitched Mr. Shep-

pards daughter and J afked him how he could goe to bewitch hir now he was keept at Salem; and he tould me that the divell was his farvant, and he fent him in his fhap to doe it, then he againe tortored me moft dreadfully and threatened to kill me for he faid J fhould not witnes againft him alfo he tould me that he had made Abigaill Hoobs a wicth and feverall more then againe he did moft dreadfully tortor me as if he would haue racked me all to peaces and urged me to writ in his book or elce he would kill me but J tould him J hoped my life was not in the power of his hand and that J would not writ tho he did kill me: the next night he tould me J fhould not fee his Two wifes if he could help it becaufe J fhould not witnes againft him: this 9$^{th}$ may mr Burroughs carried me up to an exceeding high mountain and fhewed me all the Kingdoms of the earth and tould me that he would give them all to me if J would writ in his book, and if J would not he would thro me down and brake my neck: but J tould him they ware non of his to give and J would not writ if he throde me down on 100 pichforks: alfo on the 9$^{th}$ may being the time of his examination mr. George Burroughs did moft dreadfully torment me: and alfo feueral times fence.

marce lwis uppon har oath did owne this har teftimony to be the truth before the Juriors for Jnqueft; aguft 3: 92.

*Thomas Putnam Edward Putnam v. Geo. Burroughs.*

we whofe names are under writen being prefent hard mircy lewes declare what is above written what fhe faid fhe faw and hard from the Apperifhtion of Mr George Burroughs and alfo beheld hir tortors which we cannot exprefs for fume times we wore redy to fear that euery joint of hir body was redy to be difplaced: alfo we perceived hir hellifh temtations by hir loud out cries mr Burroughs J will not writ in your book tho you doe kil me.

Thomas putnam        Edward Putnam.
Jurat in Curia.

*Simon Willard v. Geo. Burroughs.*

The Depofition of Simon Willard aged about forty two years fayth J being at y^e houfe of M^r Rob^t Lawrance at ffalmoth in Cafco Bay in Septemb^r 1689 f^d M^r Lawrance was commending M^r George Borroughs his ftrength: faying that we none of us could doe what he could doe: for f^d M^r Borroughs can hold out this gun with one hand; Mr. Borroughs being there: fayd J held my hand here behind y^e lock and took it up, and held it out, J f^d deponant faw M^r Borroughs put his hand on y^e gun: to fhow us: how he held it and where he held his hand, and faying there he held his hand when he held f^d gun out: but J faw him not hold it out then, f^d gun was about feven foot barrill and very hevie J then tryed to hold out f<sup>d</sup> gun with both hands, but could not do it long enough to take fight.                          Simon Willard

Simon willard owned to y<sup>e</sup> Jury of inqueſt, that y<sup>e</sup> above written evidence is ye truth,
     Aug<sup>st</sup> 3 : 1692.                    Jurat in Curia.

*W<sup>m</sup> Wormall.v. Geo. Burroughs.*

Cap<sup>t</sup> W<sup>m</sup> Wormall Sworne to y<sup>e</sup> above and y<sup>t</sup> he faw him Raife it from ye ground, himfelfe.
     Jurat in Curia.
The Depofition of Simon Willard aged about 42 years faith J being at Saco in ye year 1689 fome in Cap<sup>t</sup> Ed Sarjants garifon was fpeaking of m<sup>r</sup> George Borroughs his great ftrength faying he could take a barrill of molaffes out of a Cannoe or boat alone, and that he could take it in his hands or arms out of y<sup>e</sup> Cannoo or boat and carry it and fet it on y<sup>e</sup> fhore and m<sup>r</sup> Burroughs being there fay<sup>d</sup> that he had carryed one barrill of molaffes or fider out of a cannoo that had like to have done him a difplea-fure: f<sup>d</sup> m<sup>r</sup> Borroughs intimated as if he did not want ftrength to do it but y<sup>e</sup> difadvantage of y<sup>e</sup> fhore was fuch, that his foot flipping in the fand : he had liked to have ftrained his legg.
                         Simon Willard
     Simon Willard ownd to ye Jury of inqueft, that y<sup>e</sup> above written evidence is y<sup>e</sup> truth.
                    Jurat in Curia.

*Sarah Vibber v. Geo. Burroughs.*

The depofiftion of farah viber who teftifieth and faith that on the 9<sup>th</sup> day of may 1692. as J was agoeing to Salem village J faw the apperifhtion of a little man like a minifter with a black coat on and he pinched me by the arme and bid me goe along with him but J tould him J would not but when J came to the village J faw theire M<sup>r</sup> George Burroughs or his Apparance moft grevioufly torment and afflect mary walcott mercy luis Elizabeth Hubbert Ann putnam and abigaill williams by pinching twifting & almoft choaking them to death alfo feuerall times fence m<sup>r</sup> George Burrougs or his Apperance has moft grevioufly tormented me with variety of tortors and J beleue in my heart that m<sup>r</sup> George Burroughs is a dreadfull wizzard and that he has moft grevioufly tormented me and the aboue mentioned parfons by his acts of wicthcraft.

Sarah Viber declared to y<sup>e</sup> Jury of inqueft that the above written evidence is the truth. Aug<sup>st</sup> 3: 1692. the which fhe owned on her oath
Jurat in Curia.

*Eliz<sup>a</sup> Hubbard v. Geo. Burroughs.*

May y<sup>e</sup> 9. 1692. Elizabeth bubord aged about 17 yers faith that y<sup>e</sup> laft fecond day at night: There apeared a little black heard man to me in blackifh aparill J afked him his name and he told me his name was borrous, Then he tooke a booke out

Q<sup>2</sup>

of his pocket : and opened it and bid me fet my
hand to it J tould him J would not ; yᵉ lines in
this book was read as blod, then he pinched me
twife and went away : The next morning he appeared to me againe and tould me he was aboue a
wizard ; for he was a conjurar and fo went away but
fins that he hath apeared to me euery day & night
uery often and urged me uery much to fet my hand
to his book, and to run a way telling me if J would
do foe J fhould be well and that J fhould need feare
no body : and withall tormented me feuerall ways
euery time he came exept that time he told me
he was a conjuror : This night he afked me very
much to fet my hand to his book or elfe he fayed
he would kill me ; withall tortoring me uery much
by biting and pinching fquefing my body and running pins into me, alfo on the 9ᵗʰ may 1692. being
the time of his examination mʳ George Burroughs
or his Apperance did moft grevioufly affleᵭ and
torment the bodyes of mary walcott mercy lewes
Ann putnam and Abigail williams for if he did but
look upon them he would ftrick them down or almoft choak them to death alfo feuerall times fence
he has moft dreadfully affliᵭed and tormented me
with variety of torments and J beleue in my heart
yᵗ mʳ George Burroughs is a dreadfull wizzard and
that he has very often tormented me and alfo the
above named parfons by his aᵭs of wiᵭhcraft.

Jurat in Curia.

Eliz. Hubbard declared yᵉ above written evidence
to be ye truth, upon her oath, that fhe had taken :

this fhe owned before ye Jury of inqueft : Aug⁵⁵ 3. 1692.

### *Summons v. Geo. Burroughs.*

William & Mary by yᵉ Grace of God of England
    Scotland ffrance & Jreland King & Queen de-
    fendʳˢ of ye faith &cᵃ
mʳ Jnᵒ Ruck mʳˢ Eliz : Ruck mʳ Thomas Ruck
    and Samuel Ruck,
To Capᵗ William Worwood          Greeting
Wee comand you all Excufes fet apart to be and
perfonaly appear at ye prefent Court of Oyer & Termina held at Salem there to Teftify ye truth to ye
beft of our knowledge on certain Jndictmʳˢ Exhibited againft mʳ George Burrough : hereof fail not :
dated in Salem Augᵗ 5ᵗʰ 1692. and in ye fourth
year of Our Reign.

                     STEPHEN SEWAL Clee

Auguft 5ᵗʰ The perfons aboue Named where all
euery of them fumoned to appeare as aboue by me,
by me          JOSEPH NEALE Confᵗᵇ in in Salem.

### *Thos. Greenflett v. Geo. Burroughs.*

Thᵒ Greenflett aged about forty years being de-
pofed Teftifieth yᵗ about the firft breaking out of
the laft Indian warre being att the houfe of Capᵗ
Jofhua Scotts att Black point, he faw mʳ George
Burrows who was lately executed at Salem lift a
gunn of fix foot Barrell or thereabouts putting the
fore finger of his right hand into the mufell of fᵈ

gunn and that he held it out att arms end only w[th] thatt finger, and further this deponent teftyfieth that at the fame time he faw the f[d] Burrows Take up a full barr[ll] of molaffes w[th] butt two of fingers of one of his hands in the bung and carry itt from ye ftage head to the door att the end of the ftage w[th] out letting itt downe and that Liu[t] Rich[d] Hunniwell and John Greinflett were then prefent and fome others y[t] are dead.

Thomas Greenflit
his † marke. Jurat.

### Deliverance Hobbs v. Geo. Burroughs.

Deliverance Hobs Confeffion.

That they were both at the generall meeting of the Witches in M[r] Parifhes Mr. Burroughs preached and adminiftered to them.

### Hannah Harris v. Geo. Burroughs.

The depotion of Hannah Harris Aiged twenty feuen years or thare abouts Teftifieth and faith that fhe lived at y[e] hous of Georg Burros at falmouth and the aboue faid hannah harres many times hath taken notis that when fhe hath had anny Difcorfe with the aboue faid burrofs wife when the aboue faid burros was from hom that apone his Returne he hath often fcolded wife and told her that he knew what they faid when he was abroad and further faith that apone a time when his wife had Laine Jn Not aboue one weake that he fell out with his wife and kept her by Difcorce at the Dore till fhe fell ficke In ye place and grew wors at night fo that ye aboue faid hannah harres was afraid fhe would dye and thay called In thare Naibours and the aboue faid burrofes Daughter told One of ye women that was thare ye caufe of her mothers Ellnefs and ye aboue faid burros chid his Daughter for telling and y^e aboue faid burros came to the aboue faid hannah harres and told her Jf that his wif Did otherwife then well fhe fhould not tell of it & the aboue faid hannah harres told him that fhe would not be confined to any fuch thing.

Jurat in Curia.

*Benj^a Hutchinfon v. Geo. Burroughs.*

Beniemin huchenfion f^d that one the 21^st aprell 92. abegeral Wiluams f^d that there was a lettell black menefter that Liued at Cafko bay he told me fo and f^d that he had kild 3 wifes two for himfelf and one for m^r Lofen and that he had made nine weches in this plafe and f^d that he could hold out the heueft gun that is in Cafko bay w^th one hand w^c no man can Cafe hold out w^t both hands this Js about a 11 a clock and J afk her where about this lettel man ftood f^d fhe juft where the Cart wheell went along J had a 3 graned irne fork in my hand and J thru it wher fhe faid he ftud and fhe prefently fell in a letel feet and when it twas ouer Said She you have toren his coot for I herd it tare wher abouts faid I one won fide faid fhe, then we come into the houfe of left. Ingerfall and I went into the great roome and abigle come in and faid ther he

ftands J faid wher wher and prefently drood my
rapyer but he emmedetly was gon as fhe faid then
faid fhe ther is a gray catt then i faid wher abouts
doth fhe ftand ther f⁴ fhe thar then J ftruck with
my rapyer then fhe fell in a fitt and when it was
ouer fhe faid you kild hur and immedatly Sary good
com and carrid hur away, this was about 12 a clock.
The fame day after lecttor in ye faid : Jngerfolls
chamber abigaill wiliams mary walcot faid that
goody hobs of topfell bitt mary walcot by ye foot
then both falling into a fit as foone as it was ouer
ye faid william hobs and his wife goe both of them
a longe ye table ye faid huchefon tooke his rapier
ftabed gooddy hobs one ye fide as abigaill williams
and mary walcot faide ye faid abigaill and mar faid
ye roome was full of yᵐ then ye faid huchefon & Ely
putnam ftabed with their raperres at a uentor yn
faid mary and abigell you haue killed a greet black
woman of Stonintown and an Jndian that come
with her for ye flore is all couered with blood then
ye faid mary and abigaill looked out of dores and
faid ye faw a greet company of them one a hill &
there was three of them lay dead ye black woman
and the indian and one more yᵗ ye knew not.
This being about 4 a clock in ye after noone.

### *Sufannah Shelden v. Geo. Burroughs.*

The Complaint of Sufannah Shelden againft mr
burros which brought a book to mee and told mee
if i would not fet my hand too it hee would tear
mee to peeffes i told him i would not then hee told

mee hee would starve me to death then the next
morning hee tould mee hee could not starve mee
to death, but hee would choake mee that my uit-
tals should doe me but litl good then he tould mee
his name was borros which had preached at the
vilage the last night hee came to mee and asked mee
whither i would goe to the uillage to morrow to
witnes against him i asked him if he was examened
then he told hee was then i told him i would goe
then hee told mee hee would kil mee beefour
morning then hee apeared to mee at the hous of
nathanniel ingolson and told mee hee had been the
death of three children at the eastward and had kiled
two of his wifes the first hee smouthered and the
second he choaked and killed two of his own children.

*Major Brown, Thomas Ruck, Thomas Evans, Sarah
Wilfon, Martha Tyler & als v. Geo. Burroughs.*

Memorand^m in m^r George Burroughs Tryall befides ye written Euidences y^t was Sworne Seu^ll who
gave y^rs by word of mouth Majo^r Browne holding
out a heauy Gun w^th one hand.

Thomas Ruck of his fudden coming in after y^m
and y^t he could tell his thoughts.

Thomas Euans y^t he carried out Barr^els Moloffes
and meat &c out of a canoo whilft his mate went
to ye fort for hands to help out w^th y^m Sarah Wilfon Confefs^t y^t ye night before m^r Burroughs was
Executed y^t y^r was a great meeting of ye witches
Nigh Sarj^t Chandlers y^t m^r Bur. was y^r and yy had

ye Sac[t] and after yy had done he tooke leaue and bid y[m] Stand to y[r] faith, and not own any thing.

Martha Tyler faith ye fame w[th] Sarah Wilfon & Seuerall others,

### *Indictment v. Abigail Faulkner No.* 1.

Effex in the Prouince of the Maffachufetts Bay in New Englandfs. | Anno R R[s] & Reginee Gulielmi & Mariee Anglice &c QuartoAnnoq Domini 1692.

The Iurers for o[r] Sou[r] Lord and Lady King and Queen do prefent that Abigaill ffalkner Wife of ffrancis ffalkner of Andivor In the County of Effex aforf[d] Hufband[m] on or about the beginning of Auguft In the year aforefaid and divers othec dayes and times as well before as after Certaine Deteftable Arts called Witchcraft and Sorceries Wickedly Malliftioufly and fellonioufly hath vfed practifed & Exercifed at and in the Towne of Boxford in the County of Effex aforefaid in vpon and againft One Martha Sprague of Boxford aforefaid Single Woman by which faid wicked Acts the faid Martha Sprague the day and yea[r] aforefaid and diuers other dayes and times both before and after was and is Tortur[d] Aflicted Confumed Pined Wafted and Tormented and alfo for Sundry other Acts of Witchcraft by the faid Abigaill ffalkner Comitted and done Before and Since that time againft the Peace of o[r] Sou[r] Lord and Lady the King and Queen theire Crowne and dignity and the forme of the Stattute in that Cafe made and Prouided.

*Indictment v. Abigail Faulkner No. 2.*

Effex in the province | Anno R R$^s$ & Reginee Guli-
of the Maffachufetts | elmi & Marie Anglie &c$^a$
Bay in New England fs. | Quarto Annoq Domini 1692.

The Jurors for our Sou$^r$ Lord and Lady the King and Queen doe prefent That Abigaill ffalkner wife of ffrances falkner of Andivo$^r$ In the County of Effex Hufhandman in and About the begining of Auguft In the Yeare aforefaid and diuers and dayes and times as well before as after Certaine deteftable arts called Witchcraft and Sorceries Wickedly Mallitioufly and fellonioufly hath vfed practifed and Exercifed at and in the Towne of Andivor in the County of Effex aforefaid in upon and againft one Sarah Phelps daughter of Samuel Phellps of Andivo$^r$ aforefaid hufbandman by which faid Wicked Acts the f$^d$ Sarah Phellps the day and yeare aforefaid and divers other days and times both before and after was and is Tortured Aflicted Confumed Pined Wafted and Tormented, and alfo for fundry other acts of Witchcraft by the faid Abigaill ffalkner Comitted and done before and fince that time againft the peace of our Sou$^r$ Lord and Lady the King and Queen theire Crowne and Dignity and the forme of ye Stattute In y$^t$ cafe made and Prouided.

*Examination of Abigail Faulkner.*

Abig$^l$ ffolkner examined Aug$^{st}$ 11 : 1692.
M$^r$ Hauthorne : M$^r$ Corwin ; and Cap. Higgin-
R$^a$

fon preffent when fhe was brought into ye room :
ye afflicted perfons fell down. mr Ha : you are
heare aprehended for witchcraft : but anfwd J know
nothing of it : with ye caft of her eye Mary Walcot and ye reft of ye afflicted mary waren and others
fell down : it was fd to her do you not fee. She
fd yes but it is ye deuill dos it in my fhape : mary
Walcot fd fhe had feen her 2 monthes : a good
while agoe but was not hurt by her till laft night :
An Putnam fayd fhe had feen fd ffalknr but was
not hurt by her till laft night and then fhe pulled
me off my hors : mary warin fd fhe had feen her in
company with other witches : but was not hurt by
her till lately.

Mary Warin and others of ye afflicted were
ftruck down into fitts and helped up out of their
fitts by a touch of Abigl ffolkner hand : fhe was
urged to confes ye truth for ye creddit of hir Town :
her Couz. Eliz Ionfon urged her with that but fhe
refufed to do it faying god would not require her
to confefs that yt fhe was not gilty of.

Phelpfes daughter complayned her afflicting her :
but fhe denyed that fhe had any thing to doe with
witchcraft : fhe fd ffalknr had a cloth in her hand,
that when fhe fqueezed in her hand ye afflicted fell
into grevous fits as was obferved : ye aflicted fayd
Danll Eames and Capt ffloyd was upon that cloth
when it was upon ye table.

She fayd fhe was forry they were afflicted : but
fhe was told and it was obfervd fhe did not fhed a
tear: mary warin was pulld undr ye table and was

helpd out of her fitt by a touch of ſd ffaulknʳ ſhe
ſᵈ ſhe had looked on ſome of theſe afflicted : when
they came to Andovʳ and hurt them not : but ſhe
was told it was before ſhe had began to afflicte them
ſhe was told that it was reported ſhe uſed to con-
jure with a ſeiv. but ſhe ſᵈ it was not ſo that ſtory
was cleared up : and

August 30 : 92. Abigˡ ffokner before their Ma-
jeſtʳˢ Juſtices at firſt denyed witchcraft as ſhe had
done before : but afterwards ſhe owned that ſhe
was Angry at what folk ſd : when her Couz. Eliz.
Jonſon was taken up and folk laught and ſᵈ her ſiſter Jonſon would come out next and ſhe did look
with an evil eye on yᵉ afflicted perſons and did con-
ſent that they ſhould be afflicted becavs they were
yᵉ caus of bringing her kindred out and ſhe did
wiſh them ill and her ſpirit being raiſed ſhe did
pinch her hands together : and ſhe knew not but
that yᵉ devil might take that advantage but it was
ye devil not ſhe that afflicted them ; this ſhe ſaid
ſhe did at Capᵗ Chandlers gariſon : yᵉ Right after
Eliz. Jonſon had bin examined before Capt Brad-
ſtreet in ye day.

This is ye ſubſtance of what ſᵈ Abigˡ ffolkners
examination was taken out of my characters :

Atteſt,                       Simon Willard.

The abouefᵈ Examination was before John Hathorne Juſᵗ peace.

### *Roſe Foſter v. Abigail Faulkner.*

The depoſiſtion of Roſe ffoſter who teſtifieth &
ſaith J have ben moſt grevioully afflected and tor-

mented by Abigail ffalkner of Andeueour alſo J
have ſeen Abigail ffalkner or hir Apperance moſt
greviouſly affleꝗt and torment martha Sprague ſarah
phelps and Hannah Bigsbe ſence the begining Augſt
and J veryly beleue that Abigail ffalkner is a wiꝗth
and that ſhe has often affleꝗted me and the afforeſaid perſon by aꝗts of wiꝗthcraff.

The abouenamed Roſe ffoſter affirmed beffore ye
Jrand inqueſt that yᵉ aboue written evidence is truth
vppon her oath Sepᵗ 17 : 1691.

### *Mary Walcott v. Abigail Faulkner.*

The depoſiſtion of mary wàlcott who teſtifieth
and ſaith that about the 9ᵗʰ Auguſt 1692. J was
moſt dreadfully affleꝗted by a woman that tould me
her name was Abigail ffalkner but on the 11ᵗʰ of
Auguſt being the day of the examination of Abigail ffalkner ſhe did moſt dreadfully afflict me dureing the time of hir examination J ſaw Abigail
ffalkner or hir Apperance moſt greviouſly affleꝗt
and torment ſarah phelps and Ann putnam and J
veryly beleve in my heart that Abigail ffalkner is
a wiꝗth and that ſhe has often affleꝗted me and the
afforeſaid ſaid perſons by aꝗts of wiꝗthcraft.

The above named mary Walcott affirmed ye
Grand inqueſt that yᵉ aboue written Euidences is
truth vpon her oath 17 Sept. : 1692.

### *Martha Sprague v. Abigail Faulkner.*

The depoſiſtion of Martha Spreague who teſtifieth and ſaith that J haue ben moſt greuiouſly af-

flected and tormented by Abigail ffalkner of Andevor fence the begining of Auguft 1692. alfo J faw Abigail ffalkner or hir Apperance moft grevioufly torment and afflict Hannah Bigfbe and Rofe ffofter and Sarah phelps and J veryly beleue in my heart that Abigaill ffalkner is a wicth and that fhe has often afflected me and feverall others by acts of witchcraft

The aboue named Martha fprague affirmed before ye grand inqueft that ye aboue written evidence is truth vpon her oath 17 Sept 1692.

### *Mary Warren v. Abigail Falkner.*

The depofiftion of marry warren who teftifieth and faith that Abigail ffalkner of Andevor did moft grevioufly afflict and torment me on 11th Auguft 1692 dureing the time of hir examination for if fhe did but look upon me fhe would ftrick me downe or almoft choak me alfo on the day of her examination J faw Abigail ffalkner or hir Apperance moft grevioufly affect and torment mary walcott Ann putnam and Sarah phelps and J veryly beleue that Abigail ffalkner is a wicth and that fhe has often afflected me and feverall other by acts of wicthcraft

Mary Waren ownd upon her oath to ye grand Inqueft that ye above written evidence is ye truth. Sept 17: 1692.

### *Sarah Phelps v. Abigail Faulkner.*

The depofiftion of Sarah phelps who teftifioth and faith that about the begining of Auguft 1692 J was moſt greviouſly afflected and tormented by Abigail ffalkner or hir Apperance : but moſt dreadfully ſhe did torment on the 11 Auguſt being the day of her examination for if ſhe did but loock upon me ſhe would ſtrick me down or almoſt choake me : alſo ſence the begining of Auguſt J have ſeen Abigaill ffalkner or hir apperance moſt greviouſly afflect and torment mary Walcott Ann putnam and Martha ſprague and J veryly beleue in my heart that Abigail ffalkner is a wicth and that ſhe has very offten afflected me and the afforeſaid perſons by acts of wicthcraft.

The aboue named Sarah Phelps affirmed before ye Grand inqueſt that ye aboue written evidence is truth vpon her oath ye aboue written evidence is truth vpon her oath ye 17 Sep$^t$ 1692.     Jurat.

*Dorothy Faulkner, Abigail Faulkner, Martha Tyler, Johannah Tyler, Sarah Wilſon, Joſeph Draper v. Abigail Faulkner.*

dorritye fforkner and Abigale fforknor children to Abigall fforknor of Andouer now in priſon confarſed befor the honoured majaſtrats vpon theire examination heare in Salam the 16 day of this enſtant ſubtember 1692 that thire mother apared and mayd them witches and alſo marthy Tyler Johanah Tyler and Sarih willſon and Joſeph draper all acknowlidge that they ware lead into that dreadfull ſin of witchcraft by her meanſe the foreſ$^d$ Abigale forknor   The above named perſons each and euery one of them did affirm before ye Grand inqueſt that the aboue written evidences are truth : 17 ſept 1692.

### *Ann Putnam v. Abigail Faulkner.*

The depoſiſtion of Ann putnam who teſtifieth and ſaith that about the 9th of Auguſt 1692. J was affleſted by a woman which tould me her name was ffalkner : but on the 11th of Auguſt being the day of the Examination of Abigail ffalkner ſhe did moſt dreadfully torment me during the time of hir Examination alſo on the day of hir Examination J ſaw Abigaill ffalkner or hir Apperance moſt greviouſly affleſt and torment mary walcott ſarah phelps and J beleue that Abigal ffalkner is a wiſth and that ſhe has often affleſted me and ſeueral others by aſts of witchcraft.

The above named Ann Putnam affirmed before ye Grand inqueſt that ye aboue written evidence is the truth vpon her oath.

Sworne before ye grand Jury. Sept. 17. 1692.

### *Indiſtment v. Ann Foſter.*

Eſſex in the Province of the Maſſachuetts, Bay in New England ſs. } Anno R Rˢ & Reginee Guliel-mi & Mariee Angliee &cᵃ Quarto Annoq Domini 1692.

The Juriors for ouʳ Souʳ Lord & Lady King & Queen doe preſent that Ann ffoſter of Andivor In the County of Eſſex Widow Jn and vpon the fifteenth day of July in the year aforefd and diuers other days and times as well before as after Certaine Deteftable arts called Witchcraft and Sorceries wickedly and Malitioufly and fellonioufly hath vfed practifed & Exercifed at and in the Towne of Salem in the County of Effex aforefaid in vpon and againft one Eliza Hobert of Salem in the County of Effex aforefaid Single Woman by which faid wicked arts the faid Elizabeth Hobert the day and yeate aforefaid and divers other days and times both before and after was and is Tortured afflicted Confumed Pined wafted and Tormented and alfo for fundry other acts of witchcraft by the faid Ann fofter Comitted and done before and fince that time againft the peace of or Sour Lord and Lady the King and Queen theire Crowne and Dignity, and the forme of the Stattute in that Cafe made and Provided.

The examination and Confeffion of Ann ffofter at Salem Vilage 15 July 1692. after a while Ann ffofter confefed that the deuill apered to her in the fhape of a bird at feueral Times, fuch a bird as fhe neuer faw the like before, and that fhe had had this gift (viz. of ftriking ye aflicted downe w$^{th}$ her eye euer) fince, and being afk$^t$ why fhe thought y$^t$ bird was the diuill fhe anfwered becaufe he came white and vanifhed away black and y$^t$ the diuill told her y$^t$ fhe fhould haue this gift and y$^t$ fhe muft beleiue him and told her fhe fhould haue profperity, and fhe faid y$^t$ he had apeared to her three times and was always as a bird, and the laft time was a bout half a yeare fince, and fat vpon a table had two legs &

great eyes and y^t it was the fecond time of his apear-
ance that he promifed her profperity and y^t it was
Carriers wife about three weeks agoe y^t came and
perfwaded her to hurt thefe people.

16 .July. 1692. Ann ffofter Examined confefed
y^t it was Goody Carier y^t made her a witch y^t fhe
came to her in perfon about Six yeares agoe & told
her if fhe would not be a witch y^e divill fhould tare
her in peices and cary her away at w^ch time fhe
promifed to Serue the divill, y^t fhe had bewitched
a hog of John Loujoys to death and that fhe had
hurt fome perfons in Salem Vilage, y^t goody Carier
came to her and would haue her bewitch two children of Andrew Allins and that fhe had then two
popets made and ftuck pins in them to bewitch ye
faid children by which one of them dyed ye other
very fick, that fhe was at the meeting of the witches
at Salem Village, y^t Goody Carier came and told
her of the meeting and would haue her goe, fo they
got upon Sticks and went faid Jorny and being
there did fee m^r Burroughs y^e minifter who fpake
to them all, and this was about two months agoe
that ther was then twenty five perfons meet together, that fhe tyed a knot in a Rage and threw it
into the fire to hurt Timo. Swan and that fhe did
hurt the reft y^t complayned of her by fquefing
popets like them and fo almoft choaked them.

18 July 1692. Ann ffofter Examined confefed
y^t ye deuil in fhape of a man apered to her w^th
Goody carier about fix yeare fince when they made

S^a

her a witch and that fhe promifed to ferue the divill two yeares, upon w<sup>ch</sup> the Diuill promifed her
profperity and many things but neuer performed it,
that fhe and martha Carier did both ride on a ftick
or pole when they went to the witch meeting at
Salem Village and that the ftick broak : as they
ware caried in the aire aboue the tops of the trees,
and they fell but fhe did hang faft about the neck
of Goody Carier and ware prefently at the vilage,
that fhe was then much hurt of her Leg, fhe further faith that fhe hard fome of the witches fay, that
there was three hundred and fiue in the whole
Country and that they would ruin that place y<sup>e</sup>
Vilage, alfo faith ther was was prefent att that metting two men befides m<sup>r</sup> Burroughs y<sup>e</sup> minifter and
one of them had gray haire, fhe faith y<sup>t</sup> fhe formerly frequented the publique metting to worfhip
god. but the diuill had fuch power ouer her y<sup>t</sup> fhe
could not profit there and y<sup>t</sup> was her undoeing :
fhe faith y<sup>t</sup> about three or foure yeares agoe Martha Carier told her fhe would bewitch James Hobbs
child to death and the child dyed in twenty four
hours.

21. July : 92. Ann ffofter Examined Owned
her former conffefion being read to her and further
conffefed that the difcourfe amongft ye witches at
ye meeting at Salem village was that they would
afflict there to fet up the Diuils Kingdome. This
confefion is true as witnefe my hand :

the marke of<br>
Ann + ffofter

Ann ffofter Signed and Owned the aboue Examination and Conffefion before me

    JOHN HIGGINSON Jus[t] peace
Salem Septem[br] 1692.

### *Indictment v. Mary Lacey.*

| Effex in the Province of the Maffachufetts Bay in New England | Anno R R[s] Reginee Gullielmi & Mariee & Angliee & Quarto Annoq. Domini 1692. |

The Jurors for o[r] Sou[r] Lord and Lady the King and Queen doe prefent that Mary Lacey Wife of Lawrence Lacey of Andivor in the County of Effex Hufbandman vpon the Twentieth day of July In the year aforefaid and diuers other dayes and times as well before as after Certaine deteftable Arts called Witchcraft and Soceries wickedly Mallitioufly and ffellonioufly hath vfed Practifed and Exercifed at and in the Towne of Salem in the County of Effex aforefaid in vpon and againft one Elizabeth Hobert of Salem aforefaid Single Woman by which Said wicked Arts the faid Eliza : Hobert ye day and yea[r] aforefaid and diuers other dayes and Times Both Before and after was and is Tortured aflicted Confum[d] Pined Wafted and Tormented and alfo for Sundry other Acts of witchcraft by the faid Mary lacey comitted and done Before and fince that time againft the Peace of o[r] Sou[r] Lord and Lady the King and Queen theire Crowne and Dignity and. the forme of the Stattute in that Cafe made and Provided

### Examination of Mary Lacey.

21 July 1692. A part of Goody Laceyes 2<sup>d</sup> Examination and confeſſion to be added to the firſt. Befóre maj<sup>r</sup> Gedney, M<sup>r</sup> Hauthorn & M<sup>r</sup> Corwin.

When Goody foſter was upon examination the ſecond tyme, Goody Lacey was brought in alſo, who ſaid to her mother foſter, we haue forſaken Jeſus chriſt, and the devil hath got hold of us. how ſhall we get cleare of this evil one.

ſhe confeſes that her mother foſter, Goody Carryer and herſelf rid upon a pole to Salem Village meeting, and that the pole broke a litle way off from the village, ſhe ſayth further that about 3 or 4 yeares agoe ſhe ſaw miſtreſs Bradburry Goody How and Goody nurſe baptiſed by the old Serpent at newburry falls And that he dipped theire heads in the water and then ſaid they wer his and he had power over them, ſhe ſayes there were Six baptiſed at that tyme who were ſome of the chieff or heigher powers, and that there might be neare about a hundred in company at that tyme. It being aſked her, after what maner ſhe went to Newberry falls, anſwered the devil carryed her in his armes, And Sayth further that if ſhe doe take a ragg, clout or any ſuch thing and Roll it up together, And Imagine it to repreſent ſuch and ſuch a perſone, Then whatſoever ſhe doth to that Ragg or clout ſo rouled up, The perſone repreſented thereby will be in lyke manner afflicted. It being againe aſked her if what ſhe had ſaid was all true, She anſwered affirmatively, confeffing alfo that Andrew Carryer was witch.

She confeffes that fhe afflicted Timothy Swan in Comp² with miftrefs Bradbury Goody Carryer, Richard Carryer and her own daughter mary lacey, The afflicted him with an Jron fpindle and fhe thinks they did once with a tobacko pipe.

She faid fhe was in Swans chamber and it being afk't which way fhe got in anfwered the devil helpt her in at the window : She alfo remembers the afflicting of Ballards wife, and yᵗ Richᵈ Carryer was yʳ alfo,

She faid further the devil take away her memory and will not let her remember.

### *Eliz : Hubbard v. Mary Lacey.*

Eliz : Hubert affirmed to yᵉ grand Jnqueft that fhe hath feen Mary lafcy fenʳ afflict Jofeph Ballards wife of Andover fhe fayth alfo that fᵈ Mary Lafcy did at ye time of her examination afflict her fᵈ Eliz Hubbert and mercy Lewis and fhe dos beleue fᵈ mary lafcy was a witch and afflicted me and ye above fᵈ perfons by witchcraft but fhe never afflicted her fᵈ Hubberd fince fhe confeffed.

### *Mercy Lewis v. Mary Lacey.*

upon oath Septʳ 14 : 1692.

Mercy lewis affirmed to ye grand Jnqueft that he faw Mary Lafcy fenʳ afflict Jofeph Ballards wife of Andover fhe faith alfo : that mary Lafcy fenʳ afflicted her f<sup>d</sup> Lewis and Eliz Hubbert at y<sup>e</sup> time of her examination but fince fhe has not hurt her : fhe fayth fhe beleeves f<sup>d</sup> Lacy was a witch and afflicted her and ye aboue named perfons by witchcraft Sept<sup>r</sup> ye 14: 1692. upon oath.

### Mary Warren v. Mary Lacey.

Mary Warin affirmed to y<sup>e</sup> Grand Jnqueft that fhe faw Mary Lafcy fen<sup>r</sup> Afflict Eliz : Hubbert & Mercy lewis at ye time of her examination : fhe owned it upon her former oath Sept 14: 1692.

### Indictment v. Rebecca Eames No. 1.

| Effex in the Province of the Maffachufetts Bay in New England fs. | Anno R R<sup>s</sup> Reginee Gulielmi & Mariee Angliee &c Quarto Annoq Domini 1692. |
|---|---|

The Juriors for our Sou<sup>r</sup> Lord and Lady the King and Queen doe prefent. That Rebekah Eames wife of Robert Eames of Boxford in the County of Effex aforefaid In the yeare aforef<sup>d</sup> and diuers other dayes and times as well before as After Certaine Deteftable Arts called witchcraft and Sorceries Wickedly Mallitioufly and ffellonioufly hath vfed practifed and Exercifed at and in the Towne of Andivor in the County of Effex aforef<sup>d</sup> in vpon and againft one Timothy Swan aforef<sup>d</sup> by which faid wicked acts the faid Timothy Swan the day and yeare aforef<sup>d</sup> and Diuers other dayes and times both before and was and is Tortured aflicted Confumed Wafted Pined and Tormented and alfo for Sundry other Acts of Witchcraft by the said Rebekah Eames Comitted and done before and since that time against the peace of our Sou[r] Lord and Lady the King and Queen theire Crowne and dignity and the forme in the Stattute In that cafe made and provided.

(Endorfement)

She acknowledged y[t] fhe aflicted Tim[o] Swann.

*Indictment v. Rebecca Eames, No. 2.*

Effex in the province of the Maffachuetts Bay, in New England fs } An[o] R R[s] & Reginee Guliel-mi & Mariee Angliee &c quarto Anoq. Dom. 1692.

The Juriors for o[r] Sou[r] Lord and Lady the King and Queen doe prefent that Rebekah Eames Wife of Robert Eames of Boxford in ye County afores[d] About twenty fix yeares paft in the Towne of Boxford in the County aforefaid Wickedly and felloni-oufly A covenant with The evill Speritt the Devill did make in and by which Wicked Couenant Shee the faid Rebekah Eames hir Soule and body to the Deuill did giue and promifed to Serve and obey him and Keep his wayes Contrary to the Stattute of the firft yeare of ye Reigne of King James the firft in that cafe made and Provided And Againft the peace of our Soveraigne Lord and Lady the King and Queen their Crowne and Dignity

*Examination of Rebecca Eames.*

Rebecca Eames examined before Salem, Majef-trats, Aug[st] 19: 1692. She owned fhe had bin in yᵉ fnare a monthe or 2 : and had bin perfuaded to it 3 monthes and that yᵉ devil apeared to her like a colt very ugly ye firſt time but ſhe would not own yᵗ ſhe had bin baptiſed by him ſhe did not know but yᵗ yᵉ devil did perfuade her to renounce god and chriſt and ffolow his wicked wayes and that ſhe did take his Counfell and that ſhe did afflict Timo: Swan ſhe did not know but that yᵉ devil might aſk her body and foul and ſhe knows not but yᵗ ſhe did give him foul and body after ward ſhe ſᵈ ſhe did do it and that ſhe would forſake god and his works : and ye devil promiſed her to give her powr to avenge herſelfe on them that offended her after-ward ſhe ſᵈ ye devil apeared to her 7 year agoe and that he had tempted her to ly and had made her to afflict perſons but ſhe could not tell their names that ſhe firſt afflicted 2 who came wᵗ ye devil when he made you a witch A : a ragged girl : they came to gether and they perſwaded me to afflict : and J afflicte mary Warin and an other fayr face it is aboᵗ a quarter of a year agoe : J did it by ſticking of pins : but did you afflict Swan : yes, but I am forry for it : 2. where had you your ſpear A. J had nothing but an all but was it with yoʳ body or ſpi-rit you came to hurt theſe maydes : A. with my ſpirit : 2. but can you aſk them forgivnes A : J will fall down on my knees to aſk it of them : She would not own that ſhe ſignd yᵉ devils book when he aſkd her body and foul : but he would have had her done it nor to a burch Rign nor nothing : She ſᵈ ye devil was in ye Shape of a hors when he

caried her to afflict: but would not own anybody
went with her to afflict but y⁰ afflicted f⁰ her fon
Dan¹¹ went with her to afflict: 2. did you not fay
y⁰ Devil baptifed yo⁰ fon daniell.   A. he told me
fo; but; did you not touch the book nor lay yo⁰
hand on book nor paper. A: I layd my hand on
nothing without it was a peice of board: and did
you lay yo⁰ hand on ye board when he bid you. A:
yes; mary Lafcy f⁰ fhe had given her fon Dan¹¹ to
ye devil at 2 years old: and y⁰ her apertion told her
fo: but fhe could not remember it: fhe was bid to
take warin and lafcy by y⁰ hand and beg forgivnes
and did fo and they forgave her fhe f⁰ if fhe had
given her fon Dan¹¹ to ye devil it was in an Angry
fitt fhe did not know but fhe might do it nor J do
not know he is a wich but J am afrayd he is: mary
lafcy faw her fon Dan¹¹ ftand before her and f⁰
Dan¹¹ bid his mother not confefs he was a Wich:
his mother did not know fhe f⁰ but fhe might fe
him for fhe faw a burlling thing before her: Mary
Lafcy f⁰ fhe had baptized her fon Dan¹¹ and fhe had
bin babtized in five mile Pond: fhe f⁰ ye reafon
fhe feared Dan¹¹ was a witch: was becaus he ufed
dredfull bad words when he was Angry: and bad
wifhes; being afked the age of Dan¹¹ fd he was 28
years old; fhe was told fhe had bin long a witch;
then, if fhe gave her fon to ye devil at 2 years old
fhe owned fhe had bin difcontented fince fhe had
bin in league with y⁰ devil: fhe knew not but y⁰
devil might come once a day lik a mous or ratt:
fhe f⁰ fhe knew Sarah parker but did not know her

to be a wich: but fhe heard fhe had bin crofd in love and ye devil had come to her and kifd her: who was with you when you afflicted fwan : A. nobody but my fon Dan^{ll} he was there when J came theether: fhe would have Dan^{ll} perfwaded to confes but was told fhe were beft to perfwade him becaus fhe knew him to be a wich: fhe was afkt if fhe was at y^e execution : fhe f^d fhe was at y^e hous below y^e hill: fhe faw a few folk : the woman of y^e hous had a pin ftuck into her foot : but fhe f^d fhe did not doe it: but how do you afflict: A : J Confent to it ; but have you bin a wicth 26 years : A: no, J cannot remember but 7 years and have afflicted about a quarter of a year : but : if you have bin a wich fo long : why did you not afflict before feing you promifed to Sen ye devil, A : others did not Afflict before and the devil did not require it : but : doth not ye devil threaten you if you not do what he fes: A, yes he thretens to tere me in peices : but did you ufe to goe to meeting on Sabbath dayes ; yes, but not fo often as J fhould have done: what fhape did the devil com in when you layd yo^r hand on y^e board: A. J cannot tell except it was a mous,

*Indictment v. Samuel Wardwell No. 1.*

| Effex in the province of the Maffachufetts Bay in New England fs. | Anno R R^s Reginee Gulielmi Mariee Angliee &c Quarto Annoq. Domini 1692. |
|---|---|

**The** Juriors for our Sou^r Lord and Lady the King

and Queen doe prefent that Samuel Wardell of Andivor Jn the County of Effex Carpenter on or
about the fifteenth day of Auguft Jn the yeare
aforefaid and diuers other days and times as well before as after Certaine deteftable arts called Witchcraft and Sorceries Wickedly Mallitioufly and fellonioufly hath ufed practifed and Exercifed at and in
the Towne of Boxford in the County of Effex
aforefaid in upon and againft one Martha Sprague
of Boxford in the County of Effex aforefaid Single-
woman by which faid wicked Acts the faid Martha Sprague the day and yeare aforefaid and diuers
other days and times both before and after was and is
Tortured Aflicted Confumed Pined Wafted and
Tormented, and alfo for fundry other Acts of
Witchcraft by the faid Samuel Wardell Comitted
and done before and fince that time againft the
peace of our Soueraigne Lord and Lady the King
and Queen theire Crowne and dignity And the
forme in the Stattute in that cafe made and Prouided.

*Indictment v. Samuel Wardwell No. 2.*

Effex in the province of the Maffachufetts Bay, in New Eng-land fs. — An° R Rˢ & Reginee Guliel-mi & Mariee Angliee &c Quarto Anoq. Dom. 1692.

The Juriors for our Souʳ Lord and Lady the King
and Queen pʳfent Samuel Wardell of Andivor in
the County of Effex Carpentʳ About Twenty yeares
agoe in the Towne of Andivor Jn the County of

Eſſex aforeſaid Wickedly and ffelloniouſly he the
ſaid Samuel Wardell with the Evill Speritt the Devill
A Couenant did make Wherin he promiſed to honor Worſhip and beliue the devill Contrary to the
Stattute of King James the firſt in that behalfe made
and provided, And Againſt the peace of Sovareigne
Lord and Lady the King and Queen theire Crowne
and dignity.

### *Examination of Samuel Wardwell.*

The examination and Confeſſion of Sam[ll] wardwell taken Sep[t] 1st 92. before John Higginſon Eſq
of theire majties Juſtices of peace for the County
of Eſſex.

After the returneing of negative anſwers to ſeverall queſtions He ſaid he was ſenſible he was in the
ſnare of the devil, he uſed to be much diſcontented
that he could get no more work done, and that he
had been fooliſhly led along with telling of fortunes,
which ſometymes came to paſs, He uſed alſo when
any creature came into his field to bid the devil
take it, and it may be the devil took advantage of
him by that Conſtable foſter of Andover ſaid that
this wardwell told him once in the woods that when
he was a young man he could make all his cattell
come round about him when he pleaſed. The ſaid
wardwell being urged to tell o truth he proceeded
thus, That being once in a diſcontented frame he
ſaw ſome catts together with the appearance of a
man who called himſelf a prince of the aire & promiſed him he ſhould live comfortably and be a cap-

tain and requyred faid wardwell to honor him which he promifed to doe and it was about twenty years agoe: He faid the reafon of his difcontent then was becaufe he was in love with a maid named Barker who flighted his love, And the firft Apperance of the catt then was behind Capt[r] brad-ftreets houfe, about a week after that a black man appeared in the day tyme at the fame place and called hirfelf prince and lord and told him the faid wardwell he muft worfhip and believe him, and promifed as above, with this addition that he fhould never want for any thing but that the black man had never performed anything, and further that when he would goe to prayer in his family the de-vil wold begin to be angry. He faith alfo that at that tyme when the devil appeared and told him he was prince of the aire that then he Syned his book by makeing a marke like a fquare with a black pen and that the devil brought him the pen and Jnk: He faith further he couenanted with the devil untill he fhould arryve to the age of fixty years and that he is now about the age of 46 years And at that tyme the devil promifed on his part, as is above ex-preft, he faid it was about a fnight agoe fince he began to afflict, and confeffes that mary Lilly and Hannah Tayler of Ridding were of his company, Further he faith that martha Sprague was the firft he afflicted, that the devil put him upon it and threatned him y[r] unto And that he did it by pinch-ing his coat and buttons when he was difcontented, and gave the devil a commiffion fo to doe, He fayes

he was baptized by the black man at Shaw fhin
river alone and was dypt all over and beleues he
renounced his former baptifme

John Higginfon

Sam<sup>ll</sup> Wardwell owned to y<sup>e</sup> grand Jnqueft that
ye above written confeffion was taken from his
mouth and that he faid it but he f<sup>d</sup> he belyed himfelfe he alfo f<sup>d</sup> it was alone one he knew he fhould
dye for it whether he ownd it or no.

Sept<sup>r</sup> 13<sup>th</sup> 1692.

### *Martha Sprague v. Sam<sup>l</sup> Wardwell.*

Martha Spreag Aged 16 years Affirmed to ye
grand Jnqueft : that Sam<sup>ll</sup> Wardwell has afflicted
her both before his examination and at ye time of
it by pinching and fticking pinfe into her and ftriking me downe and yefterday when I had a warant
to come to court faid wardwell did grevioufly afflict me J alfo have feen f<sup>d</sup> wardwell afflict Rofe
ffofter and her mother and I veryly beleeve he is a
wizzard and that he afflicted me and ye above mentioned by acts of witchcraft,

Sep<sup>tr</sup> 14; 1692   Jurat:

### *Mary Warrin v. Sam<sup>l</sup> Wardwell.*

Mary Warin affirmd to Jury of Inqueft that
Sam<sup>ll</sup> Wardwell hath often afflicted her and that he
now before y<sup>e</sup> grand inqueft hath afflicted her alfo
fhe fd that y<sup>t</sup> on y<sup>e</sup> day and at ye time of f<sup>d</sup> ward-
wels examination he did afflict Martha Spreag and

fhe veryly beleevs f<sup>d</sup> Wardwell is a wizzard and y<sup>t</sup> he afflicted her and martha Spreag by witchcraft. Jurat Sep<sup>t</sup> : 14 : 1692 upon her oath.

### *Mary Walcott v. Sam<sup>l</sup> Wardwell.*

Mary Walcot affirmed to ye grand Jnqueſt that fhe ſaw Sam<sup>ll</sup> Wardwell or his Apperition pull Martha Spreag off from her horfe as fhe was riding out of Salem and verily beleevs he did it by witch-craft. Sept<sup>r</sup> 14 : 1692 upon oath   Jurat.

### *Ephraim Fofter v. Sam<sup>l</sup> Wardwell.*

The depofetion of Ephraim ffofter of Andover aged about thirty four years this deponant teftifyeth and fayeth that he heard Samuell Wordwell the prifoner now at the bare tell my wife that fhe fhould haue five gurls before fhe fhould have a fon ; which thing is come to pafe : and J heard him tell dority Eames hur forten and J have heard faid dority fay after that fhe belived wardwell was a witch or els he cold neuer tell what he did and J took knotes that faid wardwall would look in their hand and then would caft his eyes down upon y<sup>e</sup> ground all-ways before he told Enything this I have both feen and heard feuerall times and about feveral perfons, and y<sup>t</sup> he could make cattle come to him when he pleafed.   Jurat in Curia.

### *Thomas Chandler v. Sam<sup>l</sup> Wardwell.*

The tiftimony of Thomas Chandler aged about 65 who faith that J have often hard Samuell war-

dle of Andouer till yung perſon their fortine and
he was much adicted to that and mayd ſport of it
and farther ſaith not   Jurat in Curia.

### *Joſeph Ballard v. Sam^l Wardwell.*

The teſtimony of Joſeph Ballard of andouer eaged
about 41 yeares ſaith that my brother John
Ballard told me that Samuel Wardel told him that
J had reported that he had bewitched my wife
theſe wordes ware ſpoken before J had any knolidg
of my wife being aflicted by wichcraft after J meting with ſaid Samuel wardel priſnor at the bar J
told him that J douteed that he was gilty of hurting my wife for J had no ſutch thoughts nor had
ſpoken any ſuch wordes of him or any other perſon
and tharefore J doe not know but you are gilty, &
further y^t Sam^ll Wardwell owned to this deponent
that he had ſpoke it to my brother.

Jurat in Curia,

### *Abigail Martin, John Bridges v. Sam^l Wardwell.*

the depoſition of Abigell marten of Andavr Aged
about ſixteen years this deponant teſtifyeth and
ſayeth that ſome time laſt winter Samuel wordwall
being at my fathers hows with John ffarnom : J
heard ſaid John farnom aſk ſaid wordwall his forteen, which he did and told him that he was in love
with a gurl but ſhould be croſt and ſhould goe to
the Sutherd which* ſaid farnom oned to be his
thought ſaid wardwall further told he had like to be
ſhot with a gon, and ſhould haue a foall of from

his horfe or fhould haue, which faid farnom, after oned that he told right.

And further J heard him tell Jeams bridges his forten that he loued a gurll at forteen years old which faid bridges oned to be the truth but cold not imagin how faid wordwall knew : for he neuer fpake of it ; John bridges, father of faid ieams bridges fayeth he heard Jeam fay J wonder how wordwall cold teell fo true

Jurat in Curia, by both.

### *Indictment v. Mary Parker.*

| Effex in the Province of the Maffachufetts Bay in New England fs | Anno R Rˢ & Reginee Gulielmi & Mariee Angliee &c Quarto Annoq. Domini 1692. |

The Jurors for oʳ Souʳ Lord and Lady the King and Queen doe prefent That Mary Parker of Andivor In the County of Effex Widdow ye firft day of Septembʳ In the yeare aforefaid and diuers other dayes and Times as well before as after Certaine deteftable Arts called Witchcraft and Sorceries Wickedly Malliftioufly and fellonioufly hath vfed practifed and Exercifed at and in the Towne of Salem in ye County of Effex aforefaid in upon and againft one Martha Sprague of Boxford in aforefaid the County of Effex aforefaid Single Woman By which faid wicked Acts the faid Martha Sprague ye day and yeaʳ aforefaid and divers other dayes and times hath before and after was and is Tortured aflicted Confumed Pined wafted and Tormented

Uª

and alfo for Sundry other acts of witchcraft by the faid Mary Parker Comitted and done before and fince that Time againft the peace of or Sou<sup>r</sup> Lord and Lady the King and Queen theire Crowne and dignity and the forme of the Stattute in that cafe made and Prouided.

### Examination of Mary Parker.

2 Sep<sup>r</sup> 1692. The Examination of mary parker of Andover widow taken before Barth° Gidny John Hathorne Jona<sup>t</sup> Corwin and John Higginfon Efq<sup>r</sup> ther majefties Juftices of the peace for the County of Effex in the forth yeare of theire majefties reigne.

upon mentioneing of her name, feverall afflicted perfones wer ftruck down as mary warrin Sarah churchhill, hannah poft, Sarah Bridges Mercy ward, And when fhe came before the Juftices, fhe recovered all the afflicted out of their fitts by the touch of ther hand. She is accufed for acting of witchcraft upon martha fprague And Sarah Phelps. 2. how long have y<sup>e</sup> been in the fnare of the devil.

Anfr. I know nothing of it. There is another woman of the fame name in Andover. But martha Spreague affirmed that this is the very woman that afflicted her : The faid mary parker Lookeing upon Sprague ftruck her down, and recovered her again out of her Mary Lacey being in a fitt, cryed out upon mary parker, and f<sup>d</sup> parker recovered her out of her fitt, mercy wardwell was twice afflicted by parker and recovered again by her;

William Barker lookeing upon mary Parker faid to her face That fhe was one of his company, And that the laft night fhe afflicted martha Sprague in company with him.

Mercy wardwell faid that this mary parker was alfo one of her company and that the faid parker afflicted Timothy Swan in her company—Mary Warrin in a violent fitt was brought neare haveing a pinn run through her hand and blood runing out of her mouth She was recovered from her fitt by fd mary parker, The faid mary warrin faid that this mary parker afflicted and tormented her, And further that fhe faw the faid parker at ane examination vp at Salem Village fitting upon one of the beams of the houfe.

I under written being appointed by the Juftices of the peace in Salem to wryt down the Examination of Mary Parker above mentioned, Doe teftify this to be a true copy of the originall examination, As to the fubftance of it,

W<sup>m</sup> Murray.

### *Jno Weftgate v. Mary Parker.*

In° Wefgate aged about forty years This deponant Teftifyeth thatt about Eight years fince he being att the houfe of m<sup>r</sup> Sam<sup>ll</sup> Beadle In the company of Ino Parker and feverall others, the wife of faid In° Parker came into the company and fcolded att and called her hufhand all to nought whereupon

I the said deponent tooke her husbands part telling of her it was an unbeseeming thing for her to come after him to the taverne and raile after thatt rate w<sup>th</sup> thatt she came up to me and called me rogue and bid me mind my owne busines and told me J had better have said nothing sometime afterwards, J y<sup>e</sup> s<sup>d</sup> deponent going ffrom the house of m<sup>r</sup> San<sup>ll</sup> King w<sup>n</sup> I came over againft Jn<sup>o</sup> Robinsons house I heard a great noyce coming ffrom towards m<sup>r</sup> babage his house then there apeared a black hogge running towards me w<sup>th</sup> open mouth as though he would have devoured me, att that Inftant time, I the said deponent fell downe vpon my hipp and my knjfe runn into my hipp up to the haft w<sup>n</sup> J came home my knife was in my sheath w<sup>n</sup> J drew itt out of the sheath then imediately the sheath fell all to peaces, and further this deponent teftifyeth thatt after he gott up from his fall his stockin and shue was full of blood and that he was forc't to craule along by the fence all the way home and the hogg followed him and never left him tell he came home, and haueing a stout dog then with mee, the dog run then away from him leapeing ouer y<sup>e</sup> fence and Crying much, which at other tymes vsed to Wory any hog well or Sufficiently, which hogg J then apprehended was either y<sup>e</sup> Diuell or some euill thing not a reall hog, and did then really Judge or determine in my mind that it was Either Goody parker or by her meenes, and procureing feareing y<sup>t</sup> she is a Witch.

Sworne Salem June 2<sup>d</sup> 1692. Before John Hathorne—Affiſtᵗ Jnᵒ Weſtgate declared yᵉ aboue written and what is written on the other ſide of this paper to be a true evidence before ye Jury of Jnqueſt upon yᵉ oath he hath taken : Septemᵇ 7 : 1692. Jurat in Curia.

### *Wᵐ Barker v. Mary Parker.*

Wᵐ Barker Junʳ affirmed to ye grand Jnqueſt that mary Parker did in company with him ſᵈ Barker confeſſed which was yᵉ 1 of Sepᵗ 1692. this he owned to ye grand Jnqueſt : Sepᵗ 16 : 1692. Owned in Court.

### *Mary Wardwell v. Mary Parker.*

Mercy Wardwell owned to yᵉ grand inqueſt that ſhe had ſeen ye ſhape of Mary Parker when ſhe ſᵈ Wardwell afflicted Timᵒ Swan : alſo ſhe ſᵈ ſhe ſaw ſᵈ parkers Shape when the ſᵈ wardwell afflicted Martha Sprage but J did not certainely know that ſᵈ parker was a witch : this ſhe owned to ye Grand Jnqueſt. Sept : 16 : 1692.

### *Jno Bullock v. Mary Parker.*

Jnᵒ Bullock aged 36 years teſtifieth yᵗ aboute ye middle of January laſt paſt one of my neighboᵣs told me yᵗ mrs parkʳ did lay upon ye durt & Snow if J did not take care of her yᵗ ſhe would periſh whereupon I did deſire ſome men yᵗ were in mye hous to goe and help her : and when they came to her yᵗ they would not meddle becauſe they thought

fhe was ded there being a neighbo<sup>r</sup> by faid fhe faw
her before in fuch kind of fits : then J perfwaded
one man bye : to take her upon his fhoulders and
Carrye her home but in a little way going he let her
fall upon a place of ftones : w<sup>ch</sup> did not awake her
w<sup>ch</sup> caufed me to think fhe was really dead after y<sup>t</sup>
wee Carryed her into her hous and Caufed her
Cloaths to be taken of and while we were taking
of her Cloaths to put her into bed fhe rifes up &
laughs in o<sup>r</sup> faces.

Martha Dutch aged abo<sup>t</sup> 36 years teftifyeth to ye
above written and farthar faith that J have fene faid
parker in fuch a condition feuerall othar tims.

Jurat in Curia Sep<sup>r</sup> 7 : 92.

S SEWALL Cle.

### Sam<sup>ll</sup> Shattock v. Mary Parker.

Sam<sup>ll</sup> Shattock aged 41 years teftifieth y<sup>t</sup> in the
year 1685 : Goodwife Parker wife of Jn<sup>o</sup> Parker
mariner Came to my hous, and went into the room
where my wife and Children were and fauned upon
my wife w<sup>th</sup> very Smooth words in a Short tyme
after that Child w<sup>ch</sup> was Suppofed to haue bin under an ill hand for Seuerall years before : was taken
in a Strange and unuceall maner as if his vitalls
would haue broake out his breaft boane, drawn up
togather to the uper part of his breft his neck &
Eyes drawne Soe much afide as if they would neuer
come to right againe he lay in So Strange a maner
y<sup>t</sup> the Doctor and others did beliue he was bewitched Soom days after Som of the vifiters Cut

Som of his haire of to boyle w<sup>ch</sup> they faide altho
they did w<sup>th</sup> great tendernes ye Child would Shreek
out as if he had bin tormented : they put his hair
in a fkillet ouer a fier w<sup>ch</sup> Stood plaine on the
hearth and as fon as they were gon out of ye room
it was throwne doune and i came immediatly into
y<sup>e</sup> room and Could See no Creature in ye room
they put it on againe and after it had boyled Som
tyme the aboue faid Goodwife Parker Came in and
afked if i would buye Soom Chickens J told her
no : the woman y<sup>t</sup> were above in the Chamber faid
to me it is pitty you did not afk to See her chickens for they did beleiue fhe had none to Sell : and
advifed me to fend to her hous to buy Som w<sup>ch</sup> i did
and y<sup>e</sup> meffenger brought me word y<sup>t</sup> fhe told him
fhe had none and y<sup>t</sup> y<sup>e</sup> woman y<sup>t</sup> liued in the Same
hous told him y<sup>t</sup> ye faid Parker had not had any in
three weeks before : Soom days after She w<sup>th</sup> her
hufband and two men moor Came to mye hous. &
to anfwer their requeft i went to them : She afked
me if i faide fhe had bewitched mye Child J told
her J did beliue She had : fhe faid to me you are a
wicked man : ye lord avenge me of you ye lord
bring vengeance upon you for this wrong : one of
y<sup>e</sup> men afked her w<sup>t</sup> made you Com to this hous laft
Saturday : She faide to Sell Chicken : why did not
you let him haue y<sup>m</sup> when he fent for ym faid he :
She faid becaus fhe had fold y<sup>m</sup> he afked to
whome, She faid to fuch a one wee fent prefently
y<sup>e</sup> party and the anfwer was brought us y<sup>t</sup> he never
bought any of her well you fee faide they you have

told us y<sup>t</sup> w<sup>ch</sup> is not true w<sup>t</sup> did you w<sup>th</sup> y<sup>m</sup>  She
was at a Stand but at laft faide her fon carryed y<sup>m</sup>
to fea w<sup>th</sup> him : her hufband told her y<sup>t</sup> was not
true for her fon went to fea laft fryday : and if he
had Carryed y<sup>m</sup> to fea fhe could not brough ym
here y<sup>e</sup> Saturday following  She could not giue any
true account w<sup>t</sup> fhe did w<sup>t</sup> them : but went into y<sup>e</sup>
room where y<sup>e</sup> Child was and told my wife y<sup>t</sup> fhe
was a wicked woman for Saying foe of her : & told
my wife in thefe words J hope J fhall fee the down-
fall of you, my wife told me, and foe went away in
a great anger : and this is all true and reall to the
uttermoft of my remembrance and after this threatning or Euill wifhing the Child has Continued in a
very Sad Condition fowllowed w<sup>th</sup> very Solem fits
w<sup>ch</sup> hath taken away his underftanding.

Jurat in Curia.

*Indictment v. Mary Bradbury No.* 1.

Effex in the province
of the Maffachufetts
Bay in New Eng-
land fs.

Anno R R<sup>s</sup> & Reginee Gulielmi Mariee Angliee &<sup>c</sup>
Quarto  Annoq  Domini
1692.

The Juriors for our Sou<sup>r</sup> Lord and Lady the King
and Queen doe prefent That Mary Bradbury Wife
of Cap<sup>t</sup> Thomas Bradbury of Salifbury Jn the
County of Effex Gen<sup>t</sup> vpon the Twenty Sixth day of
July Jn the yeare aforefaid and diuers other dayes &
times as well before as after Certaine Deteftable arts
called Witchcraft and Soceries Wickedly Mallitioufly and fellonioufly hath ufed practifed and ex-

ercifed At and in the Townfhip of Andivor in the
County of Effex aforefaid in upon and againft one
Timothy Swann of Andivor Jn the county aforefaid Hufbandman, by which faid wicked Acts the
faid Timothy Swann vpon the 26th day of July
aforefaid and diuers other days and times both before and after was and is Tortured Afflicted Confumed Pined Wafted and Tormented and alfo for
Sundry other Acts of witchcraft by the faid Mary
Bradbury Comitted and done before and fince that
time againft the Peace of our Sour Lord and Lady
the King and Queen theire Crowne and dignity
And the forme of the Stattute Jn that cafe made
and Prouided.

    Witnefs.     Mary Walcott     Ann Puttnam

*Indictment v. Mary Bradbury No. 2.*

Effex in the Prouince of the Maffachufetts Bay, in New Eng-land fs.   | Anno R Rs & Reginee Gu-lielmi & Mariee Anglice &c Quarto Annoq. Domini 1692.

    The Juriors for our Sour Lord and Lady the King
and Queen doe prefent that Mary Bradbury Wife
of Capt Thomas Bradbury of Salifbury Jn the
County of Effex Genmt: vpon the Second day of
July Jn the yeare aforefaid and diuers other days
and times as well before as after certaine deteftable
arts called Witchcraft and Sorceries Wickedly Mallitioufly and fellonioufly hath ufed practifed and Exercifed at and in the Towne of Salem in the County
of Effex aforefaid in upon and againft one Sarah

Vibber Wife of John Vibber of Salem aforefaid
Hufbandman by which faid wicked acts the faid
Sarah Vibber the fecond day of July aforefaid and
diuers other days and times both before and after
was and is Tortured Afflicted Confumed Pined
Wafted and Tormented and alfo for fundry other acts
of Witchcraft by the faid Mary Bradbury Comitted
Acted and done before and fince that time againft
the peace of our Sou<sup>r</sup> Lord and Lady the King
and Queen theire Crowne and Dignity and the
forme of the Stattute Jn that cafe made and Prouided.

Wittnefs    Mary Walcott    Eliz. Booth
            Eliz. Hobard    Mercy lewis

*Anfwer of Mary Bradbury.*

The anfwer of Mary Bradbury in ye charge of
wichcraft or familliarity with ye Divell. J doe plead
not guilty. I am wholly inocent of any fuch wick-
ednefs through the goodnefs of god that haue kept
mee hitherto) J am y<sup>e</sup> fervant of Jefus Chrift and
have given myfelfe up to him as my only lord and
faviour : and to the dilligent attendance upon him
in all his holy ordinances, in vtter contempt and
defiance of the divell, and all his works as horid &
deteftible : and accordingly haue endevored to
frame my life, and converfation according to y<sup>e</sup>
rules of his holy word, and in that faith & practife
refolue by ye help and affiftance of god to contineu
to my lifes end :

for ye truth of what J fay as to matter of practifs

J humbly refer myfelf myfelfe, to my brethren ánd neighbo[rs] that know mee and vnto ye fearcher of all hearts for the truth and uprightnefs of my heart therein (human frailties, and unavoydable infirmities excepted) of which i bitterly complayne every day :                    Mary Bradbury.

### *Geo : Herrick v. Mary Bradbury.*

May 26th 1692.    Beeing at Salem village w[th] Conftable Jofp neale the perfons under written was afflicted much and Complained againft viz. Mary Walcott Ann Putnam vpon Cap[t] Bradberys wife of Salfbury and Mary Walcott Ann Putnam m[rs] marfhall vpon Goodwife Rice of Réding and Mary walcott ann Puttnam Marcy Lewis vpon Goodwife Read of Marblehead and Mary Walcott Marcy Lewis Ann Puttnam vpon Goody Fofdick y[e] fame woemen tells them y[t] fhe afflicts m[r] Tufts Negro.
                    atteft   GEO : HERRICK Marfhall.

### *Thos : Bradbury for Mary Bradbury.*

July y[e] 28 : 1692.    Cocerning my beloued wife Mary Bradbury this is that J haue to fay : wee haue been married fifty five yeare : and fhee hath bin a loueing and faithfull wife to mee, vnto this day fhee hath been wonderfull laborious dilligent & induftryous in her place and imployment, about the bringing vp o[r] family (w[ch] haue bin eleven childeren of or[t] owne, and fower grand children : fhe was both prudent and provident ; of a cheerfull fpiritt liberall and charitable.    Shee being now very aged and weake and greiued vnder her affliction may not bee able to fpeake much for herfelfe, not being fo free of fpeech as fome others may bee:

J hope her life and converfation hath been fuch amongft her neighbours, as gives a better and more reall Teftimoney of her, then can bee expreft by words

own'd by mee         Tho : Bradbury.

*Summons v. Mary Bradbury.*

W<sup>m</sup> & Mary by ye Grace of God of England L.S. Scotland ffrance & Jreland King and Queen defend<sup>rs</sup> of ye faith &cc

To Thomas Ring of Amefbury or Salfbury Timothy Swann of Andover Richard Carr & James Carr of Salfbury.       Greeting

Wee Comand you all Excufes fet apart to be and perfonaly appear at ye Next Court of Oyer & Terminer holden at Salem On Tuefday Next at Twelue of ye Clock or as foon after as poffible There to Teftify ye truth on Seuerall Jndictments to be Exhibited againft m<sup>rs</sup> Mary Bradbury and other perfones to be Tried for y<sup>e</sup> horrible Crime of Witchcraft hereof make return fail not. dated in Salem Sep<sup>r</sup> 5<sup>th</sup> 1692 and in ye fourth year of our Reign.

STEPHEN SEWALL Cler

To ye Sheriff of Effex or Conftables of Andouer Hauerhill Salfbury Amefbury Bradford or Newbury.

*James Allen, Rob^t Pike & John Pike for Mary*
*- Bradbury.*

Being defired to give my teftimony concerning
the life and converfation of m^rs Bradbury of Salifbury
amonft us, w^ch is as followeth viz—I having lived
nine years at Salifbury in the work of the miniftry
and now four years in the office a Paftour ; to my
beft notice and obfervation of m^rs Bradbury fhe
hath lived according to the rules ,of the gofpell ;
amongft us : was a conftant attender upon the miniftry of ye word : and all the ordinances of the gofpell ; full of works of charity and mercy to the fick
and poor, neither have J feen or heard an thing
of her unbecoming the profeffion of the gofpell.

James Allin.

m^r James Allin made oathe to the truth of what
is above written    Septemb^r y^e 7^th 1692.
before me     Rob^t Pike Asft.

J do alfo aferm to the truth of w^t is aboue teftifyed vpon vpward of fifty years experience and fhall
fo teftify if opertunity do prefent w^ch J fhall en-
dever            Rob^t Pike.

Having lived many years in Salfbury and been
much Converfent there according to my beft notice
and obfervation of Mrs. Bradbury muft needs affirm
to what is above written and add my oath to it if
called thereto :        John Pike

### Ann Putnam v. Mary Bradbury.

The depofition of Ann Putnam who teftifieth &
faith that J being at Andevour on the 26 day of
July 1692. J faw there Mis mary Bradbery the
wife of Cap^t Tho : Bradbery of Salifbury or hir Apperance moft grevious affleding and tormenting of
Timothy Swan of Andevor allmoft Redy to kill
him alfo feverall times before and fence that time J
haue feen mif*Bradbery or hir Apperance moft
grevioufly afflicting Timothy Swan and J beleue that
Mis Bradbery is a moft dreadfull width for fence
fhe has been in prifon fhe or hir Apperance has
com to me and moft. grevioufly afflicted me, ann
putnam ownid before the grand Jnqueft this har
evidens to be the truth one the oath that fhe hath
taken this 8 day of Septem^r 1692

### Sam^l Endicott v. Mary Bradbury.

Sam^ll Endecott aged thirty one years or there
about Teftifieth Thatt about eleven years fince being bound upon a vioage to fea w^th Cap^t Sam^ll
Smith Late of Bofton Deceaf'd juft before we Sayl'd
m^rs Bradbery of Salifbury the prifoner now att the
barr came to Bofton w^th fome ferkins of butter of
w^ch Cap^t Smith bought two, one of y^m proved
halfe way butter and after wee had been at fea three
weekes our men were nott able to eatt itt, itt ftunck
foe and runn w^th magotts, w^ch made the men very
much difturb'd about itt and would often fay thatt

they heard m^rs Bradbury was a witch and that they
verily believed fhe was foe or elfe fhe would not
have ferved the Cap^t foe as to fell him fuch butter.
And further this deponent teftifieth y^t in four dayes
after they fett fayle they mett w^th fuch a violent
ftorm y^t we loft our main maft and riggin & Loft
fifeteen horfes and thatt about a fortnight after we
fett our jury maft and thatt very night thare came
up a fhipp by our fide and carried away two of the
mizon Shrouds and one of the Leaches of the main-
faile. And this deponent further fayth thatt after
they arrived att Barbados and went to Saltitudos &
had Laden their veffell the next morning fhe fprang
a leake in the hold w^ch wafted fevrall tunns of falt
in foe much thatt we were forct to unlade our veffell
again wholy to ftopp our leake there was then four
foot of water in the hold after we had taken in our
lading again we had a good paffage home butt
when we came near the land the Cap^t fent this deponent forward to looke out for land in a bright
moone fhining night and as he was fitting upon the
Windlefs he heard a Rumbling noife under him
w^th that he the f^d deponent Teftifieth thatt he looked
one the fide of the windlefs and faw the leggs of
fome p fon being no wayes frighted and thatt prefently he was fhook and looked over his fhoulder,
and faw the appearance of a woman from her middle upwards, haueing a white Capp & white neck-
cloth on her, w^ch then affrighted him very much,
and as he was turning of the windlefs he faw the
aforfaid two leggs.

Jurat in Curia Sep^r 9^th 1692.

### *Mary Warren v. Mary Bradbury.*

The Depofiftion of mary warren who teftifieth
and faith that J haue ben a long time afflected by
a woman which tould me hir name was Mⁱˢ Bradbery and that fhe came from Salifbury but on the
2ᵈ of July 1692 : being the day of the examination
of mis mary Bradbery J then faw that fhe was the
very fame woman which tould me hir name was
Mⁱˢ Bradbery and fhe did moft grevioufly Afflect
and torment me dureing the time of hir examination
for if fhe did but look upon fhe would ftrick me
down or allmoft Choake me alfo on the day of her
examination J faw mis Bradbery or hir Apperance
moft grevioufly afflect and torment mary wallcott
Sarah vibber Eliz Hubbard and Ann putnam and J
beleue in my heart that miˢ Bradbery is a witch &
that fhe has very often afflected and tormented me
and feueral others by hir acts of wicthcraft.

mary warrin ownid this har teftimony one the
oath which fhe hath before the grand Jnqueft this
9ᵗʰ of September 92.

### *Richard Carr & Zerubbable Endicott v. Mary Bradbury.*

The depofiftion of Richard Carr who teftifieth
and faith that about 13 years agoe prefently affter
fume Diferance that happened to be between my
Honʳᵈ ffather mʳ George Carr and Miˢ Bradbery
the prifoner at the barr upon a Sabbath at noon as

we ware riding hom by the houfe of Cap^t Tho : Bradbery J faw m^is Bradbery goe into hir gate turne the corner of : ann Jmmediatly there derted out of hir gate a blue boar and darted at my fathers horfes ledgs which made him ftumble but J faw it no more and my father faid boys what doe you fe we both anfwed a blue bore.

Zorobabell Endicott teftifieth and faith that J liued att m^r George Carr now deceafed at the time aboue mentioned and was prefent with m^r George Carr and m^r Richard Carr and J alfo faw a blue boar dart out of m^r Brdbery gate to M^r George Carrs horfes ledges which mad him ftumble after a ftrange manr and J alfo faw the blue bore dart from mr carrs horfes ledgs in att m^is Bradberys window : and m^r carr jmmediately faid boys what did you fee and we both faid a blue bore then faid he from whence came it and we faid out of m^r Bradberys gate, then faid he J am glad you fee itt as well as well as J. Jurat in Curia Sep^r 9^th 92.

and they both further fay on y^r Oathes that m^r Carr difcourfed w^th them as they went home about what had happened and y^y all concluded that it was m^rs Bradbury that fo app^rd as a blue boar.

### *James Carr v. Mary Bradbury.*

The Depofiftion of James carr who teftifieth & faith that about 20 years agoe one day as J was accidently att the houfe of mr wheleright and his daughter the widdow maverick then liued there :

W^a

and fhe then did moft curtuoufly invite me to com oftener to the houfe and wondered J was grown fuch a ftranger, and within a few days after one euening J went thether againe and when J came thether againe: william Bradbery was y<sup>r</sup> who was then a futer to the faid widdow but J did not know it tell afterwards; affter, J came in the widdow did fo corfely threat the f<sup>d</sup> william Bradbery that he went away femeing to be angury; prefently affter this J was taken affter a ftrange maner as if liuing creatures did run about euery part of my body redy to tare me to peaces and foe J continued for about 3 quarters of a year by times and J applyed myfelf to docter crofbe who gave me a grate deal of vifek but could make none work tho he fteept tobacco in bofit drink he could make non to work where upon he tould me that he beleued J was behaged : and J tould him J had thought fo a good while : and he afked me by hom J tould him J did not care for fpaking for one was counted an honeft woman but he uging J tould him and he faid he did beleue that mi<sup>s</sup> Bradbery was a grat deal worfe then gody mertin : the prefently affter this one night J being a bed and brod awake there came fumthing to me which J thought was a catt and went to ftrick it ofe the bed and was geud faft that J could not ftir hand nor foot but by and by coming to my ftrenth J hard fumthing a coming to me againe and J prepared myfelf to ftrick it : and it coming upon the bed J did ftrick at it and J beleue J hit it : and after that vifek would work on me and J

beleue in my hart that mi⁵ Bradbery the prifonʳ att
the barr has often afflected me by acts of wicthcraft.
Jurat in Curia Sepᵗᵐ 9 : 92.

### *Mary Walcott v. Mary Bradbury.*

The depofiftion of mary walcott who teftifieth
and faith that J being at Andeur on the later end
of July 1692 : and on the 26 day of the fame month
J faw there Mis mary Bradbery the wife of Çapᵗ
Tho : Bradbery of falfbury or her Apperance moft
grevioufly affecting and tormenting of Timothy
Swan of Andevor allmoft Redy to kill him : alfo
before and fence that time J haue feen mⁱˢ Bradbery or hir Apperance moft grevioufly afflecting
and tormenting Timothy fwan and J doe beleue in
my heart that miſᵗ Bradbery is a moft dreadfull
wicth for fence fhe has been in prifon fhe or hir
Apperance has come to me and moft grevioufly
tormented me.

mary Walcot affirmed yᵉ truth of yᵉ aboue written evidence before yᵉ Jury of Jnqueft upon oath
Sepʳ 9 : 1691 :

### *William Carr for Mary Bradbury.*

The teftamony of william carr aged 41 or ther
abouts is that my brother John Carr when he was
young was a man of as good capafity as moft men
of his age but falling in Love with Jane Tru (now
wife of Capᵗ John march) and my father being
pfwaded by fome of the family (wᶜʰ J fhall not

name not to Let him mary fo yong : my fa-
ther woold not giue him a porfion w<sup>r</sup> vpon the
mach broke of w<sup>ch</sup> my brother Layd fo much to
hart that he grew meloncoly and by degrees much
crazed not being the man that he was before to his
dying day.   J do father teftify that my f<sup>d</sup> brother
was fick about a fortnight or three weeks and then
dyed and J was prefent with him w<sup>n</sup> he dyed and
J do aferm that he dyed peacibly and quietly neuer
maffifefting the Left troubl in y<sup>e</sup> world about any
body nor did not fay any thing of mr<sup>s</sup> Bradbury nor
anybody elfe doing him hurt and yet J was with
him till the breath and lif was out of his body.
Jurat in Curia.

*Evidence for Mary Bradbury.*

July 22<sup>d</sup> 1692.

Concerning m<sup>s</sup> Bradburies life & converfation

Wee the Subfcribers doe teftifie, that it was fuch
as became y<sup>e</sup> gofpel fhee was a louer of y<sup>e</sup> miniftrie
in all appearant and a dilligent attender vpon gods
holy ordinances, being of a curteous, and peaceable
difpofition and cariag ; neither did any of vs (fome
of whom haue lived in y<sup>e</sup> town w<sup>th</sup> her aboue fifty
year) ever heare or know that fhee ever had any
difference or falleing oute w<sup>th</sup> any of her neighbo<sup>rs</sup>
man woman or childe but was always, readie and
willing to doe for them w<sup>t</sup> laye in her power night
and day, though w<sup>th</sup> hazard of her health or other

danger more; more might be fpoken in her com-
endation but this for the p^rfent

Martha Pike

William Bufwell

Sarah Bufwell

Samuell ffelloes fen^r

Rodger Eafman

Sarah Eafman

Jofeph ffletcher and his
   wife

Jofeph ffrench

John ffrench fen^r

Mary ffrench his wife

Abigayl ffrench

John Allin

Mary Allin

William Carr

Elizabeth Carr

Sam^ll Colby

Samuell ffrench and his
   wyfe

Henry Ambros and his
   wyfe

Nathanel Stevens & his
   wyfe

Ephraim Severans

Lidia Severans

Sam^ll ffelloes jun^r

Abigail ffelloes

Sam^l Eafman

Elizabeth Eafman

Jofeph Eaton

Mary Eaton his wife

Robert Downer

Sarah Downer

Richard Long and his
   wyfe

Richard Smith and his
   wyfe

Jofeph True and his wyfe

Andrew Greley and his
   wyfe

William Hooke

Elizabeth Hooke

Benjamin Allin and Ra-
   chel his wyfe

Benj Allin and Rachell
   his wyfe

Ifaac Bufwell and his
   wyfe

William Allin

Ephraim Eaton

Ephraim Winfley

Mary Winfley his wyfe

Philip Grele & his wyfe

Richard Hubbard

Mathew Hubbard his
   wyfe

Daniel Moody
Elizabeth Moody
Jſaac Morrill
Phebee Morrill
John Maxfield
Jarves Ring
Hannah Ring
Nathanel Whitter
Mary Whitther
Jacob Morrill
Juſannah Morrill
Elizabeth Maxfield
Hanah Stevens widdow
John Stevens
Dorethie Stevens
Joanna Stevens
Sarah Hacket
Martha Carter
Elizabeth Gettchell
Benj: Eaſtman
Ann Eaſman
Benony Tucker
Ebenezer Tucker
Nathanel Brown
Hannah Brown
Tho: Evens
Hannah Evens
Nathaniel Eaſtman
Elizabeth Eaſman

John Eaſtman and
Mary Eaſtman his wife
Sarah Shepherd
Willi: Oſgood
Abigayl oſgood
Suſanah Severance
Oneſiphris Page and his
  wife
Sam^ll Gill and his wyfe
John Clough and his
  wyfe
Abraham Brown & his
  wyfe
Tho: Clough and his
  wyfe
Sarah Conner widow
John Tomſon
John Watſon and his
  wyfe
Steven Tongue and his
  wyfe
John Connor and his
  wyfe
Joſeph Page
Meres Tucker and his
  wyfe
Henry Brown Sen^r and
  his wife

*Summons v. Giles Corey.*

W^m & Mary by ye Grace of God of England
Scotland france & Jreland King and Queen
L. S. defend^rs of y^e faith and

To y^e Conftable of Salem                    Greeting,

Wee Comand you to Warn and giue notice vnto
Jn^o Derick y^e wife of Stephen Small ye Widow
Adams and Goody Golthite that they and Euery of
them be and perfonaly apear at ye p^rfent Court of
Oyer and Termina holden at Salem fforthwith there
to Teftify y^e truth to y^e beft of their knowledge On
Certain Jndictments Exhibited againft Giles Corey
here of make return fail not.

STEPHEN SEWALL Cl.

Salem Sep^r 7^th 1692.

Sep^t 7^th 1692 : J Defire m^r John Tomkins to
ferue this within Sumons and Make Returne
thereof :

by mee    PETER GSGOOD Conftable in Salem

J have warned the w^thin perfons to appeare at
the time and place within written by

JN^o TOMKINS Deputed.

*Ann Putnam v. Giles Corey.*

The Depofiftion of Ann putnam who teftifieth
and faith that on 13^th of April 1692, J faw the
Apperifhtion of Giles Cory com and afflect me
urging me to writ in his book and fo he continewed

hurting me by times tell the 19th April being the
day of hir examination and dureing the time of his
examination Giles cory did tortor me a grat many
times : and allfo feuerall times fence Giles Cory or
his Apperance has moft greuioufly afflected mee by
beating pinching and allmoft choaking me to death
urging me to writ in his book alfo on the day of
his examination J faw Giles Cory or his Apperance moft grevioufly afflect and torment mary walcott mercy lewes and farah vibber and J verly beleue that Giles Cory is is a dreadfull wizzard for
fence he has ben in prifon he or his Apperance has
com to me a grat many tims and afflected me.

An Putnam owned upon her oath that ye aboue
written evidence it ye truth to ye Jury of inqueft
Sept 9 : 92.

### Mercy Lewis v. Giles Corey.

The depofiftion of Mercy lewes agged 19 years
who teftifieth and faith that on the 14th April
1692 J faw the Apperifhtion of Giles Cory com
and afflect me urging me to writ in his book and
fo he continued moft dreadfully to hurt me by
times beating me and almoft breaking my back tell
the day of his examination being the 19th April and
then allfo dureing the time of his examination he
did afflict and tortor me moft grevioufly and alfo
feueral times fence urging me vehemently to writ
in his book and J veryly beleve in my heart that
Giles Cory is a dreadfull wizzard for fence he has

ben in prifon he or his Apperance has com and moft grevioufly tormented me.

Mercy Lewis affirmed to ye Jury of Jnqueft yᵗ yᵉ aboue written evidence is the truth upon yᵉ oath fhe has formerly taken in yᵉ Court of Oyer and terminer Septʳ 9 : 1692 :

### *Sarah Vibber v. Giles Corey.*

The depofiftion of Sarah vibber who teftifieth and faith that J haue ben moft grevioufly afflected by Giles Cory or his Apperance and allfo J have feen Giles Cory or his Apperance moft grevioufly affeting and tormenting the bodyes of mary wal-cott mercy lewes and ann putnam and J beleue in my heart that Giles Cory is a wizzard and that he has very often afflected and tormented me and the perfons above mentioned by his acts of wicthcraft : J teftifie yᵗ on yᵉ fourteenth of Auguft & ever fince at times fᵈ Cory has afflicted me by whipping me & beating me & urging me vehemently to read & write in his book : and cote me with his knife.

Sarah Vibber affirmed to ye Jury of Jnqueft yᵗ ye aboue written evidence is ye truth upon oath : Sepʳ 9 : 1692 :

### *Mary Warren v. Giles Corey.*

Mary Warin affirmed to ye Jury of Jnqueft that fhe hath been afflicted by Giles Cory or his appearition and that by beating of me with his ftaffe & by biting me & pinching & choaking me

Xᵃ

greatly torturing me & cutting me with a knife & perticulerly at yᵉ time of his examination he did grevioufly torment me alfo at the time of his examination J faw fᵈ Cory or his appearition moft dredfully afflicʒ mary Walcot An putnam mercy lewes & Sarah Vibber: Septʳ 9 : 1692

### *Eliz : Woodwell & Mary Walcott v. Giles Corey.*

Eliz : Woodwell upon yᵉ oath fhe formerly has taken in this Court : did affirm to yᵉ Jury of Jn-queft that fhe faw Giles Cory at meeting at Salem on a lecture day fince he has ben at prifon he or his apearition came in & fat in yᵉ middlemoft feat of yᵉ mens feats by yᵉ Poft : this was yᵉ lecture day before Bridget Bifhop was hanged and J faw him come out with yᵉ reft of yᵉ people : mary Walcot affirmed yᵗ fhe faw fᵈ Cory as above fit in yᵉ fame place at yᵉ fame time he or his appearance & yᵗ fhe did fe him goe out with yᵉ reft of yᵉ people : this fhe affirmed to yᵉ Jury of Jnqueft. Sepᵗ 9 : 1692

### *Eliz : Hubbard v. Giles Corey*

Eliz : Hubbard to yᵉ Jury of Jnqueft that Giles Cory hath feverall times afflected me with feveral forts of torments J veryly think he is a wizzard & afflicted me by wichcraft   Sept 9 ; 1692 : —

### *Benj. Gould v. Giles Corey.*

The depofiftion of beniamin gould aged about 23 yeares he teftifieth and faith one the 6 day of april 1692: giles cory and his wife came to my bead fide and looked upon me fum time and then went away: and emediately J had two penches upon my fide: allfo another time J faw giles Cory and John proctir and J had then fuch a paine in one of my feet that J could not ware my fhu for 2 or 3 days.         Ben: gould.

 & J doe beleiue in my: —       Jurat

### *Sufannah Sheldon v. Giles Corey.*

Sufanna Shelden faith y$^t$ y$^e$ fpectre of Giles Corey Murdered his firft wife & would haue murdered this to if fhe had not ben a witch — y$^t$ his firft wife gave him nothing but Skim Milke and J he did it & y$^t$ Goody Procters fpectre told her fhe murdered her owne child and y$^t$ it was fick & fhe did it becaufe fhe would not be troubled with it & y$^t$ fhe allfo faies y$^t$ Goody Buckley and Jn$^o$ Willard app$^d$ w$^{th}$ Hen. Wilkins app$^{en}$

### *John Dorich v. Giles Corey.*

the teftomeny of John dereth Eaged about fixten years teftefieth and fayeth that gils Cory alfo came to me and aflicted me this 5 of September as wel before as after he alfo threteneth me to kill me if J will not yeld to him he alfo came about the 20 of oges and told me that he wanted fom platers for he was gowen to a feaft he told me that he had a good mind to afk my dame but he fayd that fhe wouled not let him haue them fo he took

the platers and cared them a way being gown
about half a oure with them then he brot them
againe gowen away and fayd nothing —

alfo Sary pefe afliceth me at feueral times fhe
came to me of the faft day laft at Salem She
pinched me then and i have not feen har fencs.

*Hannah Small & Martha Adams v. Giles Corey.*

thefe howes nams are wten were there and faw
the platers were gown as John derich fayed.

hanah smal        martha Adams.

The depofiftion of Eliz: booth the wife of
George booth & Allies Booth who testifie and fay
that on the 12th of this Jfant Septr at ye widow
Shaflins houfe in Salem their appeared to us a grate
number of wicthes as neare as we could tell about
fifty: thirteen of which we knew who did Receiue
the facriment in our right amongft whicth we faw
Giles Cory who brought to us bread and wine
urging us to partake thereof: but becaufe we Refufed he did moft grevioufly afflect and torment
us: and we beleue in our hearts thas Giles Cory
is a wizzard and that he has often afflected us and
feurall others by acts of wicthcraft.

Elizabeth *Ɛ* Booth's mark.

Alice  $>\cap$  Booth's mark

*B. Martha Dutch v. Alice Parker.*

The Teftimony of martha Dutch aged about 36
yeers   This deponant Teftifieth and faith yt about

2 yeers laſt paſt Jnᵒ Jarman of Salem coming in
from ſea J This deponant & Alice parker of Salem
Both of us ſtanding Together ſaid vnto her wᵗ a
great mercy itt was for to ſee Them come home
well and Through mercy, J ſaid my huſband had
gone and came home well many Times & J this
deponant did ſaye vnto ye ſᵈ parker yᵗ J did hope
he would come whome This voyage well allſo and
yᵉ ſd parker made anſwer vnto me and ſaid no
neuer more in this world ye wᶜʰ came to paſs as
ſhe yn told me for he died abroad as J ſartinly
heare   Jurat in Curia Sepʳ 7: 92:

              atteſt STEP. SEWALL. Cli —

## *Frances Wycom v. Margaret Scott.*

The depoſiſtion of ffrances wycum who teſtifyeth and ſaith that quickly affter the firſt court at
Salne about wicthcraft margerit Scott whom J very
well knew or hir Apperance came to me and did
moſt grevioufly torment me by choaking and almoſt prefing me to death: and ſo ſhe did continue
afflecting me by times tell the 5ᵗʰ Auguſt·1692
being the day of hir examination allſo during the
time of hir examination margerit ſcott did moſt
grevioufly afflect m: And allſo feuerall times fence:
and J beleue in my heart that margert ſcott is a
wicth and that ſhe has offten afflected me by acts
of wicthcraft.

ffrances Wycum ownd to yᵉ grand Jnqueſt that
yᵉ aboue written evidence is yᵉ truth upon oath
Septʳ 15: 1692:   Jurat in Curia.

*Phillip Nelſon & Sarah Nelſon v. Margaret Scott.*

phillip Nellſon and Sarah his wife doe teſtifie and ſay that for two or three years before Robert Shilleto dyed we have often hard him complaining of margerit Scott for hurting of him and often ſaid that ſhe was a wicth and ſo he continewed complaneing of margartt ſcott ſaying he ſhould neuer be well ſo long as margerit ſcott liued and ſo he complayned of margret Scott att times untill he dyed.

Phillip Nelſon and Sarah his wife affirmed upon their oath to yᶜ grand inqueſt : that yᶜ aboue written euidence is ye truth

Sepᵗ 15 : 1692 :   Jurat in Curia :

*Thoˢ Putnam & Willᵐ Murray v. Alice Parker.*

the depoſiſtion of Tho : putnam aged 40 years and william murry aged 36 year who teſtifieth and ſaith that ſeuerall of the afflected parſons as mary walcott and mary warren and ſeuerall other were much afflected on the 6ᵗʰ Septʳ 1692, dureing the time of the examination of Elce parker and we ob-ſarved that upon the glance of hir eies they ware ſtruck down and upon hir laying hir hand on them they ware Recouered and we beleue that Elce parker the priſoner att the barr has often hurt the afore-ſaid perſons by acts of wicthcraft.

> Thomas putnam
> Wᵐ Murray

*Warrant v. Lydia Dusting.*

To yᵉ Conftable of Reading.

You are in theyr Majeftyes Names Required to Apprehend and bring before vs Lydah Dufting of Reading widdow—in yᵉ County of Midlefex on Munday next being ye fecond day of yᵉ Month of May next enfuing yᵉ date hereof, about eleven of yᵉ Clock in yᵉ forenoone att yᵉ houfe of Levᵗ Nathˡ Ingerfolls in Salem Village, in Order to hir examination, relateing to high fufpition of Severall acts of Witchcraft done or Comitted by hir upon yᵉ Bodys of Mary Walcott, Ann putnam, Mercy Lewis & Abigael Williames all of Salem Village, Whereby great hurt & damage hath bin done to yᵉ Bodys of faid perfons according to Complaint Capᵗ Jonathan Walcott & Sergᵗ Thomas putnam in behalfe of theyr Majeftys for yᵐfelves & feverall of theyr Neighbours, and hereof you are not to fayle att your perrill:

daᵗ Salem Aprill 30ᵗʰ 1692.

P vs. JOHN HATHORNE ⎫ Affifts.
       JONATHAN CORWIN ⎬

Purfeuance to a warant from yvs honrs baring date the 30 of aprill laft fore the aprihending and bringing of yᵉ perfon of Lidea Dofting in obediance ther to J haue brought the faid Lidea Dofting of Redding to yᵉ hous of .Lvᵗ Jngerfons in Salem uiledg. dated in Salem viledg the 2ᵈ day of may 1692.

Ateft. John Parker c. for Redding.

## *Warrant v. Sarah Dusting.*

Whereas Complaint hath bin exhibited before us by m<sup>r</sup> Thomas Putnam and m<sup>r</sup> Jn<sup>o</sup> putnam Jun<sup>r</sup> of Salem village In ye behalfe of theyr Majesties againſt Sarah Daſtin of Redding ſingle woman for high ſuſpition of Severall Acts of Witchcraft done or comitted by hir upon y<sup>e</sup> Boydes of Mercy Lewis, Mary Walcott, Anna putnam and Abigall Williams all of Salem Village and craved Juſtice

Therefore you are in theyer Majeſtyes Names Required forthwith to Apprehend the aforeſ<sup>d</sup> Sarah Daſtin of Redding Single woeman and hir Safely convey·unto y<sup>e</sup> houſe of Lev<sup>t</sup> Nathaniell Jngerſolls of Salem Village upon y<sup>e</sup> Ninth day of this inſtant May by Twelve of the Clock in y<sup>e</sup> forenoone in order to hir examination upon y<sup>e</sup> premiſes and hereof faille nott at y<sup>or</sup> perrill. Salem, dated May 8<sup>th</sup> 1692.

To y<sup>e</sup> Conſtable of Redding.

P vs.    JOHN HATHORNE } Aſſiſts.
            JONATHAN CORWIN

In obediance to this warant J haue brought the body of Sarah Duſtin of Redding ſingal woman to y<sup>e</sup> houſe of Leu<sup>t</sup> Nathanall Ingorſon of Salem Villeg the nint of this Inſtant Maye 1692 John Parker Conſtable of Redding

*Warrant v. Ann Sears, Bethiah Carter & Bethiah Carter.*

Whereas Complaint hath benne this day Exhibited (before vs) by Thomas Putnam and John putnam Junr both of Salem Village yeoman on behalfe of theire Majefties Againft Ann Seeres the wife of John Seeres of Woburne and Bethiah Carter of ſᵈ Towne of Woburne widdow and Bethya Carter yᵉ daufter of ſᵈ Carter widdow for high fufpition of fundry acts of Witchcraft donne by them vpon the Bodys of Ann putnam Marcy Lewis Mary Walcot &c of Salem Village whereby much hurt and wrong is donne vnto them theirfore Craves Juftice.

Thefe are therefore in theire majesᵗˢ Names to require you, to apprehend and forthwith bring the perfons of the abouenamed before vs at Salem Village at yᵉ houfe of Lᵗ Nathaniell Jngerfalls in order to theire examination Relateing to yᵉ abouefaid premifes and hereof you are not to faile Dated Salem May 8ᵗʰ 1692.

To yᵉ Conftable of Woburne

P vs.　Jᴏʜɴ Hᴀᴛʜᴏʀɴᴇ 　} Affifts.
　　　Jᴏɴᴀᴛʜᴀɴ Cᴏʀᴡɪɴ 　}

I, Ephraim bouck counftabel of Woburn haue farved this warant acording to Caza hau apurhanded the parfon of anah Sauris and of the wado cartter and hauf broit them to Laufanant ingarfons hois as warant dus expreft.

Y²

In purfuance to the within fpecified warrant J haue apprenheded the bodies of the within mentioned Anna Seers and Bethia Carter fen^r & brought them to the place within ordered this 9 May 1692.

Ephraim bock Conftabil of woburn

## *Examination of Deliverance Hobbs.*

(1) The Examination of Deliverance Hobbs 22 Apr. 1692. Ata court held at Salem village by

John Hauthorne } Efq^rs.
Jonah Corwin }

Mercy Lewes do you know her that ftands at the Bar (for the Majeftrates had privately ordered who fhould be brought in and not fuffered he name to be mentioned) Do you know her? fpeaking to another : but both were ftruck dumb.

Ann Putnam jun^r faid it was Goody Hobbs and fhe hath hurt her much.

John Indian faid he had feen her, & fhe choake him.

Mary Walcot faid, yefterday was the firft time that fhe faw her i. c. as a Tormenter

Why do you hurt thefe perfons?

Jt is unknown to me.

How come you to commit acts of witchcraft?

J know nothing of it.

Jt is you or your appearance, how comes this about? Tell us the truth.

J cannot tell.

Tell us what you know in this cafe. Who hurts them if you do not?

There are a great many Perfons hurts us all.
But it is your appearance.
J do not know it.
Have not you confented to it, that they fhould
be hurt?
No in the fight of God, and man, as J fhall an-
fwer another day
Jt is faid you were afflicted, how came that
about?
J have feen fundry fights.
What fights.
Laft Lords day in this meeting houfe and out of
the door, J faw a great many birds cats and dogs,
and heard a voice fay come away.
What haue you feen fince?
The fhapes of feverall perfons.
What did they fay?
Nothing.
What neither the birds, nor perfons?
No.
What perfons did you fee?
Goody Wilds and the fhape of Mercy Lewes.
What is that? Did either of them hurt you?
None but Goody Wilds, who tore me almoft to
peices.
Where was you then?
Jn bed
Was not the book brought to you to figne?
No.
Where were you not threatened by any body, if
you did not figne the book?

No, by nobody.

What were you tempted to under you affliction?

J was not tempted at all.

Js it not a folemn thing, that laft Lords day you were tormented, & now you are become a tormentor, fo that you have changed fides, how comes this to pafs?

Abig: Williams and Ann Putnam jun<sup>r</sup> cry out there is Goody Hobbs upon the Beam, fhe is not at the Bar, they cannot fee her there: tho there fhe ftood.

What do you fay to this, that tho you are at the bar in perfon, yet they fee your appearance upon the beam, & whereas a few dayes paft you were tormented, now you are become a Tormentor? Tell us how this change comes.   Tell true.

J have done nothing.

What have you refolved you will not confefs? Hath any body threatened you if you do confefs? You can tell how this change comes.

She lookt upon John Jndian, & then another, & then they fell into fits.

Tell us us the reafon of this change: Tell us the truth.   What have you done?

J cannot fpeak.

What do you fay?   What have you done?

J cannot tell.

Have you figned to any book?

Jt is very lately then.

When was it?

The night before the laſt.

Will the Lord open your heart to confeſſe the truth. Who brought the book to you?

Jt was Goody Wilds.

What did you make your mark with in the book?

Pen and ink.

Who brought the Pen and Ink?

They that brought the book, Goody Wilds.

Did they threaten you if you did not ſigne?

Yes, to teare me in peices.

Was there any elſe in company?

No, Sir.

What did you afflict others by? Did they bring images?

Yes.

Who brought the images?

Goody Wild and Goody Oſburn.

What did you put into thoſe images.

Pins, Sir.

Well tell us who haue you ſeen of this company?

None but thoſe two.

Have you not ſeen many?

No. J heard laſt night a kind of Thundring.

How many images did you uſe?

But two.

Nay here is more afflicted by you, You ſaid more, Well tell us the truth. Recollect yourſelf.

J am amazed.

can you remember how many were brought?

Not well, but feverall were brought.

Did they not bring the image of John Nichols his child?

Yes.

Did not you hurt that child?

Yes.

Where be thofe images, at your houfe?

No, they carryed them away again.

When?

They carred fome then, & fome fince.

Was it Goody Wild in body, or appearance?

Jn appearance.

Was there any man with them?

Yes a tall black man with an highcrown'd hat.

Do you know no more of them?

No. Sir.

*Note.* All the fufferers free from afflection during her examination after once fhe began to confeffe, tho at fundry times they were much afflicted till then.

*Note.* Wheras yefterday at Deacon Jngerfols Mary Walcot & Abigail Williams cryed there ftands Goody Hobbs, fhowing alfo where, Benjᵃ Hutchinfon ftruck at her with a Rapier, & the afflicted that is the faid Mary & Abigail faid, oh you have ftruck her on the right fide: Whereupon the Magiftrates afking her after the publick examination whither fhe had received any hurt yefterday, she faid yes in her right fide like a Prick, & that it

was very fore, & done when fhe was in a Trance,
telling us alfo in what hovfe and room it was done.
Whereupon the Magiftrates required fome women
to fearch it, who found it fo as fhe had confeffed.
Alfo a little after the faid prick in her fide, fhe had
som what in her left eye like duft, w^th agrees with
w^t the afflicted farther faid that Benj^a Hutchinfon
afterwards toucht her eye w^t_h the fame Rapier, &
faid pointing to the place there was a mark which
the Marfhall being by faid fo there was.

Salem Village Aprill the 22^th 1692. m^r Sam^ll
parris being defired to take in wrighting y^e Examination of Deliuerance hobs˙ hath deliuered itt as
aforefaid.

And vpon hearing the fame and feeing what wee
did fee together with the Charg of the afflicted
perfons againft them Wee Committed her.

John Halhorne.

### *Examination of Deliverance Hobbs.*

The firft Examination of Deliverance Hobbs in
prifon. She continued in the free acknowledging
herfelf to be a Covenant Witch, and further Confeffeth She was warned to a meeting yefterday
morning, and that there was prefent Procter and
his Wife, Goody Nurfe, Giles Cory and his Wife,
Goody Bifhop alias Oliver, and m^r Burroughs was
y^e Preacher, and preft them to bewitch all in the
Village, telling them they fhould do it gradually
and not all att once, affureing them they fhould

prevaile. He adminiftred the facrament unto them at the fame time with Red Bread, and Red Wine like Blood, fhe affirms fhe faw Ofburn, Sarah Good, Goody Wilds; Goody Nurfe, and Goody Wilds diftributed the bread and Wine, and a Man in a long crownd white Hat, fat next y^e Minifter and they fat feemingly att a Table, and They filled out the wine in Tankards, The Notice of this meeting was given her by Goody wilds. She herfelf affirms did not nor would not Eat or drink, but all the Reft did who were there prefent, therefore they threatened to torment her. The meeting was in the Pafture by M^r Parris's Houfe, and fhe faw when Abigail Williams ran out fpeak with them: But that Time Abigial was come a little diftance from the Houfe. This Examinant was ftrucke blind, fo that fhe faw not with whome Abigall fpake She further faith, that Goody Wilds to prevail with her to fign, told her that if fhe would put her hand to the book fhe w^ld give her fome Cloaths, and would not afflict her any more—Hir daughter Abigail Hobbs being brought in att the fame time while her mother was prefent was immediately taken with a dreadful fitt, and her mother being afked who it was that hurt her daughter anfwered it was Goodman Cory and fhe faw him and the gentlewoman of Bofton ftriving to break her Daughter's neck.

*Warrant v. Abigl Somes.*

To Conftable peter Ofgood.

You are in theire Mageſts names hereby required to apprehend and forthwith bring before vs Abigaile Soames Single Woman, now liveing at yᵉ houfe of Samˡ Gafkill in Salem : who ftand accufed of Sundry acts of Witchcraft, (or high fufpition thereof) donne or Committed by her Lately on the body of Mary Warren &c faile not. Dated Salem, May the 13ᵗʰ 1692.

P vs. JOHN HATHORNE } Affifts.
JONATHAN CORWIN }

I haue Apprehended yᵉ perfon Abigail Soams Acordinge to worrante exprefte on yᵉ other fide and heaue broghte hir to ye hewfe of mʳ Thomas Beadles. pʳ me Peter Ofgood conftable in Salem May yᵉ 13, 1692.

*Warrant v. Elizᵃ Colfon.*

To yᵉ Conftable of Ridding.

You are in theyr Majeftyes Names hereby Required to Apprehend & bring before us (upon Tuefday next being the feaventeenth day of this Jnftant may by Tenne of yᵉ Clock aforenoone att yᵉ houfe of Levᵗ Nathaniell Jngerfolls in Salem Village) the body of Elizabeth Colfon of Redding Single woeman, whoe ftandeth charged in behalfe of theyr Majeftys wᵗʰ high fufpition of sundry Acts of Witchcraft done or Comitted upon yᵉ Bodyes of Mary Walcott Mercy Lewis and others

Z²

in Salem Village, whereby great hurt hath bin done them : And hereof you are nott to faile.

Salem dat<sup>r</sup> May 14<sup>th</sup> 1692.

P vs.  John Hathorne ⎫ Affifts.
       ·Jonathan Corwin ⎬

May 16<sup>th</sup> 1692.  I haue made Diligent Search for y<sup>e</sup> aboue named Elizabeth Collſon and find ſhee is fled and by the beſt Information ſhee is att Boſton in. order to bee ſhipt of<sup>d</sup> and by way of Eſcape to be tranſported to ſome other Countrey whereof J make my Returne.

p<sup>r</sup> me John Parker conſtable for Redding.

### *Warrant v. Mary De Rich.*

To y<sup>e</sup> Marſhall of y<sup>e</sup> County of Eſſex or his Lawfull Deputy or Conſtable in Salem.

You are in theyr Majeſtys Names hereby required to apprehend and forthwith bring before us, Mary de Rich y<sup>e</sup> Wife of Michaell de Rich of Salem ffarmes Huſbandman, whoe ſtands charged w<sup>th</sup> Sundry Acts of Witchcraft by hir Comitted lately on the Bodys of Abigall Williames & Elizabeth Hubbard of Salem Village &c. whereby great hurt and Jnjury hath bin done y<sup>m</sup> in order to hir examination relateing to y<sup>e</sup> ſame & hereof you are not to fayle

Salem, Dat May 23 : 1692.

J ord<sup>r</sup> of ye Govern<sup>r</sup> & ⎰ John Hathorne
    Councill.            ⎱ Jonathan Corwin.

I haue apprehended y^e aboue named perfon and brought her as aboue

   p^r Jos^h Neal Conftable.

### *Warrant v. Sarah Pease.*

To the Marfhall of Effex or his dep^t or Conftables of Salem.

You are in theire Majes^ts names hereby required to apprehend and forthwith bring before vs (Sarah peafe y^e wife of Robert peafe of Salem Weauer who ftands charged with fundry acts of witchcraft by her Committed lately on y^e Body of Mary Warren of Salem village whereby great Jnjury was don her &c.) in order to her Examination Relateing to y^e fame faile not. Dated Salem May 23^d 1692.

  Pr ord^r of y^e Govern^r & } John Hathorne
    Councill.         } Jonathan Corwin.

  J haue apprehended y^e perfon mentioned within this warrant and heaue broughte hir

   p^r me Peter Ofgood conftable in Salem. May y^e 23 : 1692.

### *Warrant v. Sarah Rice.*

To the Conftables in Reding.

You are in theire Majefties names hereby required to apprehend and bring before us, Sarah Rice the wife of Nicholas Rice of Reding on Tuefday next being the 31^st day of this Jnftant moneth at the houfe of L^t Nathan^l Jngerfalls at

Salem Village aboute ten of the Clock in the forenoon, who ftand charged with haueing Committed funday acts of witchcraft on yᵉ Bodys of Mary Walcott and Abigail Williams & others to theire great hurte &c, in order to her Examination Relateing to yᵉ premifes abouefaid faile not. Dated Salem May 28ᵗʰ 1692.

P vs.    J. HATHORNE<br>
JONATHAN CORWIN } Affifts.

In obedence to this warant J haue brought the Body of Sarah Rice the wife of Nicholas Rice of Redding to the houfe of Leuᵗ Nathanal Ingerfons in Salem Viledg the 31 of this inftant: May 1692:

Ateft John Parker Conftable of Redding.

### Complaint v. Elizabeth Cary.

Salem, May 28ᵗʰ 1692. Mʳ Thomas putnam & Benjamin Hutchinfon both of Salem Village Yeomen Complaine of Elizabeth Carey yᵉ wife of Capᵗ Nathaniell Cary of Charls Towne Mariner, on behalfe of theyr Majeftyes, for fundry Acts of witchcraft by hir Comitted upon ye Bodyes of Mary Walcott, Abigall Willyams & Mercy Lewis all of Salem Village, whereby great hurt & damage is done yᵐ and therefore Craue Juftice.

Thomas putnam<br>
Beniamin Huchinfon.

### Warrant v. John Alden

To the Conftable of Salem.

Effex. fs. Whereas Complaint hath been made

vnto us John Hathorne & Jonathan Corwin Esq^rs by feverall perfons of Salem Village that Cap^t John Alden of Bofton Marrin^r is guilty of Witchcraft in cruelly torturing & afflicting feverall of ther children & others thefe are therefore in their Maj^ts Cing William & Queen Maryes name to Authorize & Comand you forthwith to Apprehend the body of the faid John Alden and Jmediately bring him before vs to anfwer what fhall be objected ag^t him in that behalfe and this fhall be yo^r fufficient warrant Given vnder our hands the 31^st day of May 1692 And in the ffourth year of the Reigne of our Sovereigne Lord and Lady William & Mary now King and Queen over England & v.

P vs.   JOHN HATHORNE   ⎫
        JONATHAN  CORWIN ⎬ Affifts.
                         ⎭

perfons Complaining viz^t   Mary Walcott
   Mercy Lewis            Elizabeth Hubbard
   Abigail Williams       Ann putnam
   Elizabeth Booth        Marry Warren

Jn obediance to the within written warant J haue Apprehended the Body of Cap^t John Alden according to the tener of this warant.

### *Eliz^a Booth v. Martha Corey.*

The teftimony of Elefebeth Booth Aged 18 yers or their about teftifieth y^t one y^e 8 of June Geiorg nedam Apeired onto me and faide y^t mattha Georie kiled him becaufe he wold not mend her Lening wheal         Elefebeth Booth.

The teftimony of Elefebeth Booth Aged 18 yers

or their about teftifieth y<sup>t</sup> on y<sup>e</sup> 8 day of June
Thomas Goold Senyer Apered vnto me & told me
y<sup>t</sup> mattha Corie kiled him becaufe he told her fhe
did not doe well by Goodman parkers Childringe.

Elefebeth Booth vpon oath.

Elizabeth Booth owned all that is aboue writ-
ten before & vnto y<sup>e</sup> Grand inqueft on ye 30<sup>th</sup> Day
of June 1692.

### Examination of Rich<sup>d</sup> Carrier.

Richard Carriers Confeffion July 22 : 1692.

Q. have you bin in ye devils fnare  A : yes.
Q. is yo<sup>r</sup> bro: Andrew enfnared by ye devils
Snare : A : Yes.  how long has yo<sup>r</sup> brother bin a
wich.  A : neare a monthe  how long have you
bin a wich :  A : not long :  Q. have you joined
in aflicting y<sup>e</sup> aflicted perfons ;  A : Yes.  Q. you
help<sup>t</sup> to hurt Timo. Swan did you  A. Yes.  Q.
how long have you bin a wich.  A. abo<sup>t</sup> five
weeks :  who was in Company when you Coun-
anted with y<sup>e</sup> devill :  A : M<sup>rs</sup> Bradbery.  did fhe
help yo<sup>u</sup> aflict.  yes :  what was y<sup>e</sup> occafion m<sup>rs</sup>
Bradbery would have to afflict Timo. Swan :  A.
becaufe her hufband & Timo Swan fell out about
a Scyth J think  Q. did they not fall out abo<sup>t</sup>
thaching of a barn to :  A : no not as J know of.
Q. who was att the Villadge meeting when you
was there  Goodwife How. goodwife Nurs. g
wildes, Procter & his wife m<sup>rs</sup> Bradbery & Gory's
wife :  Q : was any of Bofton there.  A : no :  Q.

how many was there in all : A. a duzzen J think.
was Jno. Willard there  A. J think he was

Q. what kind of man is Jn° willard : a young man
or an old man.  A : he is not an old man. he had
black hair.  Q what meeting was this meeting :
was this that that was near Jngerfals:  A : Yes. J
think.  Q. what did they do then.  A. the eat &
drank wine :  was there a minifter there.  A. no :
not as J know of :  from whence had you your
wine :  A. from Salem J think was  Q. goodwife
Olliver there,  yes I knew her.

*Warrant v. Ann Doliver*

Effex fs.  To the Sheriffe of the County of Effex
or his deputie or Conftable in Salem or Beuer-
ley.

You are in theire Magis^ts names hereby required
to apprehend and forthwith bring before vs Ann
Dalibar the wife of W^m Dalibar of Glocester who
ftands charged this day with haueing Committed
fundry acts of Witchcraft on the  Bodys of Mary
Warren & fufannah Shelden to the hurt of theire
Bodys in order to her Examination Relateing to
the premifes faile not. dated Salem June the 6^th
1692.

BARTH° GEDNEY
P vs.  JOHN HATHORNE  } Juft^cs of y^e peace
JONATHAN CORWIN

In obediance to this warant J haue aprehended
y^e perfon within Named and brought her to the

place apoynted in order to her examination as
ateft my hand.

Peter Ofgood conftabll for the town of Salem.

*Eliz<sup>a</sup> Nicholafon v. Ann Doliver.*

Elizabeth the wife of Edmond Nicolaffon will
teftify; that coming to the houfe of Samuell Dallabar; Peter Pitford and the wife of the faid Dallabar were in difcourfe before the dore in the yard:
and in theire difcourfe fhe heard Peter Pitford fay:
J merualle how that old witch knowes every thing
that is don in my houfe: Rebecca the wife of Samuell Dallabar replied oh Peter doe not fay foe: for
J belieue fhe is no Witch, foe fhe came away and
left Peter Pitford and the wife of Samuell Dallabar
in difcourfe                    Elizabeth Nicolafon.

The depofition of Sarah Jngelfon Aged about 30
yers Saith that feing Sarah Church after hur examination fhe came to me crieing and wringing
hur hands feming to be mutch trobeled in Sparet
J afked hur what fhe ailed fhe anfwered fhe had
undon hurfelf J afked hur in what fhe faid in belieing hurfalfe and others in faieing fhe had fet
hur hand to the diuells Book whairas fhe faied fhe
nauer did J told hur J beleued fhe had feat hur
hand to the Book fhe anfwered crieng and faid no.
no. no: J nauer J nauer did.   J afked then what
maed hur fay fhe did fhe anfwered becaufe they
thratened hur and told hur thay would put her into
the dongin and put hur along with m<sup>r</sup> Borows
and thus fauerall times fhe folowed one up and

downe tealing me that ſhe had undon hurſalfe in belieing hurſalf and others I aſked hur why ſhe did writ it, ſbe tould me becauſe ſhe had ſtood out ſo long in it that now ſhe darſt not ſhe ſaied allſo yᵗ Jf ſhe told mʳ Noys but ons ſhe had ſat hur hand to yᵉ Booke he wold beleue her but Jf ſhe told the truth and ſaied ſhe had not ſeat her hand to yᵉ Book a hundred times he would not beleue hur.                    Sarah Jngrſol.

*Ann Putnam Thoˢ Putnam & Robert Morrill v. Thomas Farrer.*

the depoſiſtion of Ann Putnam who teſtifieth and ſaith that on the 8ᵗʰ of may 1692. there appeared to me the Apperiſhtion of an old gray head man with a great noſe which tortored m and almoſt choaked me and urged me to writ in his booke and J aſked him what was his name and from whence he came for J would complaine of him : and he told me he came from linne and people uſed to call him old father pharoah and he ſaid he was my grandfather for my father uſed to call him father : but J tould J would not call him grandfather : for he was a wizzard and J would complaine of him : and euer ſence he hath affleᴄted me by times beating me and pinching me and all moſt choaking me and urgeing me continewally to writ in his book. we whoſe names are under writen having been converſant with ann putnam haue hard hir declare what is a bove writen what ſhe ſaid ſhe ſaw & heard from the apperiſhtion of old pharoah

Aᵃᵃ

and alſo haue ſeen hir tortors: and perceiued her
helliſh temtations by hir loud out cries J will not
writ old pharaoh J will not writ in your
book.

  Thomas putnam.      Robert Morrell.

*Mary Warren & Mary Ireſon v. Jerſon Toothaker.*

 one may the 24 mary waren being in a feet and
geeuoſly aflected then was in a trans for ſum tim
we hard her ſay who ar yᵉ what is your name and
again ſhe ſaid what to thaker Doctr toothakers
wiffe we offten herᵈ her ſay J wont i wonte i will
not touch yᵉ book and then the fet was ouer then
ſhe told us that dochter toothekers wiff brought
the book to her and a coſen and a winding ſhet
and grav cloths and ſaid that ſhe muſt ſet her hand
to the book or elſe ſhe would kill her and ſtil ſhe
urged to touch the book oʳ elſe wrapt in that ſheet
this haue ben done this day by toothekers wiff.

 mary iyerſon, wiff to benjamin iyerſon at lin
hoe in the ſame maner hau tormented almoſt to
deth and brought the book to her.

*James Kettle v. Sarah Biſhop.*

. The depoſition of James Kettle aged twenty
ſeven years or there about teſtyfieth & ſaith that J
was att Docter Grigs his houſe on the tenth of
this inſtant may & there ſaw Elizebeth Hubbard in
ſeverall Fitts: and after her ffits ware ouer ſhe told
me that ſhe ſaw my two childdren Laying before

her & that thay cry^d for vengeance & that Sarah
Bifhop bid her Look on them & faid that fhe kiled
them & and they were by her defcription much
as they were when they ware put into there Coffins
to be buried & and fhe told me that Sarah bifhop
told her that J was going to burn a kiln of potts &
that fhe would break them if fhe could: & i took
notice that while fhe was in her Fitts that fhe cried
& held her apron before her face faying that fhe
would not fe them Docter Grigs & his wife and
John hues ware thare prefent.

### *John Doritch v. Margaret Jacobs.*

The teftamany of John derech Eaged about fix-
teen years teftifieth and Sayeth that marget Jacobs
Came and aflicted me this 5 of September as
fhe hath many tims before alfo teleth me that fhe
will kill me if J woul not yield to hur fhe alfo
bringeth the book to me tempen me to fot my hand
to it fhe teleth me that i fhall be wel if i will fet
my hand to the book fhe teleth me that fhe will
run a fcuer thoraw me and threteneth me to cut
me with a knife beger than an ordnery knife is as
fhe hath don wonfe before.

### *John Porter & Lydia Porter v. Sarah Bibber.*

The Teftimony of John porter And Lidia porter
Thefe
The Teftimony of John porter, who Teftifieth
and Sayth that Goodwife Biber fom time liueing

amongſt us J did obſerve her to be a woman of an
unruly turbulent ſpirit ; And ſhee would offten fall
into ſtrange fitts when ſhee was croſt of her humor : Likewiſe Lidea porter Teſtifieth, that Goodwife Bibber and her huſband would often quarrel
& in their quarrels ſhee would call him, very bad
names, and would haue ſtrange fitts when ſhe was
croſt, And a woman of an unruly turbulent ſpirit
And double tongued.

### *Joſeph Fowler v. Sarah Bibber.*

The teſtimony of Joſeph fowler, who Teſtifieth
that Goodman Bibber & his wife, Liued at my
houſe And J did obſerve and take notice, that
Goodwife Bibber was a woman who was uery idle
in her calling, And uery much given to tatling &
tale Bareing makeing miſchief amongſt her neigh-
borˢ & uery much giuen to ſpeak bad words and
would call her huſband bad names & was a woman of a uery turbulent unruly ſpirit.

### *Thomas Jacobs and Mary Jacobs v. Sarah Bibber.*

The teſtymony of Thomas Jacob and mary his
wife doth teſtyfy and ſay that good bibbor now
that is now counted afliɕted parſon ſhe did for a
time ſurgin in our hous and good bibber wood be
uery often ſpekeking againſt won and nother uery
obſanely and thos things that were uery falls and
wichſhing uery bad wichchis and uery often and
ſhe wichs that wen hor chill fell into the reuer

that fhe had neuer pull hor child out and good
bibber yous to wich ill wichches to horfelfe and
hor chilldren and allfo to others: the nayborhud
were fhe liueued amonkes aftor fhe bered hor fuft
houfbon hes tolld us that this John bibber wife
coud fall into fitts as often as fhe plefed.

### Rich^d Walker v. Sarah Bibber.

The Teftimony of Richard Walker who teftifieth that Goodwife Bibber fometime Liueing neare
to me, I did obferue to be a woman of an unruly
turbulent fpirit, And would often fall into ftrange
fitts when anything croft her humor.

### Clement Coldum v. Eliz^e Hubbard.

The depofition of Clement Coldum aged 60
years or y^r about faith, y^t on y^e 29^th of May 1692.
being at Salem Village carrying home Elizabeth
Hubbard from y^e meeting behind me; fhe defcred
me to ride fafter, I afked her why: fhe faid y^e
woods were full of Deuils, & faid y^r are there they
be, but J could fe none; then J put on my horfe,
& after J had rid a while, fhe told me I might
ride fofter, for we had outrid them, I afked her if
fhe was not afraid of y^e Deuil, fhe anfwered me
no, fhe could difcourfe with y^e Deuil as well as
with me, further faith not; this I am ready to teftifie on Oath if called thereto, as witnefs my hand:

Clement Colddum

### *James Kettle v. Eliz^a Hubbard.*

the teftimony of James Cetel being of age who teftifie and faith i .being a^t docter grigfes one a Sabath day about the laft of may in 1692. hauing fome difcourfe with Elizabeth hubberd and J found her to fpeach feuerall untruths in denying the Sabath day and faying fhe had not ben to meting that day but had onely bean up to James houltons this J can teftifie to if called: as witnes my hand

James Ketle

### *Evidence of John Putnam & Rebecca Putnam.*

the teftemony of John putnam : Sen and rebecke his wife faith that our fon in law John fuller and our dafter rebecke Shepard did both of them dy (a moft uiolent death and did acting uery ftrangely at the time of ther death) farder faith that we did Gudg then that thay both diead of a malignant feuer and had no fufpition of witchcraft of aney nether Can wee a cufe the prifner at the bar of any fuch thing.

### *Evidence of Nath^l Ingerfoll & Hanah Ingerfoll.*

The depofiftion of Nathaniell Ingerfoll and Hannah his wife who teftifie and fay that we ware converfant with Benjamin Holton for aboue a week before he died and was acted in a very ftrange maner with moft violent fittes acting much like to our poor bewicthed perfons w^n wee thought they would haue died tho then we had no fufpition of wicthcraft amongft us and he died a moft violent death with dreadful fitts and the Docter that was with him faid he could not tell what his diftember was and he died about Two days before Rebekah Sheepard

Jurat in Curia       atteft Steph, Sewall Cle.

### *Evidence of Benj^a Wilkins & John Wilkins & Nath^l Richardfon.*

The depofition of benjamin Wilkins aged 36 years and John Wilkins aged 36 years thefe deponents teftifieth and fay that Lidia Wilkins wiffe of John Wilkins was well delivered with child and was well the next day after but the 2 day after fhee was deleivered fhee was taken with a violent feaver and flux as we fuppofed had in a little time the flux abated but the feaver continued till fhe died which was about four dayes. Nath. Richifon tells of a Nafhway man y^t fpeakes of a profound fleep y^t Willard was in

### *Evidence of Hannah Welch.*

the depotion of hanah welch the wife of Phelup welch hannah walch eaged forty foer yers thus deponian teftifieth and faith that J was with m^r Salinfton and capten eapes neer this land now in contreeuarce and they both of them agreed that the fence fhud ftand as it was and that we fhud not transgrace of one fide nor Jonathan hobs one

the other fide tel the line was run and the agreement that thay agreed tow was that if eather hade
tranfgrefed fhud make fatesfaction to the other and
the reafon of this agreement was, becaus hobs and
we was allway contending.

Jurat        Att an Jnferior Court.

### Robert Moulton v. Sufannah Sheldon.

the teftimony of Robart Moulton fener who teftifieth and faith that J waching with Sufannah
Sheldon fence fhe was afflicted J heard her fay that
the witches halled her vpone her bely through the
yearde like a fnacke and halled her ouer the ftone
walls & and prefently J heard her Contradict her
former difcource and faid that fhe came ouer the
ftone wall herfelfe and J heard her fay that fhe Rid
vpone a poole to bofton and fhe faid the diuel
caryed the poole.        Robart Mouelton.

Samuel Nurs & Jofeph Trumball faw Robert
Moulton fine this wrighting.

### *Expenfes by Abr^m Perkins.*

An Accomp^t of what was taken vpon their Majefties accomp^t in the yeare 1692.

Jmp^r by Geo. Herrick vnd^r Sheriff for himfelfe
& prifeners viz : Jn^o Jackfon jun^r Jn^o
Howard & Guard                              00-08-00

To Entertainment for y^e Confta-
bles and their prifoners from Hauerill     00-06-00

To Entertainement for y^e Confta-
bles & prifoners from Glofefter            00 : 04 : 00

To Hauerill Conftable another time    00 : 02 : 00

——————

01-00 : 00

By Abraham Perkins allow<sup>d</sup>

*Nath Ingerfolls Acct. v. Country.*

March ye 1<sup>st</sup> 169¾

Vppon a meeteing of y<sup>e</sup> Majeftrates M<sup>r</sup> Jn<sup>o</sup> Hathorne and Jonathan Corwin Efq<sup>rs</sup> in an Jnquirere after witchcraft Expences upon y<sup>e</sup> Countrys Acco<sup>t</sup> for Majeftrates Marfhalls Conftables & Affiftance at my Houfe Viz<sup>t</sup>.

| | £ | s. | d. |
|---|---|---|---|
| Jmp<sup>r</sup> To y<sup>e</sup> Majeftrate Dinner & Drink | | 8 | |
| To y<sup>e</sup> Marfhalls 2 Conftables & Affiftance & Victuals | | 3 | |
| To 43<sup>d</sup> Cakes 6 qts Cider | | 2 | |
| To 2 Conftables at 2 qts of 3<sup>d</sup> Cider one Cake | | | 9 |
| To Rum | | | 6 |
| To Majeftrates Horfes | | | 6 |
| To y<sup>e</sup> Marfhall & Conftable Herricks Horfes | | | 6 |
| y<sup>e</sup> 3<sup>d</sup> Inftant y<sup>e</sup> Marfhall Expences | | | 6 |
| y<sup>e</sup> Marfhall & his horfe 1 pott Sider | | | 6 |
| vpon examination of Goodwife Corry | | | |
| To y<sup>e</sup> Marfhall for horfes & drink | | | 6 |
| To y<sup>e</sup> Majeftrates Horfes drink and Entertainement | | | 4 |
| vpon examination of goodwife Nurfe. | | | |

To y<sup>e</sup> Marfhalls Horfe Standing, Sup-

B<sup>ba</sup>

per Lodging one night and drink for his
attendance     3   6

To Conftable Herrick & Drink &
Cake     6

To yᵉ Majeftrates Drink & Enterta-
ment and Horfes wᵗʰ yᵉ Majeftrates
Horfes     5

### Aprill 19 : 1692.

A further Accont in Examination of
witchcraft at Salem Village before yᵉ
Worfhipfull John Hathorne and Jonathan Corwin Esqʳ & Affift : for the
County of Effex

To yᵉ Majeftrates entertainemt &
horfes     6

The 22 Majeftrates Minefters & at-
tendence diners     16

The 22 for 8 Horfes Hey and Otes     4

May 2ᵈ for Majeftrates Entertainemᵗ     4

ffor Horfes hey & Qates     2

ffor yᵉ Marfhall & Affiftance Victualls
and Drink     4

ditto 3ᵈ ffor Drink for yᵉ Guard upon
yᵉ Committed perfons one night     3   0

ditto 3ᵈ ffor Victualls & Drink yᵉ next
morning for y Attendance Guard Committed woman to Bofton Goal by order
of Mittimus     3

ditto 3. for Oates for the Cart Horfes
& Marfhalls Horfe     1

May 9ᵗʰ ffor conueyance mʳ Burrows

and other prifoners ffor Victualls for the
Majeftrates & tendance & Horfes &
whole charge at this Examination is                    16

    May 18 & 19 dayes for Victuall &
drink for y^e Guard in watching J Wil-
lard Tho : ffarrier & others                          16

    Carried ouer to the other fide          5  4  9

|  | lb. | s. | d. |
|---|---|---|---|

    Brought over from y^e other fide    5  4  9

    To drink for y^e Majeftrates & Vic-
tualls for attendance & Horfes Paftering          5

    May 20 To Sider for Majeftrates &
attendance                                        ·5

    21. Vitualls & Drink to Majeftrates    2  6

    23^d To Majeftrats Horfes Meat &
Attendance                                        3

    24. To Attendance Supper & drink
next morning                                      5  6

    May y^e 21—1692 vpon the Examina-
tion of William Procter and feverall
others to their Victualls Drink to y^e
Majeftrates & and their attendance &
Horfe meat and victualls & drink to y^e
Attendance of the Prifoners                       1  10

    July 15—1692 vpon an Examination
to y^e Majeftrates Conftables an others to
attend y^e prifen^r Meat Drink & Horfe
meat                                              15

                                         £8  10  9

### *Tho* Manning Acc*t* v. County.

Thomas Manning his Accompe of work down
by him for ye County of in y*t* yare 1692.

| | | |
|---|---:|---:|
| tto mending & pouting one Rachalls fetters | 1 | 6 |
| tto John howward 1 pare of fetters | 5 | |
| tto John Jackſhon ſener 1 pare of fetters | 5 | . |
| tto John Jackſhon Juner 1 pear of fetters | 5 | |
| allow*d* | 16 | 6 |

### *Iſaac Little & John Harris acc*t* v. County.*

The County of Eſſex is D*r* 1692 :    s.
for 18 pound of iron y*t* was preſt from
Jſack Little : Alle for feetters for y*e* priſ-
iners at a 4*d* a pound        6

An account from John Harris ſherife deputy of
ſondry charges at y*e* Corts of ir an terminar held at
Sallem in ye yere 1692.

             £   s.   d.

Jtt preſing a hores & man : to aſſiſt
in carriing of Sary good from Jpſwich
goalle to Sallem          8

Jtt forgoing to Sallem to carry a return of y*e* Juriars of ipſwich & Rowly
& Attending y*t* ſiting         4

Jtt for a man & horſe yᵗ was preſt to Remoue Sary good & chilld ffrom ipſwich to Sallem        7   6

Jtt for preſſing of hores & man to gard me with yᵉ wife of John willes & ye widow pudeater from Jpſwich to Salem my ſelf & gard        9   6

Jtt for tending yᵉ Court at yᵉ ſecond ſiting        4

Jtt for prouiding a Jury to make ſearch upon Cori & his wife & Clenton Eaſty : hore : Cloiſs : & mʳˢ bradbury        4

Jtt. Tending yᵉ Court on a Jurnment Auguſt yᵉ 2ᵈ 1692 from Tueſday till Satterday        4

Jtt for expenc & Time to git 3 paire of feeters made for yᵉ two Jackſons & John howard        2

Jtt for Remoueing of howard & yᵉ two Jackſons & Joſeph emmons from Jpſwich Goall to Sallem & thare Tending yᵉ Courts pleaſure thre dayes till three of them was ſent back to ipſwich Goall by me which time of thre dayes for myſellffe & exſpenc for Thos· yᵗ aſſiſted me in yᵗ ſarues        6

for preſing of men & horſes for This deſigne        2

Jtt. for bringing of mʳˢ bradbury from

Sallem to ipswich goall & a man to affift
me                                                    4
                                            ───────────
                                              2  18  6

as atteft John Harris deputy fheref.

Att A Gen^ll Seffions of y^e peace holden at Jpfwich March 27 : 94

This account is allowed provided it be not Jn-
cluded in y^e High Sheriffs acc^o.

atteft St. Sewall Cle^r

### *Jofeph Fuller acc^t v. County.*

Jofeph fuller as cunftablle for y^e yere 1692.

for feafing of Rachall Clenton &
being of har before Juftis According to
warrant for tending y^e Court of oyer &          1   o
terminer 1s o   at Salem ten days        1   o   o

Cunftaball Choat for feafeing of goody
penne & carreing of har to Sallem & and
bring of hur back to Jpfwich Goall from
Sallem by uertu of a mittemas with one        s.   d.
man to affiftance                             8   9

for tending at y^e Court of Oyer &
turmener two weeks                       1   o   o

1692. James fuller & nathaniell fuller
thre dayes a pefe at Salem being fumoned
to giue evidence Againft Rachell Clenton        s.
at ye Court of Oyer & Termina                  12  o

### *Death Warrants.*

Warrant for execution of Sarah Good Rebecka

Nurſe, Eliz¡ How Suſanna Martin & Sarah Wildes On Tueſday 19 July 1692.

Seuerall ſent to Boſton Goale on acc$^t$ of witchcraft Salem March 1$^d$ from Ex$^m$ ſent boſton

  Sarah Oſburne     Sarah Good
      Titiba Jndian

Martha Cory   Sarah Cloyce ⎫ Aprill 12$^{th}$
Rebecha Nurce   Eliz. procter ⎬ ſent to Boſton.
Dorothy Good   John procter ⎭

 May 2$^d$ Lydia Daſting wid$^o$ of Red$^e$
    Suſanna Martin of Ames$^{br}$
    Dorcas Hoar of Beverley wid$^o$
    Sarah Murrell of Bev$^r$
    Bethya Carter ⎱ of Woburn
    Ann Seires  ⎰
    Sarah Daſting  ⎱ all ſent to Boſton.
    George Burrows ⎰

 Salem May 12$^{th}$ J mittimas w$^{ch}$ went May 13$^{th}$ to Boſton.

1. George Jacobs ſen$^r$  7. Sarah Wild
2. Giles Cory     8. Mary L$^t$ Nath put-
3. W$^m$ Hobs      nam's negro
4. Edw$^d$ Buſhop   ⎫ 9. Mary Engliſh
5. Sarah Buſhop his ⎬ 10. Allice parker
 wife      ⎭ 11. Ann pudcater
6. Bridget Buſhop alias
 Oliuer

    Jn Salem priſon
 Eaſty      Margaret Jacobs
 Del$^r$ Hobs     Abigail Soames
 Abigail Hobs    Rebeca Jacobs

Mary Warren              Sarah Buckley
Churchwell               Mary Witheridge
   Sarah procter
fent to Bofton Wedenfday the 18th May 1692.
Thomas ffarror ⎫
     ⎬ of Lyn.
Eliz : Hart   ⎭
John Willard of Salem Village
Roger Toothaker of bilrica.
  fent to Bofton munday the 23d 1692.
Mary Eafty               Abigaile Soames
Sufannah Rootes          Mary Derich
Sarah Baffett            Benjamin procter
    Eliz. Cary.
 Sent to Salem Goale ye 23d May 1692.
Sarah peafe              Sarah procter.

*Reverfal of Attainder October 17th 1711.*

Province of the Maffachufets Bay :   Anno Regni Anna Reginæ Decimo.

An Act to reverfe the attainders of George Burroughs and others for Witchcraft

Forafmuch as in the year of our Lord one
Thoufand fix hundred ninety two feveral Towns
within this Province were Infefted with a horrible
Witchcraft or pofeffion of devils : And at a Special
Court of Oyer and Termina holden at Salem in the
County of Effex in the fame year 1692. *George
Burroughs* of Wells, *John Procter, George Jacobs,
John Willard, Giles Core*, and Martha his wife, *Re-
becca Nurfe* and *Sarah Good* all of Salem aforefaid
*Elizabeth How* of Ipfwich, *Mary Eaftey, Sarah*

*Wild* and *Abigail Hobbs* all of Topsfield, *Samuel Wardell, Mary Parker, Martha Carrier, Abigail Falkner, Anne Foster, Rebecca Eames, Mary Poft* and *Mary Lacey* all of Andover, *Mary Bradbury* of Salilbury, and *Dorcas Hoar* of Beverley Were feverally Indicted convicted and attainted of Witchcraft, and fome of them put to death. others lying ftill under the like fentance of the faid Court, and liable to have the fame Executed upon them.

The Influence and Energy of the Evil Spirits fo great at that time acting in and upon thofe who were the principal accufers and Witneffes proceeding fo far as to caufe a Profecution to be had of perfons of known and good reputation, which caufed a great difatisfaction and a ftop to be put thereunto until theire Majefty's pleafure fhould be known therein: And upon a Reprefentation thereof accordingly made her late Majefty Queen Mary the fecond of bleffed memory by Her Royal Letter given at her Court at Whitehall the fifteenth of April 1693. was Gracioufly pleafed to approve the care and Circumfpection therein; and to Will and require that in all proceedings ag$^t$ perfons accufed for Witchcraft, or being poffeffed by the devil, the greateft Moderation and all due Circumfpection be ufed, fo far as the fame may be without Impediment to the Ordinary courfe of Juftice.

And fome of the principal Accufers and Witneffes in thofe dark and fevere profecutions have fince difcovered themfelves to be perfons of profligate and vicious converfation.

C$^{ca}$

Upon the humble Petition and fuit of feveral of the s<sup>d</sup> perfons and of the children of others of them whofe Parents were Executed. Be it Declared and Enacted by his Excellency the Governor Council and Reprefentatives in General Court affembled, and by the authority of the fame That the feveral convictions Judgments and Attainders againft the faid *George Borroughs, John Procter, George Jacob, John Willard, Giles Core* and *Martha Core, Rebecca Nurfe, Sarah Good, Elizabeth How, Mary Eafty, Sarah Wild, Abigail Hobbs, Samuel Wardell, Mary Parker, Martha Carrier, Abigail Falkner, Anne Fofter, Rebecca Eames, Mary Poft, Mary Lacey, Mary Bradbury,* and *Dorcas Hoar,* and every of them Be and hereby are reverfed made and declared to be null and void to all Intents, Conftructions and purpofes whatfoever, as if no fuch convictions Judgments, or Attainders had ever been had or given. And that no penalties or fforfeitures of Goods or Chattels be by the faid Judgments and attainders or either of them had or Incurrd. Any Law Ufage or Cuftom to the contrary notwithftanding. And that no Sheriffe, Conftable Goaler or other officer fhall be Liable to any profecution in the Law for anything they then Legally did in the Execution of their refpective offices.

Made and Pafs'd by the Great and General Court or Affembly of Her Majeftys Province of the Maffachufets Bay in New England held at Bofton the 17<sup>th</sup> day of october. 1711.

Whereas we the fubfcribers are Informed that His Excellency the Governour Honourable Council, and Generall affembly of this province have been pleafed to hear our Supplication and anfwer our Prayer in paffing an act in favour of us refpecting our Reputations and Eftates : Which we humbly and gratefully acknowledge.

And inafmuch as it would be Chargeble and Troublefome for all or many of us to goe to Bofton on this affair : Wherefore we have and do Authorize and Requeft our Trufty Friend the Worfhipfull Stephen Sewall Efq : To procure us a Coppy of the faid act and to doe what may be further proper and neceffary for the reception of what is allowed us and to take and receive the fame for us and to Tranfact any other thing referring to the Premifes on our Behalfe that may be requifite or Convenient.         Effex. December 1711.

John Eames in behalfe of his mother Rebecca Eames

Abigael Faulkner

Samuel Prefton on behalf of his wife Sarah Prefton

Samuel Ofgood on behalfe of his mother mary Ofgood

. Nathaniel Dane

Jofeph Wilfon

Samuel Wardwell

Charles Burrough eldeft fon

John Barker

Lawrence Lacy

Abraham Fofter

John Parker ⎰ yᵉ fons of
Jofeph Parker ⎱ mary Parker deceafed.

John Marfton

Thomas Carrier

John Frie

Mary Poft

John Wright

Ebenezer Barker

Francis Johnſon on be-
half of his mother,
Brother & ſiſter Eli-
zabeth

Joſeph Emerſon on behalf
of his wife martha Em-
erſon of Hauerhill

Ephraim Willds

John Moulton on behalfe
of his wife Elizabeth
the daughter of Giles
Coree who ſuferd

Robert peaſe on behalfe
of his wife

Annies King on behalf of
her mother

John Johnſon in behalf
of his mother Rebec-
ca Johnſon & his
ſiſter

William Barker ſen[r]

Gorge Jacob on behalfe
of his father who ſuf-
fered

Thorndik Procter on be-
halfe of his father
John Procter who
ſuffered

Beniamin Procter ſon of
the aboues[d]

Doarcas hoare

willem town

Samuel nurs

Jacob eſtei

Edward Biſhop

By his Excellency the Gouerno[r]

Whereas y[e] Generall Aſſembly in their laſt
ſeſſion accepted y[e] report of their comitte appointed to conſider of ye Damages ſuſtained by
Sundry perſons proſecuted for witchcraft in y[e] year
1692 viz[t]

| | £ | s. | d. | | £ | s. | d. |
|---|---|---|---|---|---|---|---|
| To Elizabeth How | 12 | 0 | 0 | John Procter and | | | |
| George Jacobs | 79 | 0 | 0 | wife | 150 | 0 | 0 |
| Mary Eaſtey | 20 | 0 | 0 | Sarh Wild | 14 | 0 | 0 |
| Mary Parker | 8 | 0 | 0 | Mary Bradbury | 20 | 0 | 0 |
| George Burroughs | 50 | 0 | 0 | Abigail Faulkner | 20 | 0 | 0. |
| Giles Cory & wife | 21 | 0 | 0 | Abigail Hobbs | 10 | 0 | 0 |
| Rebeccah Nurſe | 25 | 0 | 0 | Anne Foſter | 6 | 10 | 0 |
| John Willard | 20 | 0 | 0 | Rebeccah Eames | 10 | 0 | 0 |

| Sarah Good | 30 | 0 | 0 | | Dorcas Hoar | 21 | 17 | 0 |
|---|---|---|---|---|---|---|---|---|
| Martha Carrier | 7 | 6 | 0 | | Mary Poft | 8 | 14 | 0 |
| Samuel Wardwell | | | | | Mary Lacey | 8 | 10 | 0 |
| & wife | 36 | 15 | 0 | | | | | |
| | | | | | | 269 | 11 | 0 |
| | 309 | 1 | 0 | | | 309 | 1 | 0 |
| | | | | | | 578 | 12 | 0 |

The whole amounting. vnto Five hundred feventy eight poundes and Twelve fhillings.

J doe by & with the advice and confent of her Maj^{tys} council hereby order you to pay y^e above fum of fiue hundred feventy eight poundes & twelve fhillings to Stephen Sewall Efq^r who together with y^e gentlemen of y^e Comitte that Eftimated and Reported y^e faid damages are defired & directed to diftribute y^e fame in proportion as aboue to fuch of y^e faid perfons as are Liuing and to thofe that legally reprefent them that are dead according as y^e law directs and for which this fhall be your Warrant.

Given under my hand at Boton the 17 Day of December 1711               J Dudley

To M^r Treafurer Taylor By order of y^e Gouerno^r & Council Jfa Addington Secrty.

Whereas His Excellency the Governor and Generall court haue been pleafed to grant to y^e perfons who were fufferers in y^e year 1692 fome confiderable alowance towards reftitution with refpect to what they fuffered in their Eftates at that Sorrowfull time and haue alfoe appointed a Comitte viz. John Appleton Efq^r Thomas Noyes Efq^r John Burrel Efq^r Nehemiah Jewet Efq. & Stephen

Sewall to diftribute yᵉ Same to and amongft yᵉ parties concern'd as in & by yᵉ records and Court orders May appear. Now Know yee that wee Subfcribers herevnto being Either yᵉ proper parties or fuch as reprefent them or have full power & authority from them to Receiue their parts and fhares of ye money aforefᵈ and fuch of vs as haue orders from fome of yᵉ parties concerned to receive their parts and fhares doe avouch them to be real and good fo that for whomfoever wee take vpon us to receive any fuch fum wee doe oblige ourfelves to Idemnify yᵉ faid Comitte to all Jntents con-ftruction & purpofes, wee fay Recieved this 19ᵗʰ day of February anno Domi 1711-12 & in yᵉ Tenth year of

| | | | |
|---|---|---|---|
| Abram How For Mary & Abigail How | 4 | 14 | 0 |
| Ephraim Roberdes for James Martha & Sarah How children of John How | 4 | 14 | 0 |
| Abraham ᴬ fofter for mother | 6 | 10 | 0 |
| Abraham ᴬ fofter for Mary lacey by order - | 8 | 10 | 0 |
| Samuel wardei | 36 | 15 | 0 |
| Benia putnam for Sarah Good | 30 | 0 | 0 |
| William W Towne for wife widow of Willard | 6 | 12 | 8 |

Jfaac Eftey 2 9 0 for felfe   John Eafty 2 9 0 for Mary poft

| | | | |
|---|---|---|---|
| William Cleur      11 0 0 for M. Carier | | | |
| John Ames ten poundes by ord. of his mother on file | 10 | 0 | 0 |

Ephraim Wiles 14 0 0 Abigail Faulkner 20 0 0

George marke of Yorry Jacobs 46 0 0

John king for himselfe & fister 79 0 0

marke of Anne X Andrews 23 0 0

John fofter 8 7 0

Charge 1 13 0

Chriftopher marke X Read maried Eliz. Hoar.

Joana marke X Green

Jofeph Parker 8 0 0

Jofeph Parker 8 14 0

Jofeph Parker 7 6 0

Received as on y^e foregoing fide £ s. d.

Samuel Nurs for himfelfe & John Nurfe & John Tarbeu Rebeccah Prefton William Ruffell Martha Bowden & francis Nurs 21 14 0

Elizabeth marke x Richards alias Procter Benjam x Procter Ebenezer Bancraft for Martha Procter

John procter william procter

Thorndik Procter in behalfe of myfelfe and Jofeph procter and Abigill Procter and mary procter and fifter Elizabeth Very.

Sarah Munion marke x alias Procter. Elizabeth marke x Procter.

£ s. d.

Charles Burrough for myfelfe and for 4 2 0 Jeremiah Burrough and Rebeccah Fowle each of us

Hanah Fox & Elizabeth Thomas 20 0 0

John Appleton Rec^d for G^o Burrough y^e fum of ffore poundes & two fhill^s.

£ s.

23^d Abigail marke x Hoar 20 4

Rebeccah marke both x Hoar

Feb 23. 1711 William *x* Hobbs for
his fister Abigail Hobbs                    9  15  0
      cha                                      4   0
                                        ─────────────
                                          10   0   0

Leonard *x* Slue for felfe & fifter Rachel    10  4ᵈ

Mary *x* Pittman alias How
Recᵈ as aforefᵈ

for George Abbott & Hanah his wife  £   s.   d.
daughter of mary Eafty                    2   9   0

March 4, 1711 by yʳ written order forty nine
fhillings   John farnum

March 5 : Recᵈ for myfelfe forty nine fhillings
2   9   0   Jacob efti.

March 6. 1711. Received for myfelfe three
poundes 4ˢ & 6ᵈ for my owne fhare.

                        Hanah *x* Willard

March 6 Recᵈ for our daughter Margaret Willard being vnder age three pounds four fhillings 6ᵈ

William *x* Town     Margaret *x* Towne wife of fᵈ
Wᵐ Town.

March 22 Received for my daughter Mary
Burroughs four pounds 2ˢ in full for her fhare.
Mary *x* Hall alias Burroughs

March 22, 1711-12 Received for myfelfe Ten
poundes Mary *x* Hall alias Burroughs

Aprill 5 1712 Recᵈ of Stephen Sewall as aforefᵈ

6   9   0                   John *x* Willard

May 1. 1712. Recᵈ on behalf of my wife De-

borah How Two pounds Seven Shilling in full.
Iſaac Howe.

Rec<sup>d</sup> for Benj. Nurſe fifty four ſhillings & 6<sup>d</sup>
May 12, 1712. Samull nurs.

Rec<sup>d</sup> for myſelf y<sup>e</sup> ſubſcriber & for my Bro<sup>r</sup> in Law Peter Thomas in right of Elizabeth his wife & my ſiſter Hanah ffox wife of m<sup>r</sup> Jabez ffox & & Rebecca fowles four pounds Ten ſhillings.
George burrougs

Receiued for my bro<sup>r</sup> Jeremiah Burroughs & myſelfe Two pounds fiue ſhillings.
Charles Burrough.

Newbury May 22<sup>d</sup>, 1712. Rec<sup>ed</sup> for & in be- halfe of my wife Jane True & Mary Stanion daughters of Mary Bradbury & for John Buſs & Eliz<sup>a</sup> Buſs Children of Elizabeth Buſs y<sup>e</sup> Sum of nine poundes fifteen ſhillings p me Henry True

May 22<sup>d</sup> 1712. Reced. for my Brethren & Siſters being fix of vs in number children of Judah Moodey one of y<sup>e</sup> daughters of y<sup>e</sup> aforeſ<sup>d</sup> Mary Bradbury Dec<sup>d</sup>. thre pounds fiue ſhill<sup>s</sup>
Caleb Moodey.

May 22<sup>d</sup> 1712. Rec<sup>d</sup> for my fiſter Anne Allen & myſelfe children of Wymond Bradbury Dec<sup>d</sup> three pounds five Shillings
p me Wymond Bradbury.

Reced for my Two Brothers William Bradbury & Jacob Bradbury & myſelfe Three pounds fiue ſhillings in full p me Thomas Bradbury.

July 27, 1712. Rec<sup>d</sup> on y<sup>e</sup> acct aforeſaid
D<sup>da</sup>

Eleuen pounds five ſhillings for my part Rec<sup>d</sup> in
full                    Samuel <sup>marke</sup> x Proƈter.

Sep<sup>r</sup> 3<sup>d</sup> 1712. Received for my brother Joſhua &
myſelfe 4 18 0 which J ingage to produce his or-
der for & ſend to S. Sewall.      Benjamin Eſtie.

Sept 3<sup>d</sup>. 1712. Rec<sup>d</sup> for my ſiſter Sarah Gills
forty nine ſhillings which J promiſe to ſend her
receipt for                 Beniamin Eſtie.

Rec<sup>d</sup> for Joſeph Eſtie & and by his written order forty nine ſhillings   Nou<sup>r</sup> 28, 1712.

              John Commings.


Receipts of y<sup>e</sup> relations &c of y<sup>e</sup> Sufferers in y<sup>e</sup>
year 1692 taken February 19<sup>th</sup> 1711-12.

Mr Burroughs's family widow.

Charles Burroughs George Burroughs Jeremiah
Burroughs Rebecca Fowle alias Burrougs Hanah
Fox alias Burroughs Elizabeth Thomas, Mary
Burroughs.

M<sup>rs</sup> Mary Bradbury's progeny.

Wymond Bradbury Dec<sup>d</sup> has left Wymund,
Anne. Judah Moodey Dec<sup>d</sup> Caleb Moodey, Hana
Moodey, Joſhua Moody, Samuel Moody, Mary
Hale. Judith Toppen. William Bradbury dec<sup>d</sup>
William Bradbury, Thomas Bradbury Jacob Brad-
bury

Mary Stanian Jane True

Elizabeth Buſs Dec<sup>d</sup> John Buſs Elizabeth Buſs.

Families Jntereſted in ye allowance following.

Children of Elizabeth How viz. daughters
Mary How, Deborah How wife of Jſa: How of

Roxbury, Abigail How. Grandchildren James How, Martha How & Sarah How being y$^e$ children of her only fon John How Dec$^d$.

William Hoar Dec$^d$ left 3 daughters.

Dorcas Hoar family, Mary Burt widow. Elizabeth Read wife of Chriftopher Read 4 0 0 Annis King wife of John King 12 0 0 Johanna Green widow 1 0 0 Tabitha Slue Dec$^d$ left two children Leonard Rachel. George Jacobs family George Jacobs only fon 46 0 0 Anne Andrews 23 0 0 Margret Jacobs alias Fofter for her goods . . . . . . taken away 8 7 0. The Charge 1 13

Mary Eafty's family. Jfa Eafty Jofeph Eafty John Eafty Ben : Eafty, Jacob Eafty. Jofhua Eafty p$^d$ to Benj Sarah Gill daughter Hanah Abbot of Andover

Rebeccah Nurfe family, John Nurfe Sarah Bowden Rebecah Prefton, Samuel Nurfe, Francis Nurfe, Mary Tarbel Elizabeth Ruffel.

John Procters family widow alias Richards Benj. Procter John Procter, Eliz. Verey, Martha Join Mary Procter Thorndick Procter William Procter Jofeph Procter, Samuel Procter Sarah Procter Eliz. Procter Abigail Procter.

Mr. Sewall & Hon$^{rd}$ friend

S$^r$ Refpects J mifed, you$^s$ J receiued of yo$^r$ fon, bearing date y$^e$ 27$^{th}$ of this Jnftant mo$^{th}$ & according to yo$^r$ defire J haue drawne out y$^e$ names & Sums (of ye Refpective Sufferers) y$^t$ y$^e$ petition$^{rs}$ pray$^d$ for. 1$^{st}$ of thofe executed.

|  | £ | s. | d. |
|---|---|---|---|
| Elizabeth How; Mary Abigail her daughters pray<sup>d</sup> for | 12 | 0 | 0 |
| Georg Jacobs, Georg Jacobs his fon pray<sup>d</sup> p | 79 | 0 | 0 |
| Sara Wild, Ephraim Wild her fon pray<sup>d</sup> for | 14 | 0 | 0 |
| Mary Eafty. Jfaack Eafty her hufband pr<sup>d</sup> p | 20 | 0 | 0 |
| Mary Parker. Jofeph & Jn<sup>o</sup> parker her fon pr<sup>d</sup> p | 08 | 0 | 0 |
| M<sup>r</sup> Georg Burroughs, Charles Burroughs his fon pr<sup>d</sup> p | 50 | 0 | 0 |
| Elizabeth Core. & Martha y<sup>e</sup> wife of Jno Molton he pr<sup>d</sup> p | 21 | 0 | 0 |
| Rebecca Nurfe. Samuell Nurfe her fon pr<sup>d</sup> p | 25 | 0 | 0 |
| Jn<sup>o</sup> Willard. Margeret Towne his relict pr<sup>d</sup> p | 20 | 0 | 0 |
| Sarah Good. William Good her hufband pr<sup>d</sup> p | 30 | 0 | 0 |
| Martha Carrier. Thomas Carriar her hufband pr<sup>d</sup> p | 07 | 0 | 0 |
| Samuel Wardell executed & his wife Sarah condemned. Samuell Wardell their fon pr<sup>d</sup> p | 36 | 15 | 0 |
| John procter, John & Thordick his fons pr<sup>d</sup> p | 150 | 9 | 0 |
| Jfons Condemned & not Executed Mrs Mary Bradbury. Henry & Sam<sup>l</sup> Tru☉her fons pr<sup>d</sup> p | 20 | 0 | 0 |

| | | | |
|---|---|---|---|
| Abigail Faulkner for her and her children pr^d p | 20 | o | o |
| Abigail Hobs william Hobs her Father pr^d p 10^lb | 10 | o | o |
| Ann Foster. Abraham Foster her fon pr^d p | 6 | o | o |
| · Rebeccah Eames prayes p | 10 | o | o |
| Dorcas King alias whore pr^d p | 21 | 12 | o |
| Mary poft prayes p | 8 | 14 | o |
| Mary Lacy Lawrence her hufband pr^d p | 8 | 10 | o |

Elizabeth Procter & Elizabeth Johnfon. J find their names amongft y^e aboue condemned pffons & fum put to them. Pfons Jmprifon^d & not Condemned petitioned for Allowances for their Jmprifonment charges &c

| | | | |
|---|---|---|---|
| Sarah Buckley & Mary witredg for fo much they pay^d | 15 | o | o |
| John Johnfon for Rebecca his wife & daughter | 6 | o | 4 |
| · Cap^t Ofgoods wife Mary | 5 | 7 | 4 |
| Sarah Cole for hers | 6 | 10 | o |
| Edward Bifhop petitions for | 100 | o | o |
| Jn° Barker p Mary Barker his daughters expences he p^d for her | 03 | 15 | 10 |
| Rob^t peafe p his | 13 | 3 | o |
| Nath^l Dane p his | 4 | 13 | o |
| Jn° Fry p his | 4 | 17 | 4 |
| Jofeph Wilfon p his | 4 | 15 | 4 |
| Jn° Wright p his | o | 4 | o |

| | | | |
|---|---|---|---|
| Mercy Woodell yᵉ wife of Jnᵒ Wright for | 5 | 4 | 0 |
| Jnᵒ Barker prayes for his Brᵒ Wᵐ Barkers | 3 | 11 | 0 |
| Lawrence Lafy for his daughter Mary | 3 | 0 | 4 |
| Jnᵒ Marfton p his wife | 2 | 14 | 4 |
| Ebenezer Barker for his wife | 5 | 7 | 4 |
| Francis Johnfon for his wife then Sarah Hawks | 5 | 4 | 0 |
| Francis Johnfon for his mother | 7 | 12 | 0 |
| & for his fifter Elizabeth | 3 | 00 | 0 |
| Totall | 796 | 18 | 0 |

befides mʳ Englifh his demands left to yᵉ Courts Confideration & determination    Ips 28-9-1711. Sʳ yᵉ moft humble fervant NTH JEWIT.

To the Committee appointed by the Governour & Council for the diftribution of the money allowed by yᵉ Generall Court to yᵉ Sufferers in the year 1692.

Pleafe to pay my part & proportion allowed me by the faid court unto Deacon Benjamin Putnam whom J have defired to pay my part of the neceffary charge, And his receipt fhall be your full difcharge. from your fervant. Wᵐ Good *x* his mark
Salem Vill. Janua. 21 : 17

Whereas the Governour and Generall Court have been pleafed to grant a Confiderable fum towards Reftitution to thofe who were Sufferers in yᵉ year 1692, & and have appointed a Committe to diftribute yᵉ fame amongft the perfons concerned.

Wherefore in as much as J y$^e$ fubfcriber Married with Martha Procter one of y$^e$ daughters of John Procter late of Salem deced doe Requeft the gentlemen of y$^e$ committee to Deliver what part and proportion May belong to me on behalfe of my faid wife unto Cap$^t$ Ebenezar Bancroft of Lynn and his Receipt fhall be your full difcharge. from your Serv$^t$.      Nathanell Gowing

Jan$^e$y 21$^{st}$ 1711.

To the Gentelmen of the Comittee appointed by the Governer and Councell to diftribute the money allowed by the General Court to fuch as weare fufferers in the year 1692.

Pleafe to pay and deliuer unto my brother Thorndik Procter the Sume allowed unto me and his receipt fhall fully difcharge you ffrom the fame

February 18$^{th}$ 1711-12      Elizabeth Very.

Whereas we are Jnformed the Generall Couart hath a Pointed a Committee to diftrubute to the pearties Confearned what the s$^d$ Court heath alowed to make Reparation to fuch as weare fufferers in the yeare 1692. Whearfore wee doe defire and heareby order and Jmpower our brother Thorndik Procter to receive what fhall bee alowed to each of ys and to giue receit for the fame which fhall fully difchargue you thearof.

the *x* of abigaill Procter.

marke

To y$^e$ Committey appointed by y$^e$ Generall Court to diftribute what was allow$^d$ by y$^e$ s$^d$ Court towards reftitution to y$^e$ relations of thofe whoe fuffered in y$^e$ Sorrowfull times called y$^e$ Witchcraft times. pleas to pay and deliuer what fhare and proportion belongs to me on that fcore vnto my Brother m^r Samuel Nurfe of Salem & his receipt fhall be a full and fufficient difcharge from your friend &c.                    Beniamin Nurfe.

May 8^th anno Dom 1712.

Whereas we are Jnformed the Generall court hath apointed a Committe to diftribute to the parties concearned what the s^d Court hath alowed to make Reparation to the Sufferers in the year 1692. Therefore wee doe defire and hereby Jmpour our Brother Samuel Nurfe te receive what is alowed to us and to give receipt for the fame

    John Nurs          willem rufel
    John Farbell       martha bouden
    Rebaka prefton    francis nurs.

Whereas y^e Gouernour & Generall Court have been Pleafed to grant a confiderable fum towards reftitution to thofe who were Sufferers in ye year 1692 : & have appointed a Committee to diftribute y^e fame amongft y^e perfons concerned.

Wherefore J ye fubfcriber (being then a Sufferer) doe requeft y^e gentlemen of y^e Comittee to Deliver what Part and Proportion may belong to me unto my father William Hobbs, or my brother William Hobbs (both of Topffield) and either of their receipts fhall be your full difcharge from your Servant.

                       the mark of
          Abigaill *x* Hobbs.

We whofe names are hereunto Subfcribed being requefted by George Locker Deputy Sherife in

Effex by order and direction of y^e Juftices to ap-
praize and vallue a Gun & a fword of John Byfh
w^ch Gun we vallue and apprize to be worth 20^s &
y^e fword to be worth Ten fhillings as witnefs our
hands this 25^th day of auguft 1716.

Abrm Punchard          Phill^h Englifh jun.

### *Petition of M^r Englifh.*

To y^e Comitte appointed to Diftribute y^e money
allowed to the Sufferers in 1692

Gen^t  I requeft y^e favour of you to reprefent
it to y^e Gen^ll Court what a great Sufferer I have
been in my eftate by reafon of y^e fevere profecution
of me and my wife in that Dark time.  It Coft
me fifty pounds at Bofton & we were forced to fly
for our Lives at which time my eftate was feized
and Squandred away to a great Value and much of
my provifion vfed to Subfift y^e numerous Company
of prifoners  In y^e whole I am Exceedingly Dem-
nified y^e moft of my perfonal eftate to y^e Value of
many hundreds of pounds taken from me & very
little of it Reftored againe I pray to Confider my
Extraordinary Sufferings.

.         I am Gen^t yo^r humble Serv^a

an account of what John King and Annis his
wife one of y^e Daughters of Dorcas Hoare late of
Beverly Deceafed difburfed & expended on their
aforefaid Mother dureing y^e time of her imprifonment and Great Troubles in ye year 1692.

Imprimis. Subfiftance for her 9 £  s.  d.
months when fhe was in Salem prifon  9  0  0

E^ea

| | | | |
|---|---|---|---|
| tt a Journey to Bofton and money carryed to her while in prifon there | 10 | 0 |
| tt my Journey to Bofton to carry her to Ipswich & Expence while there | 15 | 0 |
| tt my wife's going two Journeys to Ipfwich and exfpence & attendance upon her | 10 | 0 |
| tt two Journeys to Bofton to procure a reprieve | 1 | 0 | 0 |
| tt a Journey to fetch her from Ipfwich to Salem | 5 | 0 |

£12  0  0

befides confiderable cloathing & other things for her neceffitys.

John king.                               Annis x King.
                                           her mark

Andover feb yᵉ 26: 1711-12  honoured Sir thes are to dezier you to deliuer to yᵉ bearer hereof John Farnum the money yᵗ falleth to my fhare of what the Cort alowed to the fufferers in 92.

J being the daughter of Goodwife Eftey of topf-feeld and now wife to George Abbut in Andover.

Geoge Abbut                               Hannah abbut

To the much honred mager fewall pray Sʳ be pleafed for to pay to the barer hearof John cummings my part of the money that the generall court did geve to the fufferers in the yeare 1692. and his recit fhall bee your defcharge

Sʳ J underftand that you have payd all of my brothers, and fo J would pray you for to pay the barer heareof fo J raft your friend and Saruent

                                      Jofeph Efti.

from Dorcheftour november the 01 day 1712 as witnes my hand.

Salem ffeb^y 19^th 1711-12    To the Honour^d Committy

The petition of Benjamin Proɛter humbly ſheweth : That

1. for as much as J your petitioner was Jm priſoned for ſeveral monthes Jn the time they called witchcraft and was by that a great ſufferer.

2. for as much as J was y^e eldeſt ſon of my father & worked hard with my father : till J was about thirty years of age : and helped bring up all my father's children, by all his wives one after another.

3. for, as much as after my fathers death J your petitioner was at great coſt and trouble in the diſpoſition of my s^d fathers affairs as to relieving his s^d family ſome of them helples : with anſwering debts charges, legaſies &c.

All which conſidered your petitioner thinketh he deſerves a greater ſhare of this that y^e country hath bin pleaſe to alow us then y^e reſt of our family doe : which J leave in conſideration of you^r hon^rs and ſhall forever remain yo^r hon^rs moſt humble ſerv^t.

Benjamin Proɛter.

To the Gentlemen of the Committee appointed by the Governo^r and Council to diſtribute the money allowed by the General Court, to ſuch as were Sufferers in the year 1692.

Pleaſe to pay and deliuer into Joſeph Parker of Andover the ſum allowed unto me, and his Receipt ſhall fully diſcharge you from the ſame.

Andover January 7. 1711-12  Thomas Carrier

Know all whom it doth or may confarn that wee Mary and Abegill How both daughters of James How of Jpfwich late deceaft being informe that ye honered Generall Court hath a-Lowed fom money for us in way of Reftitution for ye damig wee fuftained in ye yere 92 by that as was called witchcraft when our honoured mother was executed.

We pray your honours to fend us ye money alowed us, by our vncle Abraham How whom we have defired and employed to Receive ye fame for us.   dated in Jpfwich 22 of January 1711 or 12 as witnes our hands  Mary x How  Abigill x How

To the gent^m of the Committee to Diftribute the money that the Generall Court allow^d to ye Famleys of those that were Suffarers in the year of ye witchcraft.

J requeft that you would deliver my p^r of the money unto Col. John Appleton and his Receipt fhall be accept^d.

dated Jan 22 : 1711.      p^r George burouhs.

Forafmuch as it is made Manifeft that ye children of m^r George Burroughs Deced. by his former wiues did in ye time of his Jmprisonment adminifter vnto him Neceffary things & were at confiderable charge thereabout & for his Jnterment & that ye widow had moft or all of ye perfonal eftate.

In Confideration where of Wee ye Subfcribers a committee appointed by ye Generall Court & confent agree & order that ye fix pounds 6^d money yet remaing of y^e fifty pounds allowed by ye Gouernment fhall be payed to y^e s^d children in equal Shares.

January 3^d 1712.

John Appleton  Stephen Sewall
Thomas Noyes  Neh. Jewett.

Bofton New England Jan^r 16^th 1711-12.

Whereas we are Jnformed the Generall Court hath appointed a Committee To Diftribute To the Partys Concern'd what the s^d court have Allow'd to Make Repare Ation to the fufferers Jn the yere 1692. wherefore we defier and hereby order and Jmpower Our Brother Charles Burrough—To Receive what is Allowed to each of us And his Receipt fhall be a fufficient Difcharge.

Peter Thomas  Jabez Fox
Rebekah Fowle  Jeremiah Burrough.

Attelborow March the 14^th 1711-12 Loving brother my Love Remembred vnto you hoping that you eare well as I am at this prefent I make bold to wright a few lins vnto you defiring you to be fo kind vnto mee as to fend mee that which is my wright and proper due from the Jeneral court I pray you to fend it by my mother which will take fom care about itt and Let me not be forgotten by you who am your Sifter till deth.

Mary Burros.

Bofton, Decemb^r 16^th 1712. To the Honourable Gentlemen Appointed for a Committee Relateing to the Affairs of Witchcraft Jn the yeare 1692.

Gentlemen. We the Subfcribers and children

of m<sup>r</sup> Georg Burrough late of wells, who suffered att Salem in the Trouble there humbly offer for you Honours Consideration A few Lines Relateing our Case and Circomstances vpon Acco<sup>t</sup> of our Mother in Laws Conduct and Carriage Towards us, after our Father was Apprehended and Taken away Our Mother in Law laide hands vpon all she could secure (the Children were generally unable to shift for Themselves) and what she could lay hands on was her Own without any person but her own Daugh<sup>r</sup> to share with her, whom she says was to bring up, but may it Plese your Honours to Consider there was seaven children more besides That were To bring up the eldest of which was but sixteen years old att that Time, but insteed of shareing in what our father Left and she had secur'd were Turn'd to shift for ourselves without anythiug for so much as a Remembrance of Our father Tho Som of us can Remember of Considerable in the house, besides his Liberary which she sold and Rec<sup>d</sup> the money for : then Lett it out at interest and was afterward Rec<sup>d</sup> by another Husband : and not one farthing bestowed on any child but her Own. This being matter of fact we Humbly leave it with your honours to Consider wheather of what the Honourable Generall Court allow'd &c She have not already Rec<sup>d</sup> To much and the Children To Little. We Subscribe ourselves your Honours Humble Ser<sup>tts</sup>

rebaker fowl.                    Charles Burrough

The mark of ✗ Eliz Thomas      Jerimi Burrough

hannah fox

Bofton Aprill 3ᵈ Honoured Sir the fauour which i would humbly afk of your hounour at this time is that you would pleafe to let my brother George Burrough have what remains in your hands on the account of my deceafed but Honnoured Father Mʳ George Burrough Sir my requeft is that it may be don without delay for euery diffcourfe on this melloncely fubieƈt doth but give a frefh wound to my bleeding hart but i defire to fit down in filence and remain, Sir your Honnours moft obedeiⁿᵗ feruant  Rebekah Fowle.

To the Gentlemen appointed A Comittee Relateing to the affairs of Witchcraft &c | Bofton Aprˡˡ 8. 1713, Gentlemen we the fubfcribers & children of mʳ Georg Burrough who fuffered in the late Troubles at Salem in the yere 1692. offer to your confideration the conduƈt of our Mother in Laue, affter the deth of our ffather—She made fure of all that there was of houfehold Goods &c togather with our fathers Library which was off fom Value, faid Liberary was fold affterward & part of the money came afterward into the hands of a fecond Hufband, but nothing thereof nor the houfehold goods &c ever came into our hands we were Turn'd out into a wide world to Shift for ourfelves haueing nothing to truft unto but Divine Providence and the Generofity of friends (not on the fide of our mother in Law) & fom of us fo young that we can give no accoᵗᵗ of perticular Circomftances of the ffamily, nor Capeable any of us to give a perticular accoᵗ of the

wrong don us any ffurther then we are informed
by others, but can affure you we never had the
value of fixpence to Remember our ffather with
when Dead and gon. And we cannot but obferve
to you that what the Honerable Court allowed
when divided among y^e Children according to the
Direction of the fame Amou^tt to but about four
pounds a piece, which we think but a poor recom-
penfe (fetting afide the deth of our father) to make
good Our due proportion of his fubftance which
we were deprived of by means of his deth, befides
the difficulties we were put unto & the Charge of
bringing up of the Confideration of w^t we relate
which is matter of fact well known to many befides ourfelves bee motive fufficient to Engage yo^r
Confideration of us in what you have Stopt of the
above mentioned grant of the Honerable Court we
defier you to deliver what you fee caufe to allow us
to our brother Georg Burrough, if what we offer
be not worth of your Confideration or Argument
Sufficient that we fhould have what Remains in
your hands, we only defier the ffavour of a Speedy
Anfwer : for the fum as we are Inform'd is fo fmall
that much trouble in the bufinefs will furmount it
by ffarr fhould we be allowed itt at laft : fo that an
information of your refolves in the bufinefs will
Prove more of a ffavour then tedious Delays fhould
you grant it at laft. Not ffurther at prefent but
Remaine to offer—We Remaine Geutlemen your
humble Serv^tts Peter Thomas in behalf of my wife.
Jabez Fox in behalf of my wife.

Salem May 11<sup>th</sup> 1713. Majeager Seuell Sir be pleafed to let my brother Charles Burrough haue my part y<sup>t</sup> was Leaft

So you will oblige your humble Serveant.

Jeremiah Burrough.

To the Gentlemen of the Committee appointed by the Governor and Council to diftribute the money allowed by the Generall Court to fuch as were fufferers in the year 1692.

Pleafe to pay and deliver unto my fon John Eames the fum allowed unto me and his receipt fhall fully difcharge you from the fame January 7, 1711-12

rebeckah <sup>mark</sup> x Ames.

To the Gentlemen of the Committee <sup>her</sup> appointed by the Governour and Council to diftribute the money allowed by the Generall Court to fuch as were fufferers in the year 1692.

Pleafe to pay and deliver unto Samuel Wardell our Eldeft Brother, the fum allowed unto us, and his Receipt fhall fully difcharge you from the fame.

Andover January 7. 1711-12.

William Wardell     Eliakim wardell

John Right          Elizabeth wardell

Ezekiel Ofgood.

The children of Samuel Wardell deceafed.

To the honourable the Gentleman of the Commitee fitting at Salem Feb. 19. 1711-12

Whereas my mother Sarah Wardel was condemned by the court at Salem fometime in January in the year 1692, as I fuppofe will appear by the Records of the Ingalls at that Court, but her name is not inferted in the late Act of the Generall Court, for the taking of the Attainder of thofe that were condemned in that year, my mother being fince deceafed. I thought it my duty to endeavour that her name may have the benefit of that Act. J therefore humbly pray your Honours to Reprefent this cafe to the Honourable Gen<sup>ll</sup> Court, that my mothers name may be inferted in the faid Act. And whereas in the Account which J gaue to your Hono<sup>rs</sup> when you met at Salem the laft winter, J mentioned only what was feized of my Father's eftate, by the fherriffe, but gave no account of other charges which did arife from the imprifonment of my Father and mother, they having provided for their own fubfiftance while they were in. Prifon, and I fuppofe there was fomething confiderable payd to the keeper of the Prifon, though I am not able now to give a particular account how much it was. Jf your honours pleafe to allow me fomething upon that account, Jt will be thankfully acknowledged by, Your honours moft humble fervant                    Samuel wardel

Feb. 19. 1711-12.

Whereas feveral of the neer Relations of us the fubfcribers fuffered imprifonment at Salem in the year 1692. And we were put to great charges and expence to provide for them while they were in prifon, and for Prifon fees and court charges, which we were forced to pay before we could obtain their Releafe. An account of which we haue put into the Gentlemen of the Committee appointed by the Gen<sup>ll</sup> Court, we do unanimoufly agree to make our fupplication to the Gen<sup>ll</sup> Court to confider the fufferings of our Relations, and the Dammage we then fuftained and to allow us fu it, according to the accounts which we haue given to the committee to aforefaid. And to that end we humbly requeft the worfhipfull Stephen Sewall Efq to write a Petition for us to the General court at their next feffion.

Andover January 21. 1711·12

| | |
|---|---|
| Nathaniel Dane | John Johnfon |
| Jofeph willfon | John wright |
| Ebenezer Barker | Samuel Ofgood |
| ffrancis Johnfon | Sara parker. |

To the Honourable the Gentlemen of the Committee Sitting in Salem Feb. 19. 1711-12.

Whereas the Honouble Generall Court hath lately made an Act for taking off the Attainder of thofe that were condemned for witchcraft in the year 1692. J thought meet to Jnform your Honours that J was condemned by the Court at Salem in January in the year 1692, as will appear by the Records of the Tryalls at Said court, but my name is not inferted in faid act. Being very defirous of the favour of that Act, am bold humbly to pray your Honours, to reprefent my cafe to the General court at their next Seffion, that my name may be inferted in that Act, if it may be, and that the Honourable court would pleafe to allow me fome thing in confideration of my charges by reafon of my long Jmprifonment, which will be thankfully acknowledged as a great favour.

 by your Honours moft humble fervant.

    Elizabeth Johnfon jun$^{r}$

Andover Feb· 19, 1711-12.

To y$^{e}$ honourable Comittee Salem february 19$^{th}$ 1711-12

 Jentlemen. Jn ye Darke & forrowful tims in y$^{e}$ yeare 1692 when fo maney perfons of undoubted Creditt were accufed of witchcrafte owr famelue as well as others was vnder grate truble and it cofte vs veary confiderable in owur neffarey Expencue for our Honoured and tender mother Duringe hir Jmprifonment.

 Wherefore requefte of your honours to maneft itt to y$^{e}$ members of y$^{e}$ members of. y$^{e}$ Jennarall Courte that we might have fom reafonable allow-. ance for owr charge therein, which will euer oblidge your Searvent To pray.

 Peter Ofgood in y$^{e}$ name of y$^{e}$ reafte of y$^{e}$ familey

 Hampton March 24. 1711-12. Maior Sewall S$^{r}$ this is to defier you to deliuer to my Brother Henry True for my vfe that part of money that y$^{e}$ Gene$^{ll}$ Court have allotted to my wife as one of Cap$^{t}$ Bradbury's Daughters & his receipt thereof fhall be your discharge from your friends and feruants.

  John Stanyan    Mary Stanyan.

 To the Gentlemen of the Committee appointed

& the Governour and Council to diftribute the money allowed by the Gen^ll court to fuch as were fufferers in the year 1692.

Pleafe to pay and deliuer unto my Brother Jof-eph Parker the fum allowed unto us, and his receipt fhall fully difcharge you from the fame. Andover January 7 1711-12.   John Parker.

To the Gentlemen of the Committee appointed by the Governour and Council to diftribute the money allowed by the Generall court to fuch as were fufferers in the year 1692.

Pleafe to pay and deliuer vnto Jofeph Parker of Andover the fum allowed vnto me, and his Receipt fhall fully difcharge you from the fame. Andover

January 7. 1711-12   Mary ✗ poft
<br><small>mark</small>   <small>hun</small>

To the Gentlemen of the Committee appointed by the Governour and Council to diftribute the money allowed by the Generall court, to fuch as were Sufferers in the year 1692.

Pleafe to pay and deliuer vnto my brother Thorndike Procter the fum allowed unto me, and his Receipt fhall fully difcharge you from the fame. January 15. 1711-12.   mary Procter.

To the Gentlemen of the Committee fitting at Salem this 22 of January 1711-12.

Whereas I the Subfcriber fuffered Imprifonment at Salem, 17 weeks in the year 1692. And was put to great charges and Expences before I could ob-tain a Releafe. And not having an oppertunity to giue your Honours an account of my charges durng my imprifonment, when others of my neighbours and fellow fufferers, put in their accounts : J haue thought meet to do it at this time, which is as followeth.

To the keeper of the Prifon two pounds eight fhillings & four pence.

For Court charges Thirty fhillings & four pence.

For neceffary Expences while J attended the Court one pound four fhillings.

Sarah Parker of Andover.

Maj<sup>r</sup> Sewall pleafe to pay to Leonard Slue the money Comeing to y<sup>r</sup> humble Serv<sup>t</sup> Feb 23. 1711-12

Rachel R Slue.

Mary Rich of Lynn widow in y<sup>e</sup> year 1692 was Imprifoned & loft he bed & pot & other houfehold ftuffe, in about halfe year.

At a Superior Court of Indicature holden at Salem for the County of Effex the 12<sup>th</sup> December by Adjournment from the laft Tuefday in November paft.

Ordered. Whereas there hath arifen a great Charge in holding the feverall Courts of Oyer and Terminer in the County of Eftex in the year 1692. the payment of part of w<sup>ch</sup> hath been ordered by the Governour and Councill out of the publique Treafury and yet there remains due to feverall perfons for their fervice and difburfem<sup>ts</sup> one hundred and thirty pounds in money whofe Acco<sup>ts</sup> haue been examined and allowed by the Court the difcharge of which properly belongs to faid County This Court doth therefore order the Clerk therof to fignifie and make known the fame unto their Majeſt^ts Juſtices of the peace in faid County. Who are directed at their next Generall Seffions of the peace to make an Affeffment on the Jnhabitats of faid County proportionally for the payment of the faid fumm And that by an Order they caufe the fame to be paid to the County Trear—and that he pay the faid fum to the feverall perfons unto whom it is due according to the feverall Acco^ts herewith Tranfmitted.

Vera Copia Taken out of y^e Reçord of f^d Court. Atteſt. Jon^a Elaffon Cler

An account of what is due to the feverall perfons hereafter named from the publique for their refpective difburfem^ts aud fervices according to their Acco^ts Given in and & Examined by the Supereour Court holden at Salem by Adjournm^t December y^e 12^th 1693.

viz

Thomas Beadle C^r by his
acc^o of difburfim^ts    £58 11 5
 Dr to what was p^d by y^e
  Sheriff    £17 17 6
     —————
   Due to Ballance    £40 13 11
Samuel Beadle C^r by his
acc^o    £21 0 0
 Dr to what p^d by the
Sheriff    £10 0 0
     —————
     £11 0 0

Samuel Shattock C^r as p his
acc^d   £ 7 02 00
  Dr to what p^d by the
Sheriff   £ 3 00 00

       £ 4 2 0
John Cook C^r by his acc°   £ 2 13 0
Mary Gedey C^r by her
acc°   £70 00 00
  Dr by what's p^d by the
Trear & Sherriffe   £55 13 00

       £14 07 0
John Stacy Cr by his acc°
of difburfem^ts   £ 4 0 0
  Mr Thomas Newton for his
feruice   £ 2 5 0
  John Putnam Conftable 30s
& Jonathan Putnam 30^s for
their Extraordinary Seruice &
Travell   £ 3 0 0
  Jofeph Neal for his Service
and Travell   £ 2 0 0
  Cap^t Willard William Mur-
ry & Thomas Putnam for
their Seruice £5 each   £15 0 0
  Nathaniel Jngerfoll his acc°
of difburfem^ts   £ 6 0 0
  George Herrick for his
Great feruice   £25 0 0

      £130 00 11
Allowed upon the acc° aboue the feverall fumes

there amounting to the Summ of one hundred and thirty pounds Eleuen pence. $W^m$ Stoughton
ver Copia atteft $Jon^a$ Elaffon Cler.
County Eftex Deto July 92.
Ittm. for making fouer payer of Iron ffetters and tow payer of hand Cuffs and putting them on to $y^e$ legs and hands of Goodwife Cloys eftes Bromidg and Green all at one pound aluen fhillings money

|  | £ | s. | d. |
|---|---|---|---|
|  | I | II | O |

March 28th 94 A making a letter B att

|  |  | I | O |
|---|---|---|---|

£1 12 O

This work was done by order from athority Requiring me thereunto
    atteft      $Rob^{tt}$ Lord      Smith.
dedu&#x0107;t $p^d$ by $y^e$ Marfhall 6$^s$—reft is 26$^s$ allow$^d$.
$M^r$ Sewall $S^r$ I thought good to returne you $y^e$ names of feverall Jfons $y^t$ were Condemned & Executed that not any perfon or relations Appeared in ye behalfe of for $y^e$ taking of $y^e$ Attainder or for other Expences, they I fuppofed were returned to $y^e$ $Gen^l$ Courts confideration for to a&#x0107;t about according to their beft prudence. Bridget Bifhop alias Oliuer, fufanna Martin, Alice parker, Ann pudeter, Welmot Read. Marget Scott.
Sr J am $y^{rs}$ Honors to Serue      Neh Jewet.
To the Gentlemen of the Committee appointed by the Governour & Council to diftribute the
         G$g^a$

money allowed by the Gen^ll Court to such as were sufferers in the year 1692.

Pleafe to pay and deliuer vnto Abraham Fofter of Andover the fum allowed vnto me and his Receipt fhall fully difcharge you from the fame

Andover January 7: 1711-12

his mark<br>larance x lace

### *John Bradſtreet for Witchcraft* 7^th *mo* 1652.

The Court held at Ipfwich 28^th (7) 1652.
26 John Broadftreet vpon his p^r fentm^t of the laft court for fufpition of haueing familiarity w^th the devill upon examynation of the cafe they found he had tould a lye w^ch was a feconde being convi&ed once before.   The court fets a fine of 20^s or elfe to be whipt.   Edw Coborne is furety for the payments of the fine & fees of court.

### *Chriſtopher Brown for witchcraft* 24: 9 *mo* 1674.

At a County Court held at Salem the 24: 9^mo 1674.
24 Chriftopher Browne haueing reported that he had beene trafing or difcourfing with one whome he apprehending to be the Deuill. which came like a Gen^t in order to his binding himfelfe to be a fervant to him, vpon his examination his difcourfe feeming inconfiftant with truth &c: the court giueing him good councell & caution for the prfent difmifs him.

*Abel Powell for witchcraft March* 30 1680.

The Court held at Ipſwich the 30 of March
1680

30 In the caſe of Abell powell though the court
do not ſee ſufficient to charge further yet find ſoe
much ſuſpition as that he pay the charges left to mʳ
Jo : woodbridge.

### Wᵐ Morſe v. Abel Powell.

The teſtimony of Wᵐ Morſe wᶜʰ ſayth together
with his wife, aged both about 65 yeeres.   That
Thurſday night being the 27ᵗʰ day of Noʳ we heard
a grate noyſe without round the houſe of knocking
the boards of the house, & as we conceiued throw-
ing of ſtones agᵗ the houſe : whereupon myſelſe &
wife lookt out, & ſaw nobody, & the boy all this
time with vs : but we had ſtones & ſticks throwne
at vs that we were forced to retire into the houſe
againe, afterwards we went to bed & the boy with
us, & then the like noyes was vpon the roofe of the
houſe.

2. The ſame night about midnight the doore
being lockt when we went to bed, we heard a great
hog in the houſe grunt & make a noyes, as we
thought willing to gett out & that we might not
be diſturbed in oʳ ſleep I roſe to lett him out & I
found a hog in the houſe & the doore unlockt : the
doore was firmely lockt when we went to bed.

3. The next morning, a ſtick of Links hanging
in the chimney, they were throwne out o̶ their

place, & we hanged them vp again & they were throwne downe againe and some into the fire.

4. The night following I had a great awle lying in the window, the w^{ch} awle we saw fall downe out of the chimney into the ashes by the fire. 5. After this I bid the boy putt the same awl into the cupboard w^{ch} we saw done, & the doore sht too: this same awle came presently downe the chimney againe in o^r sight & I tooke it vp myselfe againe the same night we saw a little Indian baskett that was in the loft before come downe the chimney againe, & I tooke the same basket & put a piece of brick into it, and the basket with the brick was gone, & came downe againe the third time with the brick in it, & went up againe the fourth time, & came down againe without the bricke: & the bricke came downe a little after.

6. The next day being Saturday, stones, sticks, & pieces of bricks came downe so that we could not quietly dresse o^r breakfast, and sticks of fire allso came downe at the same time.

7. That day in the afternoone my thread 4 times taken away and came downe y^e chimney, againe, my awle & a gimblett wanting came downe the chimney: againe my leather taken away came downe the chimney: againe my nails being in the cover of a firkin taken away came downe the chimney. Againe the same night the door being lockt, a little before day hearing a hog in the house I rose and saw the hog to be mine. I let him out.

8. The next day being Sabath day, many ſtones & ſticks & pieces of bricks came downe the chimney: on the munday m<sup>r</sup> Richardſon & my brother being there, the frame in my cow houſe they ſaw very firm. I ſent my boy out to ſkare the fowles from my hogs meat: he went to the bowhouſe, & it fell downe my boy crying with the hurt of the fall: in the afternoone, the potts hanging ouer the fire did daſh ſo vehemently one ag<sup>t</sup> the other, we ſett downe one that they might not daſh to pieces: I ſaw the andiron leap into the pott & dance & leap out, & again leap in & dance & leap out againe, & leap on a table & there abide, & my wife ſaw the andiron on the table: allſo I ſaw the pott turne itt ſelfe over and throw downe all the water: againe we ſaw a tray with wooll leap vp & downe & throw the wooll out, & ſo many times & ſaw no body medle with it: againe a tub his hoop fly off of itſelfe & the tub turne over & nobody neere it: againe the woollen wheele turned vpſide downe & ſtood vp on its end, & a ſpade ſett on it: Steph Greenleafe ſaw it, & my-ſelfe & my wife, againe my rope tooles fell downe vpon the ground before my boy could take them, being ſent for them, & the ſame thing of nailes tumbled downe from the loft into the ground, & nobody neere. Againe my wife & boy making the bed, the cheſt did open and ſhutt the bed cloathes could not be made to ly on the bed but fly off againe.

Againe Caleb Powell came in & being affeſted

to fee o<sup>r</sup> trouble did promife me & my wife that if we would be willing to lett him keep the boy we fhould fee o<sup>r</sup> felves that we fhould be neuer difturbed while he was gone with him, he had the boy & had bin quiet ever fince.

Tho: Rogers, & George Hardy being at W<sup>m</sup> Morfe his houfe affirme that the earth in the chimney corner moued & fcattered on them that Tho: Rogers was hitt with fomewhat, Hardy with an Iron ladle as is fuppofed. Somewhat hitt W<sup>m</sup> Morfe a great blow: but it was fo fwift that they could not certainely tell what it was: but looking downe after they heard the noyfe they faw a fhooe. The boy was in the corner at the firft, afterwards in the houfe. M<sup>r</sup> Richardfon on faturday teftifyeth that a board flew ag<sup>t</sup> his chaire & he heard a noyfe in another roome, w<sup>ch</sup> he fuppofed in all reafon to be diabolicall.

Auth Morfe affirmeth that he faw the bord before tackt with nailes to the window, but his evidence is drawne at large by himfelfe. John Dole faw a pine ftick of candlewood to fall downe, a ftone, a firebrand, & thefe things he faw not what way they came till they fell downe by him.

The fame affirmed by John Tucker the boy was in one corner, whom they faw & obferved all the while & faw no motion in him Elizabeth Titcomb affirmeth that Powell fayd that he could find the witch by his learning if he had another fcholler with him, this fhe fayeth were his expreffions to the beft of her memory Steph. Greenleafe, & Edw

Richardfon affirme the motion of the woll in the tray.

Jo. Tucker affirmeth that Powell fayd to him, he faw the boy throw the fhooe while he was at prayer.

John Badgers oath is drawne out by itfelfe.

Jo. Emerfon affirmeth that Powell fayd he was brought vp vnder Norwood, and it was gudged by the people there, that Norwood ftudied the black Art.

A father teftimony of W^m Morfe and his wife.

We faw allfo a rooler of bread turne over ag^t me & ftruck me not any being neere it, & fo over-turned. I faw a chaire ftanding in the houfe & not any body neere it did often bow towards me & fo rife vp againe. My wife allfo being in the cham-ber the chamber doore did violently fly together not any body being neere it. My wife going to make a bed the bed did moue to & fro not any body being neere it. J allfo faw an Iron wedge & fpade was flying out of the chamber on my wife & did not ftricke her. My wife going into the Cellar a drum ftanding in the houfe did rowle over the doore of the Cellar & being taken vp againe the door did violently fly downe againe. My barnes doors 4 times vnpinned I know not how. I going to fhutt my barne doore looking for the pin the boy being with me. (as I did judge) the pin com-ing downe out of the aire & did fall down neere to me, Againe Caleb Powell came in as before fayd & feeing o^r fpirits very low by y^e fenfe of o^r great

affliction began to bemoane o<sup>r</sup> condition & fayd that
he was troubled for o<sup>r</sup> afflictions, &· fayd that he had
eyed this boy, & drawed neere to vs with great
compaffion. poore old man, poore old woman this
boy is the occafion of your griefe, for he hath done
thefe things, & hath caufed his good old grand-
mother to be counted a Witch, then fayd I how can
all thefe things be done by him, fayd he allthough
he may not haue done all yett moft of them, for
this boy is a young rogue, a vile rogue, I haue
watched him & fee him do things as to come up
& downe.   Caleb Powell allfo faid he had vnderftanding in Aftrology & Aftronomy, & knew the
working of fpirits, fome in one country, and fome
in another, & looking on the boy fayd you young
rogue to begin fo foone, Goodman Morfe of you
be willing to lett me haue this boy, I will vndertake
you fhall be free from any trouble of this kind while
he is with me: I was very unwilling at the firft &
my wife, but by often vrging me til he told me
whither, & what imploym<sup>t</sup> & company he fhould
goe, I did confent to it and this was before Jo:
Bedger came & we haue bin freed from any trouble
of this kind euer fince that promife made on munday night laft, to this time being friday in the afternoone then we heard a great noyfe in the other
roome oftentimes, but looking after it, could not
fee anything. but afterwards looking into the roome,
we faw a board hanged to the preffe then we being
by the fire, fitting in a chaire my chaire often would
not ftand ftill but ready to throw me backward

often times : afterward my cap allmoft taken off
my head 3 times againe a great blow in my polle
& and my catt did leap from me into the chimney
corner prefently after this cat was throwne at my
wife : we faw the catt to be ours we put her out of
the houfe & fhutt the doore : prefently the catt was
throwed into the houfe : we went to goe to bed
fuddenly my wife being with me in bed the lamp
light by o$^r$ fide my catt againe throwed at vs 5
times jumping away prefently into the floore, &
one of thofe times, a red waftcoat throwed on the
bed, & the catt wrapped vp in it : againe the Lamp
ftanding by vs on the cheft, we fayd it fhould ftand
& burn burne out, but prefently was beaten downe,
& all the oyle fhed, & we left in the darke :
Againe a great noyfe a great while very dreadfull :
againe in the morning a great ftone being 6 pound
weight did remoue from place to place we faw it :
two fpoones throwed off the table, & prefently the
table throwed downe & being minded to write my
ink horne was hid from me, w$^{ch}$ I found couered
with a rag, & my pen quite gone. I made a new
pen & while I was writing one eare of corne hit me
in the face, & fire fticks & ftones & . . . . .
throwed at me, & my pen brought to me while I
was writing with my new pin, my Ink horne taken
away, and not knowing how to write any more,
we looked vnder the table, & there found him, &
fo I was able to write againe : againe my wife her
hat taken from her head fitting by the fire by me

H$^{ha}$

the table allmoſt, throwne downe: againe my ſpec-
ticles throwne from the table, and throwne allmoſt
into the fire by me & my wife & the boy: againe
my booke of all my accounts throwne into the fire,
& had bin burnt preſently if I had not taken it vp:
againe boards taken off a tub, and ſett upright by
themſelves & my paper do what I could hardly
keep it while I was writing this relation & things
throwne at me while a wrighting preſently before
I could dry my writing a mormouth hatt rubbed
along it but I held ſo faſt that it did blott but ſome
of it: my wife and I being much afraid that I
ſhould not preſerve it for the publike vſe did thinke
beſt to lay it in the bible, & lay it ſafe that night,
againe the next I would lay it there againe, but in
the morning it was not there to be found the bag
hanged downe empty, but after was found in a box
alone againe while I was writing this morning, I
was forced to forbeare writing any more I was ſo
diſturbed with ſo many things conſtantly throwne
at me. This relation brought in deʳ 8ᵗʰ.

John Badger affirmeth that being at Wᵐ Morſe
his houſe and heard Caleb Powell ſay, that he
thought by Aſtrology, & I thinke he ſayd by
aſtronomy to with it he could find out whether or
no there were diabolicall means vſed about the ſayd
Morſe his trouble, & that the ſayd Caleb, ſayd he
thought to try to find it out.

*Sarah Hale v. Abel Powell.*

The teſtimony of Sarah Halle about 33 yeeres, &

Jofeph Mirick about 19 who affirme. That John Moores Boatfwaine of the veffell wherein Jofeph Dole was Cap$^t$ & Caleb Powell was mate, hath often fayd in their hearing, that if there were any wizards he was fure that Caleb Powell was a wizard, w$^{ch}$ he affirmed oftentimes in their houfe, Taken on oath Febr 27$^{th}$ 1679, before me

Jo Woodbridge Commifs$^r$.

### *Anthony Morfe v. Abel Powell.*

I Anthony Mores occafionally being at my brothar's Mores hows my brothar fhowid me a pece of a brik which had feuerall tims come down the chimne: I fitting in the cornar J towke the pece of brik in my hand: with in a litell fpas of tiem the pece of brik was gon from me, J knu not by what meaines Quickly aftar the pece of brik came down the Chimny: allfo in the chimny cornar J faw a hamar on the ground: thar being no parfon near the hamar itt wafs fodenly gone: by what meians J know not: but with in a litell fpas aftar the hamar came down the chimny: and with in a littel fpas of time aftar that came a pece of woud down the chimny about a fute loung. and within a litell while aftar that came down a fiar brand the fiar being out: this was about ten dayes agoe.

newbury 8 : 9 : 79. Taken on oath De$^r$ 8$^{th}$ 1679 before me

Jos. Woodbridge Com.

De[r] 3: 1679: Caleb Powell being complained of for suspicion of working with the Devill to the molesting of W[m] Morse & his family, was by warrant directed to the Constable brought in by him. The accusation & testimonyes were read, & the complaint respited till the munday following.

De[r] 8th 1679. Caleb Powell appeared according to order, & farther testimoney produced ag[t] him by W[m] Morse, w[ch] being read and considered it was determined that the sayd W[m] Morse should prosecute the case ag[t] say[d] Powell at the County Court to be held at Jpswich the last tuesday in march ensuing & in order heervnto. W[m] Morse acknowledgeth himselfe indebted to the treasurer of the County of Essex, the full summ of 20[l]. The condition of this obligation is that the sayd W[m] Morse shall prosecute his complaint ag[t] Caleb Powell at that Court.

Caleb Powell was delivered as a prisoner to Constable till he could find security of 20[l] for the answering of the sayd complaint or else he was to be carryed to prison.

Jo Woodbridge Commiss[r] •

*Mary Tucker v. Abel Powell.*

The deposition of Mary Tucker aged about 20.
She remembreth that Caleb Powell came into her house & sayd to this purpose that he coming to W[m] Morse his house & the old man being at prayer, he thought not fitt to goe in but looked in at

the window, & he fayd he had broken the inchant-
m$^t$, for he faw the boy play tricks while he was at
prayer, & mentioned fome & and among the reft
that he faw him to fling the fhove at the fayd
Morfes head. Taken on oath march 29$^{th}$ 1680
before me.

Jo : Woodbridge Commifs$^r$

Mary Richardfon confirmed the trueth of the
aboue written teftimony on oath at the fame time.

### *John Badger v. Abel Powell.*

John Badger afermeth that being at william
morfe his hous : and heard Calleb powell fay that
he thought, by Aftroligie : and I think he faid by
aftronmie too with it he could find out whither or
no ther wear diabolicoll meanes ufed about the
faid mors his trouble and that the faid Caleb faid
he thoug to try to find it out.

Vpon the hearing the complaint brought to this
court ag$^t$ Caleb Powell for fufpicion of working
by the devill to the molefting of the family of W$^m$
Morfe of Newbery, though this court cannot find
any euident ground of proceeding farther ag$^t$ the
fayd Caleb Powell, yett we determine that he hath
given fuch fuch ground of fufpicion of his fo dealing, that we cannot fo acquit him, but that he
guftly deferves to bear his owne fhame & the cofts
of the profecution of the Complaint, refered to m$^r$
woodbridge to examine & determrne w$^t$ the
charges.

*Complaint v. Margaret Read.* 29 : 4ᵐᵒ 1680.

At a County Court fitting in Salem, the 29 : 4ᵐᵒ 1680.

34 There being a complaint made by mʳ phillip Reade, againſt margarett Giffords to the court, vpon ſuſpicion of witchcraft, and pʳ ſenting ſeveral papers & euidences againſt her, & affirming ſeverall other things againſt her, which he ſaith he can produce evidence for this court hearing all that was pʳᵉſented & read as aforeſaid. The Court ſees cauſe to In-joyne the Margarett Gifford to appeer at the next court at Jpſwich, there to make further anſwer &c : & the ſaid Read is injoyned then to proſecut againſt her, & bring in what euidence he has, or can pro-cure to make good his complaint, & the whole caſe to be returned to the ſaid court :

The court held th 28 of September 1680.

34 mʳ Phillip Read appeared to Jſecute againſt mʳˢ margaret Gifford, but ſhe being legelly called did not appeare.

55 mʳ Phillip Read appeared to pʳſecute againſt mʳˢ Margrt Giffard vpon ſuſpition of her being a witch, and ſeverall teſtimony vpon oath were then brought But the ſaid Giffard being orderly called to Anſwere did not appeare.

*M. Pearſon vs Burt. NovemberI.* 1669.

The Teſtimony of Maddlene Pearſon aged fifty yeeres, or there abouts ſaith ſhe heard Sarah Pearſon

fay when her father had hur down to Goodwife
Burt to be cuered of her fore foote y$^e$ firft night
fhee was there y$^e$ faid Burt put her to bed : and
tould y$^e$ faid Sarah if fhee would beeleve in her
God, fhee would cure her body and foule : But if
fhee tould of it, fhee fhould be as a deftracted body
as long as fhee lived, and further that her hufband
did not beleue in her God and fhould not be cured
and that he maid did beleue in her God and was
cuered : this fhee faid being in her right mind fhee
being fhee being fome time in good health the
faid Burt faid to her Sarah will you Smok it and
giueing of her the pipe fhe fmoket it : and y$^e$ faid
Sarah feall into her fitts againe and faid that Goodwife Burt brought y$^e$ diuill to her to tormeante
her : further faith not.

### *Bethiah Carter vs. Burt.*

The teftymony of Bethiah Carter Aged 23
yeares or therabouts Teftifyeth that fhe herd Sara
townfan fay when fhe was a mayd and liued with
goodwife Burt that fhe faid goodwife Burt told her if
fhe could beliue in her god fhe would cure her body
and foul and farther fhe fayd goodwife burt tould her
fhe could not cure her owne hufband becaufe he
would not belue in her god : but her mayd did beliue
in her god and fhe was curd : this fhe herd Sara
townfan fay when fhe was in good helth and feve
a while after this the faid Sara townfan Being forely
afflickted with faid fitts, crying out and Rayling

agaynſt me ſayin my father carryed me to boſton But carryed her too Lin too an owld witch) and farther the s^d Sarah hath tould to me and others that ſhe hath ſen the s^d Burt apeare often at her beds feete and at diuers other places in the Day and alſo at Night, this ſhe hath often related as well in helth as in ſicknes ffarther faith nott.

### *Phillip Reed vs. Burt.*

M^r Phillip Rede Phyſiſtion aged 45 years or thereabouts teſtifyeth that he being ſent for 3 feuerall times too ſe the above s^d Sara townſan and her ſiſter Carter: being both very il but eſpeſſially ſhe s^d Sara townſan being in a more ſadder condittion he had noe oppertunyty, too examine her condittion but did playnly perceiue there was noe naturall caus for ſuch unnatural fitts but being ſent for the 4^th time and finding her in a meat capaſſity to give iufomation of her agreuanc and cauſe of her former fitts ſhe tould me the abous^d Burt had afflicted her and told her if euer ſhe did relate it to any one ſhe would afflict her wors one hower after ſhe had a ſadder fit than any euer ſhe had afore: then i aſkt her whoe afflict her now and what the matter was ſhe replide with a great ſcrich ſhe had tould me alreddy and that ſhe did now ſuffer with it much more not related at p^rſent.

Witneſs my hand 15^th 9^mo 69.

Phillp Reade.

Thomas ffarar aged aboue fifty years faith that my daughter Sarah & my daughter Elizabh were in

former time forely afflicted and in their greateft
extremity they would cry out & roare & fay that
they did fee goody Burtt & fay ther fhe is doe you
not fee her kill her ther fhe is & that they faid
feuerall times and I haue a fon now in extrem
misery much as the former hath bin and the docter
fays he is bewiched to his vnderftanding.

*John Pearfon & Mary Burnop vs. Burt.*

The Teftimony of John Pearfon aged about
ninetene years and Mary Burnop aged about 26
yeres teftifieth that Goodwif Burt coming into the
Roome wheare Sarah Pearfon was afked her how
fhee did : fhee faid the worfe for her : the faid Burt
feat down, and laughed at y$^e$ faid Sarah fhee coming towards her faid douft thou laugh and know-
eth thou heath don me a mifchefe I could find in
my heart to bafte thy fids the faid Burt faid doe if
thou durft, and I will pay thy fids. ffurther y$^e$
aboue faid John Pearfon faith that he heard goodwife Burt aboue faid did fay that the aboue faid
Sarah fhould fpake as much againft her friends as
eure She did againft her. furthermore that the
aboue faid Mary Burnop faith fhe heard the abouefaid Sarah fpake telling Bethyah Cerrter that her
father had her to Boftown : but carryed me to Lin
to an ould witch further faith not.

*John Knight vs. Burt.*

The teftimony of John Knight about fourty

I²

feaven yeares of age faith he was goinge to fetch
fome things for his wife and he faw old goody burt
coming out of a Swamp and fhe was in her fmok
fleeves and a blacke hancather and black cap of
her head and he looked up and fuddenly fhe was
gone out of fight and I looked aboute and could
not fee her foe when I cam into the houfe I found
her in the fame habit as I faw her and he faid vnto
her did I not fee you in the fwamp even now and
fhe s^d noe I was in the houfe and he told her then
fhee was a light headed woman and further faith
not.

### *Jacob Knight vs. Burt.*

The teftimonye of Jacob Knight aged about 24
or 25 yeares: I boarded in the houfe of Mr Cobit
with my brother wormwood: in which houfe widdow Burt liuen at that tyme, my brother, & fifter
being gone to Boftone: there being noe fire in my
brothers roome, I went into widdow Burts roome
to Lite, my pipe, & tould her I had a paine in my
head, & foe went into my Lodging roome: which
was through five dores (& ftooping downe to
Loofe my fhoee looking vpward there was widdow
Burt with a glaffe bottle in her her hand, & fhee
tould mee, there was fumething would doe my head
good, or cure my head, & gaue mee the botle in
my hand, & when I had drunke of it, I was worfe
in my head) but Concerning the five doeres I
paffed through into my Roome, I thinke they were

all fhutt after mee, but however ther is one fflore,
y$^t$ muſt be paſſed over to come into my Roome,
that was foe Looſe y$^t$ it would make ſuch a noyſe
y$^t$ might, in an ordinarye waye be heard when any
paſſed over it, but I heard nothing & her ſudden
being with mee put mee into affright, & foe remained while the next morneing though ſhee
p$^r$fentlye Left mee, & foe the next morning but one,
I being to goe to Salem, intended to tell my ſiſter
wormwood of it, before I went, but widdow Burt
coming into my ſiſter wormwoods Roome, s$^d$ I
hade a minde to faye fomething to my ſiſter ag$^t$
her y$^t$ I would not haue her heare, & this was before I had ſaid any thing, & foe went out of the
the houſe & then I tould my ſiſter, and going to
Salem, I faw a Catt, which being out of ſight againe,
I p$^r$fentlye faw faw a dogg it being, Likewiſe p$^r$-
fentlye out of ſight, I faw one before mee, Like-
unto widdow Burt goeing before mee downe a hill
as I was goeing vp it, & foe I loſt ſight of her, the
night following I Lodged at my brother knights at
Salem, I Looking out of the chamber, it being a
cleare moone light night, I faw widdow Burt vppon
a graye horſe or mare in my brothers yard, or one
in her ſhape, & foe I waked my Cozen John knight
y$^t$ Lodged with mee, & tould him of it, then
neither he, nor I, could ſee any thing, fo when he
was a ſleep againe, ſhee appeared to me in the
chamber, &. then I tooke vpp a piece of a barrell
head & threw it at her, & as I think hit her on
the breſt : & then could ſee her noe more that
tyme.

Eſſex ſs. Clerk's office, October 22, 1859.

I Aſahel Huntington, Clerk of the Supreme Judicial Court and of the Superior Court and the Court of County Commiſſioners for ſaid county, do hereby certify, that the foregoing except the words in red ink are true copies of original papers on file in ſaid office, and that the ſame were made by direction of ſaid County Commiſſioners, under the authority of a law of the commonwealth, paſſed May 15, 1851.

Atteſt,

A. Huntington, Clerk.

Eſſex ſs. Clerk's office October 22, 1859.

The words in red ink in the foregoing pages are to be taken as conjectural readings, where, from the loſs, decay or obliteration of the manuſcript, the original writing has become illegible.

Atteſt,

A. Huntington, Clerl

CPSIA information can be obtained
at www.ICGtesting.com
Printed in the USA
BVHW041810180621
609919BV00002B/3